IRAQ

Second Edition

Hot Spots in Global Politics Series

Samer Abboud, *Syria*
Christoph Bluth, *Korea*
Alan Dowty, *Israel/Palestine*, third edition
Kidane Mengisteab, *The Horn of Africa*
Amalendu Misra, *Afghanistan*
Gareth Stansfield, *Iraq*, second edition
Jonathan Tonge, *Northern Ireland*
Thomas Turner, *Congo*

IRAQ: PEOPLE, HISTORY, POLITICS

Gareth Stansfield

Second Edition

polity

First edition published in 2007 by Polity Press
This edition published in 2016 by Polity Press

Polity Press
65 Bridge Street
Cambridge CB2 1UR, UK

Polity Press
350 Main Street
Malden, MA 02148, USA

ISBN-13: 978-0-7456-4929-0
ISBN-13: 978-0-7456-4930-6(pb)

A catalogue record for this book is available from the British Library.

Library of Congress Cataloging-in-Publication Data

Names: Stansfield, Gareth R. V., author.
Title: Iraq : people, history, politics / Gareth Stansfield.
Description: Second edition. | Malden, MA : Polity Press, 2016. | Includes bibliographical references and index.
Identifiers: LCCN 2016002781| ISBN 9780745649290 (hardback) | ISBN 9780745649306 (pbk.)
Subjects: LCSH: Iraq–Politics and government–1991-2003. | Iraq–Politics and government–2003-
Classification: LCC DS79.7 .S73 2016 | DDC 956.7044/3–dc23 LC record available at http://lccn.loc.gov/2016002781

Typeset in 10.5 on 12 pt Sabon
by Toppan Best-set Premedia Limited
Printed and bound in Great Britain by Clays Ltd, St. Ives PLC

For further information on Polity, visit our website:
politybooks.com

For Amélie, Nathan and Robyn

Contents

Maps

Acknowledgements

Writing the second edition of a book on a subject as complex and topical as the politics of modern Iraq has proved to be a difficult and at times frustrating task, but one made infinitely more enjoyable and straightforward by the advice and counsel of several colleagues and friends who I have engaged with since the first edition was published. While I have benefited from the input of those I mention below, any errors remain solely my responsibility, of course.

As ever, there are many colleagues who have remained crucial for my generating of knowledge of events unfolding in Iraq, and how to read unfolding developments. Sajjad Rizvi and Robert Gleave continue to correct my views on Shi'i politics and society, and I have also valued the input of Ahab Bdaiwi (St Andrews) on these matters. Tim Niblock, Faleh Abd Al-Jaber, Brendan O'Leary and Toby Dodge have each informed or challenged my opinions many times over, and I have had the good fortune of being able to turn to the expertise of Ali Ansari and Michael Axworthy when trying to delve into the complexities of Iran's role in Iraq, and Greg Shapland provided me with the view of Iraq from the vantage point of the UK Foreign and Commonwealth Office on many occasions. Through my own research background, I have been able to call upon the assistance of a range of very knowledgeable people on the Kurdish question in Iraq, and I would like to thank in particular Hashem Ahmadzadeh,

Mohammed Ihsan, Falah Mustafa, Latif Rashid and Salar Amin. In addition, the advice of two anonymous reviewers undoubtedly improved the quality of the book. The advice of all of these figures has proved to be invaluable.

In Exeter, Zoe Humble ensured that I had the stretches of time needed to complete this project, shouldering the burden of managing diaries, meetings and expectations, for which I am very grateful.

At Polity Press, thanks to Louise Knight and Nekane Tanaka Galdos, who have shown astonishing resilience as deadlines were extended and have been a pleasure to work with, always on hand with advice and encouragement, and to Helen Gray for all her copy-editing work.

Lastly, I would like to thank my family for their love and support. Putting up with the blinkered nature of book-writing academics is not an easy task, but is one that Melissa, along with my children Amélie, Nathan and Robyn, continues to endure with grace and humour.

Abbreviations and Glossary

ADM	Assyrian Democratic Movement. Political party representing Chaldo-Assyrian community, headed by Younadam Youssef Kanna.
Al-Qaeda (Iraq)	Sunni Islamist organization attacking foreign influences in Muslim countries. Headed by Ayman al-Zawahiri following the death of Osama bin Laden. Al-Qaeda Iraq (AQI – or *tanzim qa'idat al-Jihad fi bilad al-Rafidayn*) headed by Abu Musab al-Zarqawi until his death in 2006, and formed basis of the Islamic State of Iraq (ISI) that led to the formation of the Islamic State of Iraq and al-Sham (ISIS), then the Islamic State (IS).
Anfal	Codename of Government of Iraq campaign in 1987–88 for systematic depopulation of rural Kurdistan. *Anfal* refers to the eighth *sura* of the Quran.
Ansar al-Islam	Partisans of Islam. Kurdish Islamist group that formed part of the *Ansar al-Sunnah* group that emerged in the years following regime change.

Asa'ib Ahl al-Haq	League of the Righteous. Shiʿi militia group led by Qais Al-Khazali. Formed in 2006 as splinter of *Mahdi* Army and fought against US forces. Close relationship with Iranian IRGC, and, since 2014, part of the *Hashed al-Sha'abi*.
Ayatollah	Literally, 'Sign of God'. Highest clerical rank in Shiʿi religious establishment.
Badr Organization	Originally the military wing of SCIRI then ISCI. Operates independently as a Shiʿi militia headed by Hadi Al-Amiri. The *Badr* organization is part of the *Hashed al-Sha'bi*.
Baʿth Party	Arab Socialist Baʿth Party. Founded in 1947 as a secular Arab nationalist party by Michel Aflaq. Came to power in Iraq in 1963 coup, then again in 1968 when Saddam Hussein quickly became the leading figure.
Caliphate	An Islamic government led by a caliph (*Khalifa* in Arabic). The caliph has to be recognized as a successor to the Prophet Mohammed and would then lead the worldwide Muslim community. Abu Bakr al-Baghdadi proclaimed himself caliph in Mosul in July 2014, but has not received global recognition among Muslims as being a legitimate caliph.
CIA	(US) Central Intelligence Agency.
CPA	Coalition Provisional Authority. Replaced ORHA. Headed by Ambassador L. Paul Bremer III.
Daʿwa	*Hizb al-Daʿwa Islamiyya* (Party of the Islamic Call). Shiʿi party formed in late 1950s under guidance of Ayatollah Mohammed Baqr Al-Sadr. Fractured into several wings. Prominent figures include Haidar Al-Abadi, Nouri Al-Maliki and Ibrahim Al-Jaʿfari.

Hashed al-Sha'abi	People's Mobilization Forces (PMF). Umbrella Shiʿi militia organization formed in 2014 in response to rise of ISIS. Overall Chairman is Dr Falih Al-Fayyadh. Most prominent components include *Asaib Ahl al-Haq*, *Badr* Organization, Peace Companies and *Kata'ib al-Imam Ali*.
hawza	More fully, *hawza al-marja'iyya*. The religious establishment surrounding the leading clerical figures of Shiʿism.
GDP	Gross Domestic Product.
GNP	Gross National Product.
IAEA	International Atomic Energy Agency.
ICP	Iraqi Communist Party. Formed in 1934.
IGC	Iraqi Governing Council. Appointed by CPA to provide advice on governing Iraq between 13 July 2004 and 1 June 2005.
IIG	Interim Iraqi Government. Formed after the elections of 30 January 2005. Replaced on 3 May 2005 by the Iraqi Transitional Government. Dr Iyad Allawi served as prime minister with Ghazi Al-Yawer appointed president.
IIP	Iraqi Islamist Party. Sunni Arab Islamist party. Headed by Muhsin Abdel Hamid until July 2004, then by Tariq Al-Hashemi.
IKF	Iraqi Kurdistan Front. Political front of leading Kurdish parties in Iraq formed in the late 1980s.
IMK	Islamic Movement of Kurdistan. Kurdish Islamist party.
INA	Iraqi National Accord. Opposition political party from the 1990s, representing dissident figures from the Baʿth Party and the Iraqi military. Led by Dr Iyad Allawi.

INC — Iraqi National Congress. Opposition political party from the 1990s, forming an umbrella movement. Headed by Dr Ahmed Chalabi.

IRGC — Iranian Revolutionary Guards' Corp, otherwise known as *Sepah* or *Pasdaran*.

IS — Islamic State, or *al-Dawla al-Islamiyya*. Proclaimed in June 2014 by Abu Bakr al-Baghdadi as the Caliphate.

ISF — Iraqi Security Forces.

ISI — Islamic State of Iraq, or *Dawlat al-Iraq al-Islamiyyah*. Formed in October 2006 from AQI and other Sunni insurgent groups. Led at first by Abu Omar al-Baghdadi, then Abu Ayyub al-Masri, and then Abu Bakr al-Baghdadi, from 2010.

ISIS — Islamic State of Iraq and al-Sham, or *al-Dawla al-Islamiyya fi al-Iraq wa al-Sham*, formed in 2013, following an announcement by ISI leader Abu Bakr al-Baghdadi of the merger of ISI with the ISI off-shoot in Syria, *Jabhat al-Nusra*.

ISCI — Islamic Supreme Council of Iraq, previously SCIRI (the Supreme Council for the Islamic Revolution in Iraq), and consistently known as 'al-majlis' (the Council). Formed in Tehran in 1982 to bring together Shiʿi opposition groups in Iraq. Headed by Sayyed Ammar al-Hakim.

JRTN	Jaish al-Rijal al-Tarika al-Naqshabandiyya. Translated as the Army of the Men of the Naqshabandiyya Order, the JRTN emerged as one of several Baʿthist insurgency groups established in the summer of 2003 following the invasion of Iraq. They came to public prominence in 2006, following the execution of Saddam Hussein. Linked to Saddam's former deputy, Izzet Ibrahim al-Douri, the group entered an uneasy alliance with ISIS.
KDP	Kurdistan Democratic Party. Established 1946 and remains one of the two main Kurdish political parties. Led by Massoud Barzani.
KIU	Kurdistan Islamic Union. The mainstream Kurdish Islamist party. Formed in 1994.
KNA	Kurdistan National Assembly. The 111-seat parliament of the Kurdistan Region of Iraq.
KRG	Kurdistan Regional Government. The executive authority of the Kurdistan Region of Iraq, based in Erbil.
KRI	Kurdistan Region of Iraq. The federal autonomous region established in 1991 and enshrined in the Constitution of 2005, subsequently expanded in the summer of 2014.
Mahdi Army	The militia movement of Muqtada al-Sadr in 2003 and disbanded in 2008. Replaced by the Peace Companies (*Saraya al-Salam*) in 2014.
marja' al-taqlid	'Source of Emulation'. Honorific name given to the most important religious figures in Shiʿism.

MNF-I	Multi-National Forces Iraq. The name of Coalition forces in Iraq following the 2003 invasion.
mujtahid	A scholar of Islam qualified to interpret Islamic law.
neo-cons	Neo-conservatives. Right-wing ideological grouping in US in early 2000s that advocated interventionist strategies in the Middle East.
OECD	Organization for Economic Cooperation and Development.
OIP	(UN) Office of the Iraq Program.
OPEC	Organization of Petroleum Exporting Countries.
ORHA	Office of Reconstruction and Humanitarian Assistance.
pasdaran	The Iranian Revolutionary Guard Corps, otherwise known as the IRGC.
peshmerga	Kurdish fighters in general, but most often used to refer to the military organizations of the KDP and PUK, and now the Kurdistan Army nominally under the command of the KRG. Literally means 'those who face death'.
PKK	*Parti Karkaren Kurdistan* or Kurdistan Workers' Party. Formed in 1970s by Abdullah Ocalan against the Turkish state.
PUK	Patriotic Union of Kurdistan. One of the two main parties of the Kurdistan Region of Iraq. Formed in 1975 and led by Jalal Talabani, with factions led by Hero Ibrahim, Kosrat Rasoul, and Barham Salih.
PYD	*Partiya Yekitiya Demokrat* or Democratic Union Party. Syrian Kurdish political party formed in 2003 and becoming prominent from 2011. Led by Salih Muslim and Asya Abdullah.

RCC	Revolution's Command Council (Ba'th Party). Highest legislative and executive authority in Iraq before 2003.
SCIRI	Supreme Council for the Islamic Revolution in Iraq, an Iraqi Shi'i opposition movement established in Tehran in 1982, and led by Ayatollah Mohammed Baqr al-Hakim.
SOFA	(US) Status of Forces Agreement.
TAL	Transitional Administrative Law. Interim constitution signed on 8 March 2004 by the IGC.
TNA	Transitional National Assembly. The TNA was elected in January 2005 to legislate during the 'transitional period' during which the permanent constitution of Iraq would be drafted. The TNA remained in place until the formation of the sovereign government of Iraq in May 2006.
UAE	United Arab Emirates.
UAR	United Arab Republic, formed by union of Syria and Egypt in 1958. Collapsed in 1961.
UIA	United Iraqi Alliance. Alliance of Shi'i parties support by Ayatollah Sistani to contest the elections of January 2005.
UNMOVIC	UN Monitoring, Verification and Inspection Commission.
UNSCOM	UN Special Commission.
vilayet	Ottoman territorial division.
WMD	Weapons of Mass Destruction.
YPG	People's Protection Units (*Yekineyen Parastina Gel*). Syrian Kurdish militia of the PYD, operating in the post-2014 period in the KRI. Led by Sipan Hemo.

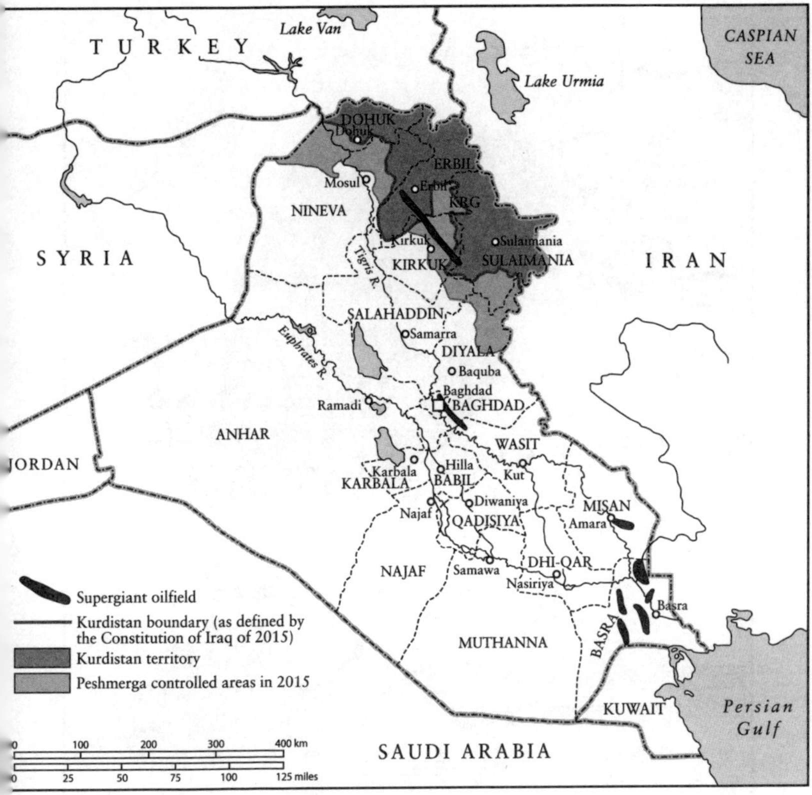

Map 1 Iraq: Governorates and the Kurdistan Region

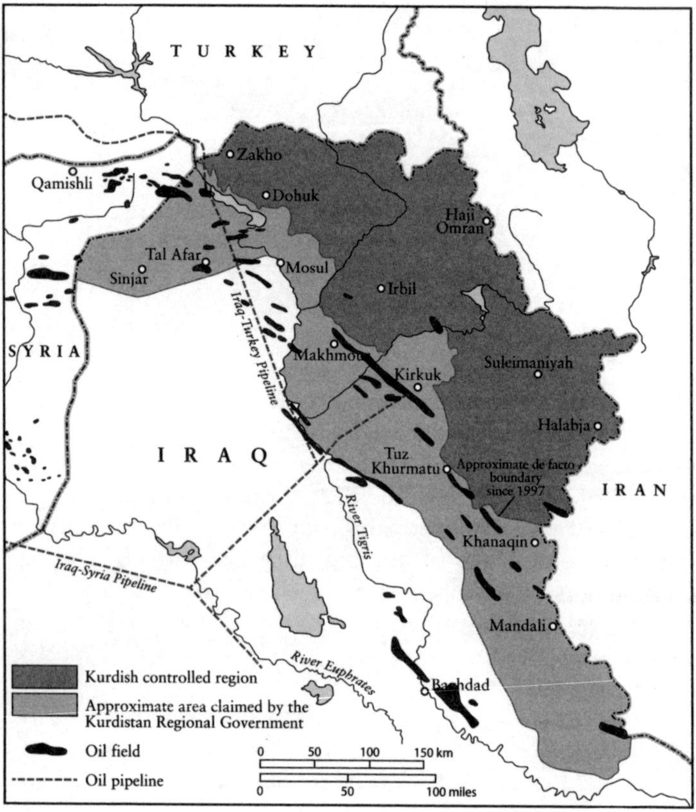

Map 2 The Kurdistan Region of Iraq and the disputed territories, until 2014

Introduction: Artificiality, Identity, Dictatorship and State-Building

The first edition of *Iraq* was published in 2007, at a time when the country was witnessing an unprecedented level of sectarian violence, between Sunnis and Shiʿis. The conclusion to the first edition was bleak, and understandably so, noting the impact on society of the high levels of violence then being inflicted, and the consolidation of patterns of ethno-sectarian political mobilization – dynamics that had been largely kept at bay by Saddam Hussein's invidious and oppressive methods of governing Iraq. In the 'new' Iraq, this new form of mobilization – enshrined in the political elites' approach to dividing power between communities (known as *muhasasa*) – had resulted in the marginalizing and ostracizing of the Sunni Arabs, the empowerment of certain Shiʿi groups, and the protection and relative advancement of the Kurds. The manifestation of this approach was a Sunni insurgency against the state, a backlash by Shiʿis against Sunnis, and the continued isolationism of the Kurds. Together, these dynamics gave credence to a conclusion that pointed to a future for Iraq that would continue to be unstable, dangerous for its inhabitants, and potentially transformative for the wider region.

For a period between 2008 and 2012, however, it seemed that my pessimism had been unwarranted. Recognizing the very real chance that Iraq could collapse further, the US had no choice but to refocus their intervention. They did this by building upon domestic developments that had been happening among certain Sunni tribes. By 2007, the Islamic State of Iraq (ISI) organization had appeared as the latest manifestation of al-Qaeda in Iraq (AQI).[1] Starting in Anbar province, several important Arab tribes and nationalist militias rose up against what was seen as the foreign-fighter dominated ISI. What became known as the Awakening Movement (*harakat al-sahwat al-Iraq*), or the Sons of Iraq (*abna al-Iraq*), presented the US with conveniently placed local allies that could be co-opted to provide local solutions for local problems. Combined with a 'surge' of US forces into Anbar province and Baghdad and the unrelenting targeting of 'irreconcilable' insurgents by the US military (see Woodward 2008), it seemed that the objective of the US government – to establish a 'democratic federal Iraq that can govern itself, defend itself, and sustain itself, and is an ally in the War on Terror' was being achieved.[2]

For a time, specifically between 2008 and mid-2011, it seemed that Iraq had perhaps turned a corner and at last was beginning to develop in the way envisaged by US planners. Insurgent attacks had lessened, and the institutions of the state seemed to be re-establishing their presence and projecting their authority across the country. But it was not to last. From 2012 onwards, and following the withdrawal of US forces from Iraq at the end of 2011, developments in political life indicated that my bleak analysis of 2007 was more durable than were the short-term realities generated by the much-vaunted US surge and the Sunni Arab awakening. Indeed, it could even be suggested that the long-term consequence of the short-term actions of the US and their Iraqi government counterparts only served to further undermine any remaining sense of cohesion that may have existed between Iraq's communities. Rather than honouring the promises made to the Sunni Arabs by the now departed US, Iraqi Prime Minister Nouri al-Maliki instead began to pursue policies that could be viewed as being sectarian, with Sunni Arab elites across Iraq's northern governorates being targeted for arrest, and with demonstrations being suppressed, often with lethal force. More than any other individual, Maliki has been blamed for the deterioration of Iraqi security and political life in the period following the quelling of the ISI-led insurgency, and his actions created a political and social environment in which a new manifestation of Sunni militancy – this time in the form of the Islamic State of Iraq and al-Sham (ISIS) – would flourish.[3] Not only were Sunni Arabs – many of whom had accepted US patronage and fought against ISI – left marooned by the US withdrawal; they were now targeted by Maliki as potential threats. Meanwhile, those insurgents who had been arrested by the US and entered prison camps such as Camp Bucca – including the future Abu Bakr al-Baghdadi – had become more focused in their aims and networked with each other. They had also become clever – they had learned the reasons for their defeat and what it would take to succeed in the future, not only by reflecting upon their own failings but by understanding the tactics that had been used against them. While the government of Iraq, and even the US and coalition members, had quickly forgotten the counter-insurgency lessons developed in the 2007–8 period, the remnants of ISI had not. Their bringing together of different components – from *jihadists* to Baʿthists to disaffected tribes – combined with a new strategic vision, and benefiting from brutal tactical efficiency, enabled them to return with incredible success in 2014 as ISIS seized control of a vast swathe of land across Sunni-dominated Iraq.

Updating *Iraq* in 2015, there is even less reason to be optimistic than there was in 2007. The integrity of the country has become largely a fictional presentation that is interestingly most tightly adhered to not by Iraqis, but by Western governments that remain wedded to the neat notion of Iraq as it was, rather than what it has become. Inside Iraq, there are at least three distinct regions that exercise de facto if not *de jure* sovereignty. In the north, the Kurdistan Region of Iraq (KRI)[4] has continued with its trajectory of moving from autonomy through to virtual independence, even though the Kurds had still not resolved their difficult economic questions and were very nearly defeated by a ferocious Islamic State (IS) assault that threatened Erbil in August 2014. Then there is the reality of IS. Far from being an ephemeral development that could be quickly defeated, IS has proved to be much more durable, with their operations across Iraq and Syria giving them strategic depth, and with their message of regional and then world domination seemingly resonating loudly among Sunnis of a particular disposition who continued to volunteer to serve the self-proclaimed Caliph. And then there was the Shiʿi south. Largely removed from the troubles north of Baghdad, the Shiʿi-dominated areas increasingly viewed events to the north as taking place in a different country, experiencing considerable discontent that their sons in the Iraqi Security Forces (ISF) and the many different militias were being deployed against IS forces, and being slaughtered in the process. While the ISF struggled against IS, Shiʿi militias re-established themselves not only as powerful military forces in the struggle against the Sunnis, but as political actors in what had now become a highly fragmented Shiʿi political landscape. With their strong links to the Iranian Revolutionary Guards Corp (IRGC), the militias swiftly filled the void left by the collapse of the ISF. In effect, the government of Iraq, now led by Prime Minister Haider al-Abadi, was the government of the country ranging from the northern and western environs of Baghdad, to Basra on the Gulf coast – and even in these places the government did not enjoy sole authority over what should have been competences of the state, and especially with regard to security provision. Across the rest of Iraq, the government was even more challenged, and it could no longer project its power into the domains of IS or the KRI. The question of whether Iraq would devolve into three entities had by now largely been answered – it had done so in a chaotic and violent fashion. Three regions – the Kurdistan Region, the Islamic State, and Baghdad-Basra – had become established around core communal areas and with the borders of them being sharpened by the terrible effects of ethnic cleansing. What was less easy to answer was 'what would happen next'? Would these three regions survive, consolidate and became the de facto reality going forward, or would one or more of them collapse? Would external pressure see a new, federal Iraq emerge in an imagined post-IS landscape, or would IS, against all the odds, survive and become a reality that Baghdad-Basra and the Kurdistan Region would have to accept? If these possibilities seemed far-fetched, they were slightly less so than the prospect of Iraq returning to how it was before the rise of ISIS, with the Shiʿi-dominated government controlling the Arab parts of the country, and the Kurds left to their own devices in the north.

Four Key Debates

How did Iraq get into this position? Why were communities that once lived in relatively peaceful harmony, according to the historical literature on Iraq's society, now subjecting each other to ever increasing levels of brutality and indiscriminate violence?[5] What possible bonds could those attempting to stabilize the situation appeal to in the face of such actions? Unfortunately, the answers to these questions have proved elusive.

Some observers, particularly those who were opposed to the invasion of Iraq in the first place, focused upon the period immediately following the downfall of Saddam's government. For them, the actions of post-Saddam Iraqi governments were responsible for the chaos, but the blame for creating the situation in the first place could be laid squarely on the US and UK for invading Iraq without adequately considering what the consequences of such an action would be. In so doing, the occupying powers were forced to act in an increasingly reactive and myopic manner as they struggled to cope with the post-invasion dynamics. Their reactivity was responsible for the creation – wittingly or unwittingly – of a political system whereby religious and ethnically based parties could thrive (see, for example, Rangwala 2005).

Others, while considering the US government to be responsible for the problems of post-2003 Iraq, viewed the real problem as being an innocent but disastrous failure to implement a pre-designed plan for the 'interim' period during the occupation (see Klingner and Jones 2005: 146).

A further approach was to contextualize what was happening within a wider historical analysis. With regard to recent historical events, the impact of UN-imposed sanctions in the 1990s rightly received attention, with prescient observers warning before 2003 that the profound damage inflicted upon Iraqi society made it difficult to imagine a democratic transition being feasible in the foreseeable future (see Niblock 2001: 219). Casting the historical net further back in time, other commentators delved into Iraq's history to see whether the reasons behind Iraq's turbulent post-Saddam existence could be traced to the policies of the occupiers, or to something deeper, perhaps found within the pathology of the Iraqi state construct itself (see Anderson and Stansfield 2005).

Rather than pursue any one of these foci at the expense of all others, the analytical theme of this book is assembled around four (very) interrelated debates that have been and remain prominent in the expansive discussion about Iraq's formation, history, society, politics and, indeed, future. I refer to these as: (1) the *artificiality debate*; (2) the *identity debate*; (3) the *dictator debate*; and (4) the *state-building and democratization debate*. To expand a little on these titles:

1 The *artificiality debate* focuses upon whether Iraq, at its founding, was an 'artificial' state or not, and, if it was, how the implications of any suggested 'artificiality' at the time of state-building nearly a century ago have affected state-building nearly a century later.
2 The *identity debate* revolves around the nature of identity in Iraq – in essence, what it meant in the past and now means in the present to 'be' an Iraqi. How powerful, as a mobilizing force, is the concept of 'Iraqi nationalism', compared to the power of religious association and ethnic solidarity? What were the causative factors of the reappearance of communal identities? Indeed, had they ever been hidden, or had they been merely glossed-over by the combined effect of the transformative nature of modernity with the confining strictures of Saddam's government?
3 The *dictator debate* addresses the nature of political authority in Iraq, and questions how and why the modern history of Iraq has been characterized by the involvement of the military in political life, and the reasons behind

Iraq's succumbing to an authoritarian method of governance that culminates with the totalitarian Ba'thist regime dominated by the person of Saddam Hussein. Is the authoritarian/totalitarian state merely an unfortunate, anomalous, development in the history of Iraq and need not have happened? Is there something that predisposes the Iraqi state to being dictatorial in nature, or was this development a reaction to external pressures and influences? Perhaps the most important question to ask is what was the impact upon Iraqi society of decades of non-democratic politics and, at times, brutal and omnipotent state control?

4 The *state-building and democratization debate* in effect attempts to synthesize the arguments presented in the preceding three debates, and focuses upon the mechanics of state-building in plural societies and/or countries emerging from under the shadow of authoritarianism.

Together, the four debates inform our understanding of why, since the removal of Saddam's regime, Iraqi political life has been dominated by actors and organizations that are mobilized in terms of religious affiliation, ethnic origin or tribal association (and, at times, combinations of two or more of these), rather than secular nationalism or class-based identities that encompass all of Iraq's peoples inclusively. They also allow us to understand how and why the building blocks of civil war began to coalesce in the post-2003 environment, and why they re-established themselves so powerfully in the post-2011 period. It is now clear that the prevailing political forces in Iraq would seem to be those associated with (a) Shi'i religious trends, (b) the Kurdish nationalist agenda and (c) a 'Sunni Arab' position that has formed mainly in reaction to the first two forces, and which has now been overshadowed by IS. Other communal poles are also apparent within the Turkmen and Christian (Chaldo-Assyrian communities). None of these groups may be considered cohesive in terms of internal dynamics and even aims (with the Shi'i religious establishment divided between different poles of authority; the Kurds notoriously politically divided; and the Sunni Arab insurgency split between ex-Baʿthists, neo-Baʿthists and an array of Islamist groups), but, even so, their very existence is evidence of different conceptions existing within Iraq's society that promote contending, and at times exclusive, visions of the future of the country. The four debates give a sense of the arguments that have been forwarded to explain how these visions have been formed, and why Iraqi political life developed as it has.

Book Outline

The purpose of this book is to provide a 'thematic' political history of Iraq. As such, the chapters proceed in chronological order, but with one of the four 'key' debates appearing at the appropriate moment.

The 'modern' history of Iraq commences in Chapter 2 with an outline of the *artificiality debate* – i.e., what is meant by the phrase that 'Iraq is artificial'? The chapter investigates the first episode in state-building in Iraq, and considers the reasons why Iraq was created in the aftermath of the First World War, how its territorial parameters were identified, and how the British set about constructing the state. It is argued that many of the attributes of the Iraqi state can be understood by considering how the British structured it to begin with, and then how British advisors attempted to influence Iraqi affairs in subsequent years. I contend that the British designed a political system that had the potential to nurture increasingly authoritarian approaches to government. But it was also the British that acted to make this potential into a reality, by continually meddling in Iraq's affairs and provoking a reaction in the form of a nationalist movement.

Chapter 3 investigates what is one of the most contentious of issues when discussing modern Iraq, and that is how Iraqis identify themselves, and how they are identified by others. The *identity debate* considers how political mobilization in Iraq has been discussed primarily in Western academic literature, and presents the two most prominent models – the first focusing upon vertical cleavages in society (i.e., forwarding the saliency of communal association, whether sectarian or ethnic), and the second contending that horizontal cleavages of class and socio-economic status are more powerful forces that manage to transcend the ties of religion and ethnicity. Again, I contend that a middle ground, which is in effect a combination of these two approaches to conceptualizing political mobilization in Iraq, has greater explanatory value than either model applied in isolation. The chapter considers the interplay between Iraqi and Arab nationalism, before analysing the nature of the Sunni–Shiʿi divide, the emergence of Kurdish nationalism, and the situation of the Assyrian and Turkmen communities.

The growth of the authoritarian state is taken up in Chapter 4. Beginning with the *dictator debate*, definitions from the political science literature on non-democratic regimes are discussed in order to provide a framework by which Iraq's transition from authoritarianism, to totalitarianism in the 1980s, and back to authoritarianism in the 1990s, can be understood. The essence of the debate itself focuses upon statements made by US government officials, including President George W. Bush, in the run-up to the invasion of Iraq in 2003. An implicit (and, at times, explicit) assumption made at this time was that Saddam Hussein and his immediate circle of supporters were all that stood in the way of Iraq being democratic. Saddam was, therefore, an anomaly that needed to be removed. The counter to this argument is that, far from being anomalous in the history of Iraq, Saddam's regime was, in fact, a product and, logically, the conditions remain for Iraq to continue being governed by authoritarian/totalitarian regimes in the future. The chapter considers the role of the military in political life following the creation of Iraq, and how the military, with a distinctly Arab nationalist world-view, served to further 'communalize' Iraqi society. The reaction of the military to the seemingly omnipresent British imperialist presence is considered, and viewed as a primary causative factor in the rise and consolidation of anti-imperialist and increasingly nationalist sentiment. The chapter concludes by considering the impact of increased oil revenue and the rise of the Baʿth Party – both of which would be important factors in the Iraqi state moving from being authoritarian to totalitarian in nature.

The continued rule of Saddam Hussein is addressed in Chapter 5, which focuses upon the events that would lead to Iraq coming into conflict with Western powers in the 1990s. Iraq's invasion of Iran in 1980 sees the beginning of a period which is still arguably ongoing, as a state of war has hung over the country since 23 September 1980 – the date that Iraqi forces entered Iran. The complexity of the causative factors of Iraq's invasion of Iran are investigated, including the history of the 'trigger' cause of the war – the status of the Shatt al-Arab waterway – and the role played by Kurdish rebel movements that had continued with their sporadic insurgency against the central government since the formation of the state itself. The chapter concludes with an assessment of the political and economic impact of the conflict, and how the invasion of Kuwait can be seen as being a consequence of the problems generated by the inconclusive but hugely destructive war with Iran.

The 1990s are considered in Chapter 6. The reasons why Saddam ordered the invasion of Kuwait are assessed, building upon the findings presented at the end of the previous chapter. The uprisings that then occurred following the expulsion of Iraqi forces from Kuwait by the US-led 'Coalition of the Willing' are then considered, followed by an assessment of the opposition groups that formed in the 1990s. The impact of the brutally comprehensive UN-imposed sanctions upon Iraq are then described, followed by how Saddam managed to survive several US-sponsored coup attempts. The emergence and institutionalization of the Kurdistan Region is also addressed, and the chapter concludes with the events that would lead to the US invasion of Iraq in 2003.

Chapter 7 addresses the political development of Iraq since the removal of Saddam's regime and up until the commencement of the sectarian conflict of 2007. The *state-building and democratization debate* is used to provide a framework for understanding how political scientists and observers viewed the chances of Iraq successfully democratizing after Saddam's demise, and whether the empirical evidence points to a future

Iraq being democratic, authoritarian or even in existence. The chapter covers the major issues that have characterized post-2003 Iraq, including the political process started by the US that culminated with elections in December 2005, the communalization of political life, the emergence of insurgent groups from within the Sunni community, the strengthening of the Kurdistan Region and the appearance of a radical movement in the Shi'i community.

Chapter 8 covers the period in which Iraq could well have been 'saved' following the final roll of the military dice of the US – in the form of 'the surge strategy' that partly led to the defeat of ISI and Sunni Arab insurgencies, and quelled the worse excesses of the Sadr militia, the *Jaish al-Mahdi*. From this point, Iraqi elites could have embraced a new political compact, and perhaps even have recognized the weight of Sunni opinion following the parliamentary elections of 2010 in which *Iraqiyya* – a Sunni-associated block – secured a marginal victory over the *dawlat al-qanun* (State of Law) coalition of incumbent prime minister Nouri al-Maliki. The failure to acknowledge the results of this election – which saw Maliki remain as premier – led to the further and rapid deterioration of inter-communal relations, giving ISIS an atmosphere of grievance that it would then spectacularly exploit. The final substantive chapter addresses the rise of ISIS, presenting it not only as a logical progression of Sunni Arab militancy, but as a learned, informed and considered outcome. The rise of ISIS and then the formation of the Islamic State is considered, before a detailed evaluation of IS actions in the remainder of 2014.

Before all of this, however, it is necessary to delve into history and reflect on Iraq 'before Iraq'. The modern state was not created out of thin air – indeed, the region that was brought together to form Iraq has perhaps the longest and richest civilizational history of anywhere in the world, with events of global importance taking place within its boundaries. To understand Iraq's modern history, we need to appreciate the legacies of ages past.

1 Legacies of Civilizations and Empires

The modern state of Iraq, crafted by imperial powers following the defeat of the Ottoman Empire in the First World War, is merely the latest in a long line of political structures to have existed in and around the watersheds of the rivers Tigris and Euphrates (see Map 1 on page xix for the boundaries of the modern state, and the internal boundaries of the provinces and the Kurdistan Region). Along with China, Egypt and India, Iraq has the oldest heritage of any state in the world. It is home to some of the earliest examples of agricultural activity, and its cities and rural areas alike display the remains of a palimpsest of ancient civilizations. Later, Iraq was the imperial centre of the Abbasid Caliphate, recognized as being the apogee of Islamic civilization and, before becoming part of the territories of the expansive Ottoman Empire, famed for its cosmopolitan sophistication.

Three 'elements of the past' have been most important in forming collective memories in modern Iraq, those being the civilizations of ancient Mesopotamia, the Arab-Islamic conquests and heritage, and the Ottoman Empire (Marr 2004: 3–8). The mechanisms by which these elements have impacted modern Iraq varies, with the most 'direct' influences that have coloured, even structured, modern Iraq being those of Islam and the Ottoman Empire. The Arab-Islamic heritage continues to shape social contours more so than any other dynamic, particularly as its customs and traditions remain the most powerful of the forces governing social activity and interaction. The Ottoman Empire is now consigned to history, but over a period of five centuries was responsible for ordering modern Iraq's political structure, leaving an indelible imprint on Iraq's social and political structures. The influence of ancient civilizations is not so prominent as that of Islam or the Ottoman Empire, but these were and remain a potent force in the building of myths of nationhood. For the classically educated British civil servants and military officers tasked with working in Iraq in the aftermath of the First World War, the ancient civilizations of the region were often better known to them than the living communities they had to deal with. Later, ancient Mesopotamians were also referred to by the architects of the modern Iraqi state as proof of Iraqis' unique heritage, and used as myths in the construction of a nationalist discourse, supporting the contention that it was *primus inter pares* among the Arab states (Davis 2005: 9). Even the US occupiers/liberators of 2003 were not averse to reminding Iraqis of their own heritage. Speaking to cadets of the Police Academy in Baghdad on 1 April 2004, the US 'Administrator' of Iraq, L. Paul Bremer III, opened with an immediate 'civilizational' flourish with '[t]he men and women before me are the line between civilization and barbarism' before going on to inform them that '[c]ivilization started here, in what is now Iraq'.[1]

Ancient Civilizations

This region's emergence as a cradle of civilizations was determined by the geographical conditions of what is now southern and central Iraq. As in the valleys of the Nile and Indus, conditions on the floodplains of the Tigris and Euphrates made cultivation of crops possible (Morozova 2005: 401). But the presence of essential materials – water from the rivers and fertile land deposited by them – was only one part of the equation which would see civilizations emerge and grow. The other part consisted of the challenges presented by the environment, which included extremes of temperature, localized rainfall and the proximity of an arid landscape surrounding the relatively narrow areas adjacent to the rivers. The existence of materials in a region characterized by localized extremes necessitated the development of innovative techniques of environmental management, leading to the growth of civilizations.

The principal collective activity of ancient Mesopotamian societies was the creation and management of an irrigation infrastructure, bringing water from the rivers to cultivable land. How such activities then impacted upon societal development is a subject of debate. The orthodox view envisaged societies dependent upon irrigation ('hydraulic' societies), giving rise to despotic regimes, as a centralized administration was needed to ensure the survival and maintenance of the infrastructure and to enforce the procedures necessary for managing the environment (Wittfogel 1981). However, more recent archaeological investigations contend that irrigation schemes in Mesopotamia were smaller than originally supposed. Instead, it is speculated that Mesopotamian cities came about because of the economic impact of wealth creation from more localized irrigation schemes, rather than the need to manage larger systems (Fernea 1970; Pollack 1999). Cities then drew in residents from the rural areas in waves of rural to urban migration to work in the agricultural sector, producing a surplus that allowed the development and expansion of other non-agricultural activities. Specialists in other fields emerged, including those with high levels of technical skills, those with administrative expertise and those of a more spiritual orientation (Crawford 2004: 18). These city-states became religious centres and locations of important shrines, and provided military protection from predatory neighbours living in the desert areas to the west, or the mountains to the north and east (Yoffee 1995: 284).

Four groups are commonly referred to in the context of Iraq's ancient civilizations. These are the Sumerians, Akkadians, Babylonians and Assyrians. They are mentioned with good reason, as they invented and refined many of the building blocks of modern civilization, including writing, mathematics, accountancy, astronomy, legal codes, organized religion and models of government. A brief outline of the most notable periods and peoples of ancient Mesopotamia will be provided in the following sections. The first section of this overview commences with the Uruk, Sumerian and Akkadian periods. The second section addresses the Babylonian, Assyrian and neo-Babylonian periods. The final section considers the Medes, particularly because Kurds in Iraq view them, however contentiously, as 'their' ancient civilization.

Uruk, Sumeria and Akkad

The antecedents of the ancient Mesopotamians can be found in the agrarian-based societies that appeared in the lower Tigris-Euphrates valley in the sixth millennium BC. Within this region, first referred to by the name Mesopotamia (land between the rivers) by the Greek scholars Polybius and Strabo, physical conditions combined with the ingenuity of the ancient inhabitants to produce an agrarian-based society across Mesopotamia, south-western Iran, the piedmont of the Zagros Mountains and the western shores of the Persian Gulf. This period, known as the Ubaid, was approximately 7,000 years ago and the settlement pattern was characterized by small village communities and, later in the millennium, towns. From the Ubaid developed the wide-ranging Uruk culture between 4,000 and 3,000 BC. This period witnessed advances in agriculture, the invention of writing and the establishment of the first legal systems (Simons 1994: 113; Marr 2004: 4). Other equally important developments that occurred during this period include the emergence of armies and of organized warfare (Crawford 2004: 17). The period culminated in the rise and then expansion of Uruk culture into areas of modern northern Iraq and Syria, the foothills of north-eastern Iraq, and neighbouring parts of modern Turkey and Iran in the fourth millennium BC (Rothman 2001 5–9).

Urbanization increased throughout the period, and city-states were founded in the land of Sumer, in Babylonia, and even west of the Euphrates towards the Mediterranean Sea. The Sumerian city-states that emerged from 3,000 BC onwards included Ur, Eridu, Uruk, Larsa, Lagash, Nippur and Nisin. These cities were composed of large urban centres with a surrounding hinterland, and were ruled by hereditary dynasties which also had associated religious authority. Sumerian scholars developed the science of mathematics and astronomy, and invented the wheel, but perhaps their greatest contribution was the further development and codification of writing. Their 'cuneiform' system, whereby clay tablets carried wedge-shaped imprints made by a stylus, facilitated the accumulation of a wide body of knowledge and literature.[2]

Despite these advances, the political scene on the Mesopotamian plain was characterized not by a unified political structure, but by 'individual city-states forming alliances and breaking them in an ever-changing kaleidoscope' (Crawford 2004: 28). Each of these cities was wholly dependent upon securing a reliable water supply, thus competition and conflict ensued over access to resources. Fractured and politically disparate, the Sumerian city-states fell to the Akkadian king Sargon in 2370 BC, who then unified Mesopotamia under his rule. But the Sargonic period of centralized authority ended as abruptly as it began. Following internal decline and chronic rebellions, centralized control over Mesopotamia collapsed following the infiltration of the land by foreign tribes, and particularly 'the hordes of the Gutium' (possibly the 'Quti' – the speculated antecedents of the Kurds) from the Zagros Mountains (Postgate 1994: 41; Crawford 2004: 34).[3] The final episode in the history of the Sumerian period is the dominance of the city of Ur from 2100 BC. Under the Ur dynasty (known as 'Ur III'), a vast trading network again evolved with links into Anatolia, Persia, Armenia, India, Egypt and Lebanon (Bossuyt et. al. 2001: 375). In addition to being the imperial centre of the age, Ur was also the starting point for the monotheistic religions of the modern era when, in approximately 1850 BC, Abram (later to be known as Abraham) left with his followers for the land of Canaan, in today's Israel, believing that God had promised it to him and his descendants.

Babylonia and Assyria

The Ur dynasty fell primarily due to the resistance of the peoples of the city-states to the 'enormous bureaucratic pyramid' which had been established to control communal and private action, and opposition was further fuelled by declines in agricultural production (Yoffee 1995: 295). Individual city-states reclaimed their local authority, but no supreme political power emerged. Instead, the region was characterized by shifting alliances and the emergence of two power centres in what is known as the 'Old Babylonian' period (*c.*2000–1600 BC). In the north, the Akkadians exercised control from Babylon, while in the south Larsa was the predominant city among the city-states. The Babylonian king Hammurabi unified the two regions, but, again, a centralized bureaucratic structure struggled to maintain its mastery over the entire realm. The Babylonians continued with the Sumerian and Akkadian practice of monarchical rule and also introduced taxation and military conscription as part of a wider process of administrative centralization. Unlike the previous Sumerian system, which was characterized in its latter years by a patchwork of authority held by individual city-states, power and authority were taken from individual city-states and invested in the monarch, and Hammurabi subjected his provincial governors to rigid royal control (Roux 1980: 189).

Following the sacking of Babylon by the Hittites in 1595 BC, a period of instability again plagued Mesopotamia until the ascendancy of the Assyrians. A Semitic people from the northern areas of Mesopotamia, the Assyrians had previously attempted to form an independent entity, only to be ruthlessly crushed by Hammurabi (Yoffee 1995: 299). From approximately 1300 BC to 600 BC, the Assyrian state controlled the trading networks of Mesopotamia from four cities – Assur, Arbela (modern-day Erbil), Kalakh (Nimrod) and the capital Nineveh (near Mosul) – and ultimately dominated the Middle East from Iran to Egypt (Bagg 2000: 302). The Assyrians have the reputation of being the 'bad boys' of ancient Mesopotamian history, which stems from the value placed by Assyrian leaders on the pursuit of warfare, and the manner in which the Assyrians have been depicted in the Bible (Machinist 1983: 722). Assyria's small armies certainly enjoyed unprecedented success on the battlefield. However, this martial proclivity was also matched by developments in the civil arena. New settlements were founded, with canals and water-supply features requiring more advanced technological approaches than had been needed in Sumer and Babylon (Bagg 2000: 309–10).

However, the management of the empire proved to be problematic, with the Assyrian state ultimately collapsing under the pressure of attacks from an alliance of the Medes (to the north) and the Babylonians (to the south) in 609 BC. The previously subordinated kingdom of Babylonia became the dominant power of Mesopotamia, with the Medes establishing their hegemony in the Zagros Mountains and the Iranian plateau (Zawadzki 1988; Brown 1986: 108). While this neo-Babylonian era was short-lived, lasting little more than a century, it produced the most famous of the kings of Mesopotamia, Nebuchadnezzar (605–562 BC), noted primarily for the construction of the hanging gardens of Babylon and the conquest of Judah in 586 BC.

Media and Persia

When considering the legacies of ancient civilizations, it is necessary to make an addition to the regular canon of Sumer, Babylon and Assyria. For the Kurds of Iraq, the civilizations of the Zagros and Taurus mountain ranges are of more relevance in terms of legacies and myths of nation than those of Mesopotamia. But the origins of the peoples of the Zagros are again vague and we are dependent upon much of what we know from evidence found in the archaeological records, and in the writings of Mesopotamian empires that had contact with these peoples. The 'Quti', which may be the earliest version of the word 'Kurd' (Elphinston 1946: 92), existed as one of several kingdoms in the Zagros, and by the end of the third millennium BC had succeeded in uniting many of the city-states of the mountains, launching attacks against Akkad and Sumer. By around 1500 BC, a new homogenizing force was arriving from the east with the westward movement of Indo-European tribes, bringing with them a new language from Central Asia and the Indian subcontinent.

These tribes were the forerunners of the Medes and the Persians (Diakonoff 1985: 48–9).

As the Assyrian empire expanded north into the Zagros, it came into contact with these Median tribes from *c.*835 BC (Brown 1986: 110). However, the Medes proved a force to be reckoned with. A chiefdom centred on Ecbatana and led by Cyaxares moved to unify the Medes and, in alliance with the Babylonians, crushed the Assyrians. The history of the Medes then becomes merged with that of the Persians, following the rise of Cyrus the Great, the founder of the Persian Empire. Originally a vassal of the last king of the Medes, Cyrus organized a power-base in Persia among his ruling family, the Achaemids, and formed alliances with other Persian tribes before defeating the Medes (Young 1988: 29–31). Within twenty-five years (550–525 BC), the Persians had conquered the rest of the region, including Babylon and, by 486 BC, controlled a region ranging from Macedon to Egypt and across Mesopotamia to India, with the largest empire the world had ever seen.

The Islamic Conquest

On the eve of the Muslim conquest of the third decade of the seventh century AD, Iraq's population reflected the diverse legacies of previous empires. Governed by the Persian Sasanids for centuries, semi-autonomous Arab tribes roamed the deserts, the descendants of the Medes – the Kurds – lived in the mountains, and pockets of Greeks, Indians and Africans were scattered across the region (Donner 1981: 168). Religious beliefs were equally diverse. The majority religion was Nestorian Christianity, but Jewish communities were found throughout the country, and Zoroastrianism was common among the Persians and Kurds (Abdullah 2003: 3). Islam, with its revelations in Arabic, was a strongly homogenizing tendency both in terms of belief structure and language. Indeed, perhaps because the conquest turned out to be permanent, the event is seen as an historical watershed between the ancient and medieval histories of Iraq (and, indeed, the wider western Asian region). But the watershed is perhaps not as absolute as is often depicted. Rather than a whole-scale change occurring in a short period of time, many of the patterns of socio-political and economic interaction established before the rise of Islam continued to exist under Muslim rule (Morony 1984: 4).

This section will address four aspects of the first half-century of Iraq's Islamic history. First, the rise of Islam and the subsequent conquest of Iraq are outlined. Second, the schism of Islam into its Sunni and Shiʿi components – one of *the* defining moments in the history of both Islam and Iraq – will be described, laying the foundation for discussion in later chapters regarding the nature of sectarian divisions in the modern state. The third area to consider is the rise of the Abbasid Caliphate and the re-emergence of Iraq as the imperial centre of a vast and wealthy empire. The final aspect of Iraq's Islamic history considers the rapid decline of the Abbasid Caliphate and the devastation wrought on Iraqi society by the Mongol invasion of the thirteenth century.

The rise of Islam

The origins of Islam can be traced to the Arabian town of Mecca at the end of the sixth century. Here, Mohammed was born into the small clan of Banu Hashim, which was part of the prominent tribe of the Quraysh (Lapidus 2002: 20). At the age of around forty (*c.*610), Mohammed experienced visions whereby he received the revelations of the word of God, containing the basis of the system of religious and ethical teachings of Islam (Donner 1981: 52–3). Due to opposition in his home town, Mohammed and his followers fled to Medina in 622 (this journey is called the *hijra*, and is the first year in the Muslim calendar) and it is here that the new Islamic state was founded. When compared with the strength of surrounding empires, including those of Byzantium and Persia, the new state was insignificant in size and influence. However, the tying of social and political organization with Mohammed's teachings, combined with an understanding and exploitation of Arab tribal organization, unleashed 'the expansive military potential of the peninsula and generated the Islamic conquest – a phenomenon that transformed the face of the ancient world profoundly and irrevocably' (Donner 1981: 53).

By the time of Mohammed's death in 632, the Muslim state dominated the political affairs of the Arabian peninsula and was increasingly encroaching north into Mesopotamia. Under the leadership of Mohammed's successor, Abu Bakr, the Islamic state consolidated its position among the Arab tribes of Arabia (the *ridda* wars). After this, Muslim armies moved to extend the dominion of Islam over all Arab tribal groups in the region, including those in Syria and Iraq (Donner 1981: 89). Islam's domains expanded not only through conquest. Indeed, the more common method of advancement was through an appeal to Arab kinship and the promise of riches and paradise and, while the progress of the conquest of Iraq included a series of sporadic engagements with Persian Sasanid forces, the more common occurrence was the voluntary conversion of Arab tribes to Islam. The death of Abu Bakr was followed by the accession of Umar as caliph (literally 'successor') in 634. Umar reorganized and reinforced the Muslim forces in Iraq, while the king of the Persians, Yazdegird, was also doing the same with his army. The Persians drew up in battle order against the Muslim army at Qadisiyya in 637, but were comprehensively defeated. With the Persians routed, and Yazdegird forced to flee, Mesopotamia and the mountains beyond quickly succumbed to the victorious Muslims.

The schism in Islam

For as long as the Prophet Mohammed remained alive, his charismatic appeal and strength of character made the issue of who should succeed him irrelevant. However, his sudden death in 632, with no heir apparent immediately obvious, heralded a power struggle in Islam that would ultimately rend the new creed apart. Two groups emerged in the aftermath of Mohammed's death. The first group, who became known as the Sunnis, favoured the election of a caliph by seeking consensus among leaders of the community. The second group believed that only those related to the Prophet could lead the community, and therefore demanded the direct appointment of the Prophet's son-in-law, Ali, due to his ties to Mohammed by blood and marriage. Ali's followers were known as *Shi'at Ali* (supporters of Ali, simplified to Shi'i).

It would take several decades for the Shi'i to see Ali recognized as caliph and he secured the position as late as 656, only to be murdered five years later. The Caliphate then passed out of the Prophet's family to Muawiya, a figure despised by the Shi'i due to his earlier opposition to Ali's reign as caliph (Lapidus 2002: 46–7). After Ali's slaying, the political hopes of the Shi'i focused upon his sons, Hassan and Hussein. The power struggle between the two wings of Islam continued, with Hassan, venerated by the Shi'i as the 'Second Imam' (the first being Ali), being poisoned by the supporters of Muawiya. Following the succession of Muawiya by his son, Yazid, in 680, the Shi'i of Kufa in Iraq seized the opportunity to attempt to restore the Caliphate back to the house of Ali. Messages were sent to Hussein in Mecca, encouraging him to lead his followers in revolt. Unfortunately for the Shi'i, he never reached Kufa. Instead, he and his small band of followers were intercepted by Yazid's forces at Karbala, in present-day Iraq, where Hussein was killed.

Leadership of the Shi'i community remained with Hussein's descendants, known as 'Imams', and the line of the Imams numbers twelve since the death of Mohammad (hence their name of 'Twelver' Shi'i). The Shi'i believe that the 'Twelfth Imam' (Mohammad al-Mahdi) was taken by God in 874 and concealed in order to prevent his murder by the Sunnis. The Hidden Imam, according to Shi'i teaching, will then return as the *Mahdi* – the one guided by God – who will bring about the final judgement (Pinault 1992: 6). In the temporary absence of the Hidden Imam, responsibility for leading the community fell to the *ulama* (religious community). Respected individuals recognized by the *ulama* as significantly learned continue to bear the title of *mujtahid*, denoting their capability to apply Islamic law to specific issues. Shi'i believers follow the teaching and guidance of prominent *mujtahids*, who are known as the *marja' al-taqlid* (source of emulation).

These figures sit at the pinnacle of the Shi'i religious establishment, bearing the title Ayatollah (literally, sign of God).

The Abbasid Caliphate

The early notion that Islam would introduce a new and better society based upon Muslim credentials, rather than upon the pre-Islamic distinctions of tribal status and wealth, was rapidly forgotten in the years following the conquest of Iraq. Instead of equality existing in all parts of the Caliphate, a situation emerged which marginalized those in the periphery. The seizure of the Caliphate by the Umayyad family moved the focus of power in Islam away from the Arabian peninsula and to Damascus where fortunes were made by old elites, with questionable Muslim credentials, from the expansion of the empire (Kennedy 1981: 35–6). Arab and non-Arab Muslims alike began to oppose the dominance of the Umayyads. Objections to their rule ranged from corruption and mismanagement, through to the fact that they were not related to the Prophet. Following a series of rebellions in Iraq, the Abbasid family emerged as the main focus of opposition to the Umayyads. Benefiting from being linked to the Prophet's family, with a strong following in Khurasan and Persia, and having had a prominent position in pre-Islamic Arabia, the Abbasids defeated the Umayyads first at Kufa, and then definitively in February 750 at a battle held near the banks of the River Zab in northern Iraq. With the rise of the Abbasids, Iraq was no longer the marginal periphery of the Islamic caliphate. Instead, it became its dynamic core (Kennedy 2004: 10).

The Abbasid period lasted until 945, and is considered to be a golden age in the history of Iraq. An indicator of the levels of prosperity enjoyed in this period is the fact that after only 150 years of Abbasid rule, the population of Iraq had grown to 20 million, which is comparable to today's estimates. Perhaps the greatest achievement of the Abbasids is that of Baghdad itself. Planned by Caliph Mansur and founded in 762 on the banks of the Tigris, Baghdad was built for several reasons. First, there was a need to construct a fortress – Iraq remained a troubled place even in this golden age. Second, there was a desire to build a new capital to demonstrate the identity and prestige of the dynasty and, third, a new city was needed in order to accommodate the many non-Arab Khorasani and Persian loyalists of the Abbasids, who could not be accommodated elsewhere (Kennedy 1981: 86). Also, the fact that Iraq had earned a reputation for opposing the deposed Umayyad dynasty, and supporting the succession of the family of the Prophet, heightened the desire to locate the new capital in Iraq. By the end of the century, it is estimated that Baghdad's population had already reached half a million and had increased to a million and a half by the end of the tenth century, making it the imperial centre of a vast and wealthy empire.

The golden period of the Abbasid Caliphate was, however, short-lived. From a position of unparalleled prosperity and security under the rulership of Caliph Harun al-Rashid, the empire was torn apart by a struggle for power between his sons, Amin and Ma'mun, following his death in 809. Problems caused by the pressures of a rapidly growing urban population also undermined the cohesiveness of Abbasid society. Fragmented and weakened, resurgent neighbouring powers began to challenge the hegemony of the Abbasids with increasing and notable success. In 945, Iraq again fell under the control of a Persian power (the Buwayhids), which heralded the break-up of the Abbasid empire and the ascendancy of a range of dynasties governing different parts of Iraq. While the Caliphate remained (until 1258, and then, in a diluted form, based in Cairo, until 1516), it would never again be the pre-eminent power. Although the successor dynasties were still Islamic, they now represented local powers previously subordinated under the Abbasids. However, thousands of miles away to the east, the Mongol empire was advancing across the Asian continent. It posed a threat that the now fractured power of the Islamic world could not counter, and eventually visited untold death and destruction upon Iraq and Baghdad.

By the thirteenth century, the Mongols had reached the boundaries of Iraq following the dispatching in 1253 of Ghengiz Khan's brother, Hulago, with instructions to conquer the Islamic lands of the Middle East (Abdullah 2003: 40). Obviously unaware of the brutality visited upon conquered peoples by Mongol invaders, the Abbasid Caliph al-Mustasim snubbed Hulago's demand for his submission. Unperturbed, the Mongols entered Iraq in 1257, reaching Baghdad in January of the following year. After the caliph surrendered the city, following a siege and artillery bombardment, Baghdad was subjected to an orgy of death and destruction in which as many as 100,000 inhabitants were killed and the once shining symbol of the power of the Islamic Empire reduced to ruins. The fall of Islamic Baghdad to a pagan force constituted a watershed in the history of Iraq and of Islam. It was not just the actual defeat that was significant. It was the psychological impact of it that was perhaps even more important. From being an imperial centre, Iraq entered a dark period in which it was no longer the centrepiece of an extensive empire. Instead, it was a defeated backwater and an object of imperial competition.

The Arrival of the Ottoman Empire

Following the sacking of Baghdad in 1258, Iraq became the domain of a medley of different powers of Mongol, Turkic or Persian origin. Under the Mongol 'Il-Khanate', Iraq was part of a region governed from Tabriz in modern-day Iran. Following the demise of the Khanate due to internal factional disputes, Iraq was invaded by Tamer of Samarkand, with Baghdad again subjected to a devastating attack in 1401, even surpassing that of the Mongols in terms of its brutality and destructiveness. In the aftermath of Tamer's assault, a new federation of Turkmen tribes, the Qara Qoyunlu ('Black Sheep'), seized Iraq, and were quickly succeeded by a rival Turkmen federation, the Aq Qoyunlu ('White Sheep').

Imperial competition

Iraq was therefore a region in chaos, but it had also become a geopolitically important prize that attracted the two growing regional powers – the Shiʿi Safavids of Persia, and the Sunni

Ottomans of Anatolia. The Safavid movement emerged in Azerbaijan in the fourteenth century. After capturing the Aq Qoyunlu capital of Tabriz in 1501, the Safavids then conquered Baghdad in 1508, thereby bringing them into contact with the Ottomans, the self-proclaimed leaders of Sunni Islam and the inheritors of the Abbasid's legacy. The Safavids were decisively defeated by the Ottomans at Chaldiran in Azerbaijan in 1514, with northern Iraq falling to the victors soon after. It would still take another twenty years before Baghdad itself fell to the Ottomans but, when Sultan Suleiman the Magnificent entered the city in 1534, three centuries of socio-economic deterioration, political fragmentation and Shi'i predominance were brought to an end. Iraq was about to embark upon nearly four centuries of Ottoman, Sunni-dominated, rule (Abdullah 2003: 60–4).

The period preceding the bringing of Iraq into the Ottoman Empire was one characterized by political instability, with no one power managing to exercise unchallenged control and with changes of rulers occurring often. How the Ottomans therefore managed to break this pattern and maintain their hold not only over Iraq, but the rest of their extensive dominions, over a period of centuries, is therefore an important question to address. Quite simply, the Ottoman Empire owed its longevity to the manner in which it exercised control over its component regions and their subjects. Controlling such a vast empire, stretching from Eastern Europe, across North Africa and the Middle East, and including the seaboards of the Arabian peninsula, strategies appropriate to each localized geopolitical situation had to be pursued in order to maintain the overall integrity of the realm. The empire's durability stemmed from its implicit recognition of the diversity apparent within the realm.

Devolved authority

With regard to Iraq, the Ottomans were concerned about two principal issues. The first was economic, necessitating the continued flow of tribute, taxes and subsidies from Baghdad to Istanbul. The second was geopolitical and was concerned with blocking Safavid penetration into the south-western parts of the empire. These two considerations were influenced by the effects of geography. The immense territorial size of the empire necessitated power to be devolved to controlled (or at least trusted) elites. As such, the Ottoman Empire (before the nineteenth century) was characterized by a strong central state apparatus, and a variable and inconsistent level of influence in the provinces (Nieuwenhuis 1982: 169). This pattern was also mirrored at the level of the regions of the empire, known as *vilayets*. While the sultan was content to leave power in the hands of local elites (including the *mamluks* in Baghdad and prominent families in Mosul), the policy was tempered by the necessity of preventing power centres emerging in the empire, which could potentially threaten the authority of the sultan in the peripheries.[4] The Ottomans therefore operated a shifting system of appointments (to restrict the influence of ambitious regional governors), and stimulated rivalry between groups, including tribes, ethnic actors and social strata. One distinctive product of this approach to governing the empire was the emergence of a diverse and cosmopolitan society and, under the Ottoman *millet* system, religious minorities were able to maintain their unique characteristics, which led 'to a mosaic of strong, distinctive community groups throughout the Mesopotamian region' (Preston 2003: 24–5).

The durability of the Ottoman Empire was undoubtedly assisted by the decentralizing of administrative responsibilities, and the acceptance of societal diversity. However, the Ottomans faced problems other than those of a domestic nature. Particularly from the eighteenth century onwards, European powers, with their large armies, centralized bureaucracies and vigorous economies were perceived by the Ottomans to be covetous of the empire's territory. The Ottomans' attempts to match the advances made by European powers, and their failure to do so, ultimately resulted in the decline of the empire and the exposure of its former territories to the organizing principles of Europe.

2 State Formation, Monarchy and Mandate, 1918–1932

The modern state of Iraq was created after the defeat of the Ottoman Empire in the First World War, but its foundations were rooted in the legacies of preceding centuries. Structures of political authority, patterns of human geography, the interactions of communities and the origins of a class structure are but a few important examples of the Ottoman endowment to the modern state of Iraq.

If Iraq's societal characteristics were founded in the Ottoman period, the development of the relationships between groups would be governed by the new state, and an understanding of the balance between the 'pre-state' and 'state' characteristics and linkages during the formative moments of modern Iraq's establishment is crucial in explaining Iraq's subsequent political development. In many respects, the date of the formation of the Iraqi state provides a division in the academic literature, between those who consider that the modern state merely 'veneered' over tribal and communal identities, and those who contend that the modern Iraqi state 'wrought profound changes' in terms of political culture (Khoury 1997: 308). This is, in essence, the *artificiality debate*.

The Artificiality Debate

The impact of the British in shaping modern Iraq, until now, is second only to that of the Ottomans (Marr 2004: 21). It was the British who invented the state of Iraq and introduced the trappings of a modern government. Along with the creation of the institutions of state, the British also demarcated Iraq's geographical limits, bequeathing its boundaries, which continue to survive into the twenty-first century. Without Britain's interest in the region, itself spurred on by competition with other European powers, it is unlikely that Iraq as we know it today would feature on the map. Indeed, it is fair to say that 'Iraq...owes its existence almost entirely to the constellation of forces among the European imperialist powers at the end of the war' (Wimmer 2002: 172–3).

Even if this is accepted as factually accurate, it still needs to be nuanced; just as Iraqi society following the Islamic conquest continued to be coloured by the legacies of previous decades and centuries, the same could be said for the new state. The British architects were still heavily influenced by the legacies of the previous Ottoman systems of government and administration. But, while the British operated in a 'post-Ottoman' environment, they also were responsible for introducing concepts of political organization and approaches to governance previously unheard of in the region. The imposition of what was, in effect, a European model of a centralized state upon the three former Ottoman *vilayet*s (provinces) was in stark contrast to the earlier model of administrative and political organization. With its dual associations of sovereignty and territory, the European concept of 'the state' was something quite different from 'Eastern' conceptions, which viewed the state as being more closely related to the identification of people rather than territory (Kelidar 1993: 317). The imposition of a Western model of governance created significant stresses and strains, particularly with regard to identities and nationalism, and how communities interacted with the institutions of the new state.

Political scientists tend to view the emergence of the state and nationalism as being a distinctly modern phenomenon, with its origins in the melting pot of Western European political developments from the early modern period onwards. The logical progression of Western nation-building then starts out from 'the state', goes through the constitution of a political nation inclusive of all citizens irrespective of class and geographic location, and finally yields cultural homogeneity and cohesion (Péteri 2000: 369). Inherently Eurocentric as a concept, such a progression can only rarely be found in the Middle East region, and not so in Iraq. Instead, modern Middle East states developed not out of the logic of socio-economically driven conditions, but belatedly out of the ruins of empires. They also developed not as a 'melting pot' of peoples brought together within a cohesive national identity, but more as a powder keg of competing aspirations.

Iraq was a powder keg of considerable dimensions, and was certainly not a logical construct in a domestic sense. Indeed, the political and economic lives of the communities of the Ottoman *vilayet*s remained loosely focused upon their major towns of Mosul, Baghdad and Basra, with a strong rural–urban divide being evident, and each of these towns existing within quite separate geo-economic and political spheres, with Mosul being linked with Anatolia, and acting as a bridge with Iran; Baghdad looking westward towards Arab lands; and Basra having a notably 'Gulf-centric' identity (Visser 2005: 35). It is clear that the boundaries of Iraq were not drawn by 'some irreducible essence of Iraqi history'. Instead, Iraq was created because of the logics of colonial and imperial power (Tripp 2003 quoted in Gregory 2004: 145). Rather than emerging from the natural interaction of the communities of the region, the Iraqi state was imposed from afar.

Because of this, Iraq is often described as an 'artificial state', one 'cobbled together' by imperial powers. This description is then commonly used as the starting point to explain Iraq's twentieth-century development and, as a logical conclusion to such explanations, that it is Iraq's existential fate to suffer under a succession of non-democratic governments. The territory of Iraq, so this argument tends to go, was brought together in the aftermath of the First World War because of the geopolitical and economic needs of victorious Western powers, and most notably Britain. From a constellation of disassociated peoples living in different geographical spaces, the modern state of Iraq was doomed to succumb to various manifestations of authoritarian rule because this was the only mechanism by which the fractious country could be held together. Taken at face value, and considering recent events, the 'artificiality' argument that Iraq was predestined to fail when authoritarian regimes were no longer heading the state is persuasive.

But it is also contentious, as virtually all states are to some extent, as human-made constructs, artificial. The argument also presupposes that social and political characteristics in twentieth-century Iraq remained in a state of stasis, rather than one of dynamism and development. Why should it be presumed that just because Iraq was 'artificial' in the 1920s, nearly a century of existence as a state has not endowed it with some form of societal cohesiveness? Commenting on this, Hala Fattah acknowledges that the Iraqi state was 'first established under colonial rule and shaped by British design', but then considers that it has 'endured and developed indigenous roots in fertile soil' (Fattah 2003: 49). In other words, the modern state of Iraq has existed for nearly a century, and has created its own realities irrespective of its beginnings. This idea forms the basis of arguments that criticize analyses that focus upon differences in post-Saddam society – with Kamil Mahdi's claim that 'the perceived ethnic tensions are based entirely on the outlook of the occupiers – an outlook that is based on the false notion that Iraqi society is divided and on the verge of civil war' being a particularly good example of this (Mahdi 2005). Fattah's insight into the development of the 'indigenous roots' of the Iraqi state is particularly persuasive, but to then go on to consider the post-2003 ethnic tension to be 'perceived' rather than 'real' is simply counterfactual. Indeed, such claims are difficult to reconcile with the unremitting wave of sectarian and ethnic-based violence that has characterized post-Saddam Iraq.

The question of whether Iraqi society is in fact divided into distinct ethno-sectarian communities keen to exact revenge on each other for centuries-old grievances, or whether the outlooks of the occupiers have been acting in a catalytic manner inducing inter-communal violence in post-2003 Iraq will be more fully addressed in the next chapter, addressing political mobilization in Iraq. The purpose of the present chapter is to analyse and assess the formative forces that resulted in the conception of the state of Iraq in the early twentieth century, and identify how decisions made a hundred years ago may or may not be impacting upon events today.

The Decline and Fall of the Ottoman Empire

It had not gone unnoticed in Western capitals that the once mighty Ottoman Empire had been struggling to compete with neighbouring powers in Europe for some time. Similarly, the sultan also viewed the aspirations of European powers as covetous of his empire's territory. Indeed, his concerns were well-founded. The proximity of the empire to Europe and to European imperial possessions (and especially British India) raised geopolitical interest and concerns among European capitals, as changes in the political map of the Ottoman Empire could have profound ramifications for the balance of power in Europe itself. Of particular interest to the British were the overt aspirations of Russia. Intense competition between Britain and Russia had developed over the question of influence in Central Asia in the nineteenth century. The suspicion engendered by this competition was quickly transferred to the Middle East as Russian interest in a Mediterranean–Persian Gulf railroad concession and a trans-Persian railway to the Gulf became apparent (Patton 1963: 9). By the turn of the twentieth century, Britain's stated policy was to dominate the Gulf to prevent Russia securing a warm-water port on its shores. The possible demise of the Ottoman Empire was an event that the British could therefore not ignore.

The political organization of the Ottoman Empire was of a complex and fragmented nature, and this was particularly so in Iraq. Existing in the borderlands between two competing empires (the Ottomans and the Safavids), the political landscape was shifting and unfixed, and power in these remote areas was often localized (Tripp 2000: 8). From the sixteenth century, while the sovereignty of the Ottoman sultan was acknowledged, the political and military elite of the provinces of Basra, Baghdad and Mosul (and particularly the *mamluk* pashas) existed virtually autonomously from their imperial masters. By the end of the seventeenth century, power throughout the empire was exercised by local, rather than central, powers partly due to political realities within the empire, but also due to the interaction of the empire with European powers. Caught in draining competitions in Europe, the Ottoman government was unable to maintain loyal military forces across the empire's provinces, the result being that local leaders, with local interests and local militias, filled the vacuum (Nieuwenhuis 1982: 34; Salman 1992: 43). European powers, viewing what they considered to be a chaotic devolution of power within the Ottoman Empire, formed the opinion that it was weak, internally divided and on the verge of collapse. Imagining what would happen if it ceased to exist as a political entity became an increasingly common pastime in the capital cities of Europe.[1]

From the seventeenth century onwards, the Ottoman state was struggling to maintain its authority over the diverse peoples and regions of its empire, while attempting to match the advances of European states and counter their territorial designs at the fringes of the empire. The Ottomans had good reason to be worried. By the mid-nineteenth century, the British presence in the Gulf was looking ominously northwards towards Basra and Baghdad. Royal Navy warships patrolled the Gulf, and many local sheikhdoms had signed protective agreements with the government of British India (Çetinsaya 2003: 194). Even more sensitive for the embattled Ottomans was the competition over Balkan lands, with the 'First Serbian Uprising' (1804–13) and the Greek Revolution (1821–30) both bringing the empire into confrontation with a range of rapidly industrializing European powers, while Russia remained determined to secure access to the Mediterranean by annexing the Straits of the Bosphorus (Meriage 1978; Hurewitz 1962).

It was a distinctly uneven competition and, by the nineteenth century, the Ottoman Empire was seen as being increasingly weak when compared with the powerful European states, with their centralized administrations, large armies and extensive overseas possessions. In a bid to redress this perceived weakening, the Ottoman government of Sultan Mahmud II (1808–39) embarked upon a reform of the administrative structure of the empire alongside a reordering of its military forces (Tripp 2000: 13–14).[2] Known as the *Nizam-i Cedid* (New Order), and developing upon earlier reforms undertaken in the eighteenth century, these reforms sought to centralize power in the hands of the sultan and curb the activities of provincial governors, including those in the provinces of Iraq (Karpat 1972: 245). By 1834, Ottoman authority was firmly re-established in its imperial outposts, ending the rule of the *mamluks* in Baghdad and Basra, and removing the Jalili family of Mosul from its position of dominance. The Ottoman government then embarked upon a series of extensive reforms (the *Tanzimat*), in an attempt to rationalize landholding, administration, conscription, law and public education, again in response to the perceived weakness of the empire when confronted by European powers. However, rather than unifying the empire, the piecemeal manner in which the reforms were implemented served to further fragment political and social structures (Tripp 2000: 14–17).

Serious though these domestic problems were, the Ottoman government still had to contend with acute external threats. With regard to the territories of the northern Gulf, the continuing spread of British influence caused serious concern in Constantinople. Sultan Abdulhamid remained suspicious of British designs on Iraq and, following the Ottoman defeat in the 1877 war with Russia, Britain's perceived failure to assist the Ottomans was taken as proof that Britain had designs upon Ottoman territory, and particularly on the three provinces of Iraq. Following serious confrontations with the British over Kuwait (1896–1902) and disputes in the Red Sea, the Ottoman government was firmly of the belief that Britain wished to annex Iraq and make it into 'a permanent source of wealth for the British Empire, like Egypt' (Çetinsaya 2003: 195–200).

The presence of British forces in the Gulf and the appearance of British representatives in Baghdad were concomitant with the increasing influence of the French in the Levant. Both developments suggested the emergence of a significant geopolitical threat to the continued existence of the empire, but in reality these two European powers viewed the survival of the Ottoman Empire as essential in containing what was perceived to be an expansionist Russia. For France and for Britain, it seemed that the only possible beneficiary of the Ottoman Empire's collapse would be Russia. However, the close links that developed between Constantinople and Berlin in the late nineteenth century, combined with the Ottoman Empire's tense relationship with Russia and inherent suspicion of Britain, made it impossible for them to remain neutral when war was declared in 1914 between Germany and Russia. In October, the Ottoman Empire entered the war as one of the Central Powers, making any notion held by the Entente Powers of seeking to maintain the territorial integrity of the empire redundant.[3] Now, the British in particular realized that the political map of the Middle East would have to be withdrawn, if the Central Powers were defeated, if only to reach some form of accommodation with Russia.

Planning the Carve-Up

The rapid collapse of Europe into war in 1914 changed how the Ottoman Empire was viewed by the British (and, indeed, by other European powers). From merely talking about scenarios and attempting to find ways to shore up its continued existence as a means to prevent Russian expansion, the British now moved to defeat the empire. With the onset of war, Britain moved quickly to defend its position in the Gulf and occupied the Fao peninsula and Basra in November 1914. In a situation which would be mirrored nearly a hundred years later as US forces advanced in Iraq, the British forces proved militarily able to occupy the region, but received relatively little guidance from their political masters in London as to what the political aims were. However, whereas the US military would occupy Iraq in a matter of weeks in 2003, it took the British significantly longer, perhaps because the Mesopotamia campaign was a mere sideshow, in military terms, when compared to the British actions in Europe against Germany and at Gallipoli against Ottoman forces. After taking Basra in 1914, Baghdad only fell to the British in 1917, with Kirkuk succumbing by the summer of 1918. With the capitulation of the Ottoman government, the Armistice of Mudros was signed in 1918, which demanded the surrendering of all Ottoman forces to the British. With this, the British occupied Mosul in November 1918, thereby placing the armistice line on the boundary of the Mosul *vilayet* (Tripp 2000: 32; Busch 1976: 11).

While the British army was in the process of pushing the Ottomans out of Mesopotamia, a game of diplomatic chess was being played between Entente capitals as London, Paris and St Petersburg competed among themselves to gain advantageous strategic positions in order to influence how the spoils of an Ottoman collapse would be distributed. The rapidity with which Europe found itself at war forced the Entente powers into hurried negotiations. The Constantinople Agreement of 1915 was the first of several secret agreements that would be made during the war for the partition of the Ottoman Empire. Russia, which initiated the meetings that led to the agreement, stated her desire to annex Constantinople and the straits in the event of an Entente victory. The British and French accepted this claim, with Britain counter-claiming Persia, the Arabian peninsula and other parts of the Ottoman Empire (Hurewitz 1979: 17).

The negotiations behind the Constantinople Agreement were of considerable concern to the British, as they made it painfully clear that not enough thought had been given to a post-Ottoman scenario, when compared with that of their French and Russian allies. The de Bunsen Report of 1915 was an attempt to rectify this imbalance and laid down the guidelines for later negotiations with allied powers (Hurewitz 1979: 27). The report identified three areas of particular importance, with all of them to some degree related to Britain's control of India (Cohen 1976: 2–3). First, there was a need to maintain Britain's supremacy in the Gulf. Securing Basra was particularly important in this regard, and preventing Baghdad and Mosul from falling under the control of non-Turkish powers was also deemed necessary. Second, Britain had developed extensive commercial interests across Mesopotamia. The British presence in Arabia and the Gulf had become a virtual monopoly by the 1830s, and a large proportion of the trade of Mesopotamia was with British India (Çetinsaya 2003: 194). The de Bunsen Committee saw the preservation of the trade of the region for British merchants, the retention of petroleum rights and the use of the region as a granary for India all as British interests (Cohen 1976: 2). The third area focused upon the political organization of Mesopotamia, stating that the Arab inhabitants of the region should not be permitted self-government, but should instead fall under some form of British indirect supervision.

The de Bunsen Report set out the British vision for a post-war Middle East. Later agreements would attempt to make this vision a reality. The report itself still clung to the view that the continued existence of the Ottoman Empire might be in the interests of Britain. However, with the empire now firmly rooted in an alliance with Germany, there was a need to identify new strategies to further Britain's interests in the event of an Entente victory. Under the guidance of the Foreign Office, the British embarked upon an initiative to draw Arab rebels loyal to the Sharif of Mecca, Hussein, into an alliance with Britain against the Ottoman Empire. The initiative, known as the Hussein-McMahon correspondence, culminated in a 'mutually acceptable military alliance but an ambiguous political understanding' (Hurewitz 1979: 47), but was enough for the Arab revolt against the Ottomans to begin.

The Husayn-McMahon correspondence was matched, and even contradicted, by secret tripartite diplomacy between the British, French and Russians in October 1915. On 3 January 1916, Sir Mark Sykes, François Georges-Picot and Sergei Sazonov signed an agreement that planned for the full-scale partition of the Ottoman Empire. The Sykes-Picot Agreement, as it became known, saw Syria and the Mosul *vilayet* ceded to French control. As was the case for the British, France had need of Mosul's speculated oil reserves, and now had an agreed diplomatic claim to the area (Fitzgerald 1994: 697). Indeed, Britain's acceptance of France's claim to Mosul suggests that British policy was driven more by the 'traditional' interests of maintaining Persian Gulf security, and particularly against any expected Russian expansion, than by economic factors. However, with Russia withdrawing from the war (and the Sykes-Picot Agreement) due to the internal upheavals caused by the Bolshevik Revolution, the need to have a 'buffer' in between Mesopotamia and an expected Russian-occupied Anatolia had evaporated, and British policymakers soon realized the error of having granted the oilfields of the Mosul *vilayet* to the French (Kent 1976: 13–14). Faced with the reality of a British-occupied Mosul in 1918, the Sykes-Picot boundaries were reworked, with France ceding control of Mosul to the British to ensure an untroubled relationship with Britain in the difficult post-war period, while consolidating her hold over Syria and Lebanon – areas considered by France to be of more strategic importance (for a comprehensive account of this period, see Fromkin 1991: 449–54).

Occupation and Uprising

If we briefly move forward nearly a century to 2003, when the Coalition forces entered Iraq they soon found themselves caught in an inextricably dense web of internal Iraqi political considerations, with regional powers manoeuvring for their own geopolitical gains, and their own policy needs as decided upon in Washington DC and, to a lesser extent, London. Within a matter of months, the presence of Coalition forces was deemed more damaging than beneficial, and the most advanced military forces in the world soon struggled to exert control over Iraq, to the extent that Coalition policymakers were increasingly reduced to reacting to events as they happened, rather than following their own plans and policies. In many ways, the situation was not new but had much in common with the British experience in Iraq during the 1920s, when the British had moved from being, at best, reluctant occupiers following the demise of the Ottoman Empire, to becoming administrators of the three former *vilayet*s of

Baghdad, Basra and Mosul, while facing resistance from considerable segments of Iraq's society, and most notably among the Shiʿi and Kurdish communities.

A further similarity exists between that original event in the 1920s and the twenty-first-century episode of attempted state-building in Iraq. Just as the actions of the US could be viewed as the product of a struggle occurring in Washington between different offices of the US government, most notably the Pentagon on the one hand and the State Department on the other (see Chapter 7), so too could the development of the earlier British policy be similarly viewed. Within Whitehall, several government departments had involvement in foreign-policy construction and the administering of Britain's overseas empire. The two most important of these departments were the Foreign Office (with T. E. Lawrence of the 'Arab Revolt' fame being very influential), advocating some measure of Arab autonomy and supporting the claims of the family of Sherif Hussein of Mecca, and the India Office (with Arnold Wilson, the acting civil commissioner in Baghdad between 1918 and 1920, being particularly prominent) promoting imperial control and sponsoring Sherif Hussein's rival, Abd al-Aziz ibn Saʿud, for hegemony over Arabia (Rothwell 1970: 276–7; Paris 1998: 773).

The differences between the two approaches had a profound effect upon Iraq in the immediate post-First World War years. The views of the India Office, which was the organization tasked with governing Iraq in the aftermath of the war, were formed with reference primarily to India rather than the Arab world, and with a view to incorporating Mesopotamia within the 'Indian' segment of the empire. Due to many Indian Muslims considering Sherif Hussein's revolt against the Ottoman Caliph as apostasy of the worst sort, British viceroys in India pursued a policy aimed at pacifying Indian Muslim sentiment, with attention to Arab sentiment being somewhat secondary to this concern (Paris 1998: 776–7). The result saw India Office officials posted in Iraq pursuing a policy of direct control over the newly occupied territories, with administrative structures based largely upon those refined in India. Previous Ottoman structures of governance were dismantled, and the commonly held belief in the ineptitude of local Arabs in governing themselves led to few of them being appointed to positions of responsibility. Instead, Mesopotamia was divided into political districts, with British political officers administering them. Indians were brought into the army, and the Indian rupee was even introduced as the new unit of currency (Marr 2004: 22). Furthermore, the British set about re-tribalizing Iraqi society. Following the Ottoman *Tanzimat* reforms in the nineteenth century, the prominence of the tribes had been drastically reduced. However, the British experience in India had involved dealing with tribes as a means to create order at relatively little expense, and an identical policy was pursued in Iraq, in both Arab and Kurdish areas. Pliant Arab sheikhs and Kurdish aghas were identified and empowered by British political officers to be responsible for law and order in given regions. But it was a stop-gap measure, with the British desperately hoping that these strategies would stabilize what already appeared to be a very ominous situation. As Kamal Salman poetically notes, '[t]his complex [tribal] system was repaired and improved, much like rebuilding the engine of an old car to allow the owner time to obtain a new one' (1992: 222). However, the British were operating in an environment in which they were not fully familiar. Rather than shoring up the political system, their tinkering had the opposite effect as some Arab sheikhs and Kurdish aghas were empowered, and others were not. The resulting competition that emerged between different tribes created cleavages and enmities between them which only added to the difficulties of governing the region.

This manipulation of the existing socio-political landscape was matched with a misrepresentation to London of the preferences of the indigenous population regarding their own future. The British Civil Administrator, Arnold Wilson, who was himself part of the India Office, pursued a range of measures designed to maintain and extend British control over Iraq, including the conducting of a survey (erroneously referred to as a 'plebiscite') aimed at assessing the opinions of notables regarding Iraq's future (Tripp 2000: 37; Yaphe 2004: 26). Wilson presented highly selective, even misleading, findings indicating that there existed a general acceptance of British control. These findings proved unacceptable to Wilson's highly regarded Oriental Secretary, Gertrude Bell, who became a voluble advocate of Iraqis governing themselves, but with British tutelage. Bell, whose influence upon Iraq's political development in the early years of the state is difficult to exaggerate, advised that Arab nationalism was spreading with an unstoppable momentum, and that the British should work with the Sunni nationalists rather than the more reactionary Shiʿi clerics (Yaphe 2004: 27).[4] In so doing, she assisted in creating a pattern of Sunni-dominated governments which would characterize Iraq throughout the remainder of the century.[5]

Sheikh Mahmoud's rebellion

It should have come as no surprise that these approaches to governance did little to endear the British to their new charges. The presence of an occupying force that was perceived to be supercilious in its approach to governance and condescending in its interaction with local communities, which brought in Indian bureaucrats and soldiers to assist in occupying the area while overturning delicate indigenous administrative structures developed over centuries, would soon lead to the local population turning against it. In actuality, opposition to the British presence had existed in Iraq since the first appearance of British forces in 1914. In the north, British forces were initially welcomed by the Kurds. Then, following the occupation of Mosul in 1918, Arnold Wilson was empowered to administer British-controlled Kurdistan. At first, Kurdistan was a relatively unknown quantity for the British and their political and military position in this border region was far from secure. Therefore, as a matter of policy, the British had to gain the support of the local population and take advantage of the anti-Turkish sentiment that characterized the region. But they were not in a position to invest significant resources in this strategy as they were militarily and financially stretched following the exertions of war and, rather than embark upon a full-scale occupation of Kurdistan, the

British instead sought to empower local Kurdish leaders and provide them with political and administrative advice (Eskander 2000: 141). The most notable of these leaders was Sheikh Mahmoud Barzinji. With a history of fighting Turkish forces, and having made notable attempts to negotiate with the British (and also the Russians) during the war on behalf of the Kurds, Sheikh Mahmoud was the obvious candidate for the British to support. He himself had high expectations of the British, believing that they would support Kurdish autonomy, and welcomed to Kurdistan several political officers who counselled their superiors not to ignore the existence of nationalistic sentiments among the Kurds.

However, the plan for an autonomous Kurdistan fell foul to the machinations of the India Office and Commissioner Wilson. As with the Arabs, the British administrators on the ground in Baghdad and Basra (if not in the Mosul *vilayet*) did not believe that the Kurds had the ability to govern themselves, and Wilson embarked upon a strategy of discrediting the notion of an autonomous Kurdish entity to London. Major Noel, the pro-autonomy political officer for Kurdistan, was replaced with Major E. B. Soane, who quickly brought in Indian and Arab officials to replace those of Kurdish origin, while moves were afoot to weaken Kurdish authority in Kirkuk, Suleimaniyya and Erbil. In a bid to preserve his authority in Kurdistan, and to ensure that the forthcoming peace conference would have to discuss the situation in Kurdistan, Sheikh Mahmoud led a revolt against the British, starting on 22 May 1919 in Suleimaniyya. The revolt was quickly suppressed, and Kurdistan was amalgamated with the rest of British-administered Mesopotamia, but the fire of Kurdish nationalism had been ignited and would remain a perennial problem for successive Iraqi governments in the decades to come.

The 1920 revolt

Meanwhile, in Mesopotamia, many Arab tribes, and particularly those of the mid-Euphrates, objected to the existence of a non-Muslim administration in the region, and Turkish agitators were highly effective in encouraging these tribes to liberate themselves from the British by promising them autonomy when the authority of the sultan was restored (Salman 1992: 242–4). Such feelings of resistance were not only the preserve of the tribes, however. In Baghdad, a secret Arab nationalist organization had formed, with its support base consisting of Arab military officers of the former Ottoman army. Known as *al-'Ahd al-Iraqi*, it was founded in 1918 and sought the outright independence of Iraq (which they defined as the provinces of Basra, Baghdad and Mosul), within a framework of Arab unity and headed by Sharif Hussein (Tripp 2000: 36).

Considerable antipathy therefore existed against the British and could be found in many segments of Iraq's society. The spark which ignited these sentiments into a full-scale revolt was the announcement in April 1920, at the San Remo Conference, that the League of Nations had assigned a mandate for Britain and France over the lands of the ex-Ottoman Empire, with Britain's responsibility being the territory of Iraq. The mandate system was, in effect, a codification of the 'white man's burden' (see Davidson 1933 for a contemporary view of the mandate system), with Article 22 of the League of Nation's Covenant describing a mandate system as dealing with:

> those colonies and territories which as a consequence of the late war have ceased to be under the sovereignty of the States which formerly governed them and which are inhabited by people not yet able to stand by themselves under the strenuous conditions of the modern world.

To many of those peoples living in such colonies and territories, including those in Iraq, the mandate system appeared to be a ploy by which the imperial (non-Muslim) powers of Britain and France could consolidate their colonial dominance and integrate these newly occupied lands fully into their respective empires. The fact that the League of Nations as the awarding body was itself dominated by Britain and France only served to strengthen this belief.

The Iraqi Revolt of 1920 is often considered to be the debut of modern Iraqi nationalism, and a '"primitive", but genuine, national response to fundamental dislocations in the political and socio-economic adaptation of the tribally organized rural Iraqis' (Vinogradov 1972: 125). Rather than being a singular revolt, however, it is perhaps more correct to refer to plural happenings of rebellion against the British. There were, in effect, three interrelated cores to the revolt, these being Arab nationalist, a Shi'i *ulama*-led component (though still Iraqi and Arab nationalist) and disaffected tribal groupings. While having different reasons for rebelling, all were unified against the British occupation, irrespective of their communal affiliation or ideological colouring. As the details of the San Remo Conference became known in Iraq, the different groupings of Iraqis gradually became more coordinated in their activities. Nationalists met with Shi'i *mujtahids* in Najaf (who were committed to the independence cause), and leaflets printed in Najaf and Baghdad were distributed among the tribes to prepare them to rebel against the British.

Despite these activities, opposition in Iraq to the British occupation was still fragmented and localized in nature, although nationalist activity was now extensive and growing daily since the announcement at San Remo. However, in the atmosphere characterizing Iraq in 1920, it took only an insignificant dispute to begin a revolt that lasted three months, cost 6,000 Iraqi and 400 British lives, and drained £40 million from the British coffers (twice the annual budget allocated for Iraq). It also forced the British to hastily adopt a new policy for the governing of Iraq.

The revolt commenced in the mid-Euphrates area on 2 June when a prominent sheikh refused to pay his taxes to the British and was imprisoned by the local Political Officer (Marr 2004: 23). His imprisonment saw his own tribe revolt, storm the prison and free him, before declaring a rebellion. Fighting quickly spread and, far from being disorganized, the tribal rebels 'displayed courage, coordination and ingenious military tactics', leading British officials to believe that ex-Ottoman officers must have been assisting them (Vinogradov 1972: 136). The British were forced to withdraw quickly from Najaf, with the rebels engaging them across the rural areas of Iraq. Recognizing the severity of the revolt, the British War Minister, Winston Churchill, ordered the Royal Air Force to bomb rebel positions, heralding the beginning of the end for the rebels. Meanwhile, Wilson, increasingly seen as a problematic figure due to his uncompromising policies in Iraq, was replaced on 1 October by the more accommodating Sir Percy Cox. By the end of the year, Karbala and Najaf had surrendered to British forces, as had the rebelling tribes.

Although ultimately unsuccessful, the revolt succeeded in forcing the British to reconsider their position in Iraq. With the approach of the India Office discredited, Cox was now tasked with the terminating of the military administration, the drafting of a constitution and the establishing of a provisional government with an Arab head of state. He quickly established the latter, naming it the Council of State, appointing ‘Abd al-Rahman al-Kaylani as its head. Other notable figures, such as Ja‘far al-Askari, a former Ottoman army officer with a considerable following among Iraq's nationalist groupings, were also selected to be part of the Council (Eppel 2004: 13). This was only a temporary measure, however, with the blueprint for Iraq's future being decided at the Cairo Conference of 1921. It was in Cairo that the ‘three pillars of the Iraqi state were conceived’ (Marr 2004: 24), these being the monarchy, the treaty which would codify Britain's position in Iraq, and the Constitution designed to integrate the peoples of the new state. Although seemingly an understandable approach, aimed at resolving the problems faced by the British in occupying Iraq while also providing a framework in which the interests of both Iraq and Britain could be satisfied, with hindsight the 1920 revolt forced the British to enact a solution which simply did not serve to forge the various segments of Iraqi society into an organic nation, but instead created an entity that would need to be maintained by force for nearly forty years (Vinogradov 1972: 123).

The Cairo Conference

A conference of senior British officials was held in Cairo in March 1921 under the leadership of Winston Churchill, who by now held the senior position of Colonial Secretary. This conference was perhaps the most formative event in creating modern Iraq, but the primary driving force ordering discussions was not the domestic concerns and issues of the peoples of the region, but rather the management of Britain's imperial territories in a time of acute financial difficulty following the exertions of the First World War, and the potential effort involved with administering troublesome territories such as Mesopotamia and Kurdistan. For Churchill, the relative rights or wrongs of having a Hashemite as monarch were secondary to finding a solution which would allow the numbers of troops in Mesopotamia to be reduced, thereby saving millions for the Treasury. However, the commonly held view at the conference, which included Percy Cox, T. E. Lawrence and Gertrude Bell as participants, was that the Hashemite Emir Faisal was the best candidate for the job of ruling Iraq because of his history of leading the Arab Revolt against the Ottomans and his expected ability to galvanize Iraqis, Sunnis and Shiʿis alike, if not Kurds, under his leadership, thereby reducing the need for the British to maintain a large presence to secure the territory. This policy, it was believed, 'would enable the British Army to withdraw and save millions without leaving chaos behind' (Catherwood 2004: 129–30).

The thirty-six-year-old Faisal accepted his nomination, but he still had to go through a process of being elected by Iraqis in order to give him some vestige of legitimacy. The first of many flawed electoral processes in Iraq's modern history occurred in July 1921. A plebiscite was held to impart legitimacy to Faisal's rule, which indicated an astonishing 96 per cent supported his accession. Faisal's real support could not have been anywhere near this figure, particularly as the Kurds did not support him, the Shiʿi *mujtahid*s favoured a theocratic government and the towns of the north, and especially Mosul, remained pro-Turkish in their political outlook (Marr 2004: 25). But Faisal remained from the perspective of the British the best candidate available and, on 27 August 1921, he was installed as Iraq's first king. The real power behind the throne was aptly illustrated, however, by the fact that the national anthem performed as the Iraqi flag was raised was none other than the British anthem 'God Save the King' (Anderson and Stansfield 2004: 15).

King Faisal's position was precarious. With a limited support base in Iraq, and with the Shi'i and the Kurds distinctly unimpressed by the new monarch, Faisal had little choice but to staff his government with those who had served under him during the Arab Revolt against the Ottomans. This cadre of Sharifians were ex-Ottoman army, Arab nationalist and predominantly Sunni, and their appointment to the key offices of the state and military marked the beginning in the Iraqi state (or continuation, if the Ottoman period is considered) of the prevalence of Arab Sunnis in key positions of legislative, executive, judicial and military affairs.

Iraq now had a king, a treaty with Britain and institutions of government, but the precise territorial configuration of the new state had yet to be determined. It was clearly accepted that the provinces of Baghdad and Basra were components of the fledgling Iraqi state, and the borders between Iraq and Najd (to the south) were identified in the Muhammara Agreement of 1922, the Uqair Protocol of 1923 and the Bahra Agreement of 1925. The border with Kuwait was also defined in 1923, even though Iraq continued to claim that Kuwait was in fact part of the *vilayet* of Basra, and therefore part of Iraq (Eppel 2004: 13–14). However, the northernmost of the three former Ottoman *vilayet*s – Mosul – raised a number of important strategic concerns. First, it was readily apparent that the majority population, the Kurds, were far from enamoured with the prospect of being included in the Iraqi state. After enjoying autonomy under the government of Sheikh Mahmoud between 1918 and 1920, then to have their claim for an independent state recognized in the Treaty of Sèvres, the Kurds had begun to realize that the imposition of direct control over their territories by the British, and the lack of recognition of the validity of their demands in European capitals, did not bode well for the future. The final nail in the coffin of Kurdish independence was the emergence of Mustafa Kemal Ataturk's nationalist movement in Turkey, which resulted in the abolition of the Sultanate in November 1922 and, with it, the rejection of the Treaty of Sèvres (Beck 1981: 256).

Replacing Sèvres, the Treaty of Lausanne of July 1923 did not discuss Kurdish independence, but instead saw 'northern' Kurdistan (i.e., the areas north of the Mosul *vilayet*) incorporated into Turkey, with the Mosul *vilayet* falling under the de facto control of British-mandated Iraq (Stivers 1982: 141). The resurgent Turkish government questioned the armistice settlement at the Lausanne Conference and demanded the restoration of the Mosul *vilayet* to Turkey (Lloyd 1926: 104). The situation was complicated by the fact that the British were by now beginning to realize the scale of the oil reserves around Kirkuk, as was the Kemalist government. There was also a strong military logic for including the mountainous province as the northern region of Iraq. Britain, having fought a brutal war, did not have the military resources to defend the flat plains of Mesopotamia from attacks from the north (whether from Turkey, or even Russia). However, it would be much easier to defend Mesopotamia from the mountains, and less costly in terms of manpower (Lloyd 1926: 104). Turkey disputed the inclusion of the Mosul *vilayet* into Iraq, and the matter was referred to the League of Nations. A commission was created to investigate the validity of the cases made by each of the claimants, and it reported its findings in December 1925. Mosul *vilayet* was awarded to Iraq, leaving the League of Nations open to the accusation that it was little more than the plaything of the British and French governments. The commission also finalized the boundary of Iraq and Turkey as running through the heart of Kurdistan, removing the possibility of a Kurdish state materializing in the post-First World War restructuring of the Middle East. By doing so, it encumbered Iraq with a non-Arab population which could not subscribe to the prevailing Arab nationalist tendencies emerging in Baghdad, and which successive Iraqi governments would struggle to either assimilate or coerce into submission.

The New State and Enduring Pathologies

The patterns which would characterize Iraq's political development over the next eighty years could therefore be traced to the immediate post-war period. The introduction of a centralized system of governance and administration was something that went against the experience of the decentralized Ottoman system. The mistrust engendered by the imposition of a new system was compounded by the fact that the majority of the population viewed with suspicion the staffing of the Iraq state with an urban Sunni elite that enjoyed a prominent position due to their involvement in fighting against the Ottoman Empire. The dominance of Iraq by Sunni Arabs was striking. For example, between 1921 and 1936, only five out of fifty-seven ministers were either Shiʿi or Kurdish, and during the entire period of the monarchy (to 1958), the prime minister and ministers of finance, interior, defence and foreign affairs were almost exclusively Sunni (Simons 1994: 195; Anderson and Stansfield 2005: 20). This pattern of Sunni Arab dominance was replicated at the governorate and district level, meaning that the Sunnis dominated out of all proportion to their population size.

Within the military, it is indeed true that many Shiʿi could be found in all branches of the armed forces, yet if the breakdown of the officer corps is considered, the predominance of Sunni Arabs in positions of authority is clear. Again, this was a continuation of the Ottoman pattern, with military officers being trained in specialized military colleges which were located in prominent Sunni cities, and especially Mosul. However, the prevalence of Kurds and Shiʿi in the ranks of the Iraqi army certainly served to imbue a sense of it as being a non-communal organization and symbol of Iraq's unity. It also offered a means of social mobilization. Of the ten Kurds who became significant political actors between 1920 and 1958, all of them owed their success to being associated with the military (Marr 2004).

The British introduction of a policy of empowering pliant tribal leaders to assist the securing of Iraq in the chaotic post-war period saw the tribes emerge as important actors in the new state. The British, and then Faisal, proved to be particularly adept at targeting tribes in order to fracture political opposition to them, and especially within the Shi'i community. By increasing the representation of tribal leaders in parliament (with as many as a fifth of seats reserved for tribal leaders), and by patronizing them with land and resources and empowering them to act as local leaders, a wedge was driven between the Shi'i tribes and the religious establishment, ultimately strengthening the monarchy (Anderson and Stansfield 2005: 21). Driving this policy was the experience of the 1920 revolt, which witnessed the union of the Shi'i religious establishment and Shi'i tribes, and also the bridging of the Sunni–Shi'i cleavage to some extent. These factors, combined with a distrust of the still rebelling Kurds in the north, pushed the Iraqi government into building support bases upon which it could rely, while pursuing a policy of divide-and-rule among communities it viewed with suspicion.

But Iraqi nationalism continued to exist after the ascension of Faisal and during the early years of the state's history. The cause of this nationalism also remained the same, which was the continued involvement of Britain in the affairs of Iraq. The treaty discussions of 1920 and the election of a Constituent Assembly to ratify the treaty were both considered by many to be the machinations of a perfidious imperial power that had no intention of allowing Iraq to ever be independent. The king, the assembly and the treaty were all considered to be creations and impositions of Britain. As such, a vigorous Iraqi nationalism developed in opposition to these developments. The early focal points of nationalist opposition in Iraq were centred upon Shi'i religious leaders. Sunni nationalists felt alienated by the overt Shi'i discourse emanating from the *mujtahid*s, and they preferred the establishment of a secular state, with strong Arab nationalist credentials, which could even exist under temporary British control (Marr 2004: 32). The British, ever more concerned with the ability of the Shiʿi *mujtahids* to cause them serious trouble, exiled the most troublesome clerics to Persia, thereby handing the leadership of the nationalist movement to the Sunnis.

Sunni Arab opposition began in earnest in 1924 and focused upon weakening the power of the king vis-à-vis the cabinet, with the leaders of the opposition objecting to the high proportion of tribal members sitting in the Constituent Assembly. In a move designed to question the sincerity of Britain's commitment to Iraq's development, the nationalists introduced an amendment to the Constitution, requiring members of the Constituent Assembly to be literate. Such a move would have skewed the membership of the assembly heavily over to urban rather than rural Iraqis, thereby weakening the tribal component. Needless to say, the amendment did not pass but the struggle for the control of the assembly continued unabated until the end of the monarchy (Marr 2004: 32).

The End of the Mandate

By the end of the 1920s, opposition towards the government had become more vocal and broadly based than ever before. The new Iraqi prime minister, Nuri al-Saʿid, represented the ascendancy of the Sunni Arab military elite within Iraq. Enjoying the support of the British, Nuri and his cohort of military officers tightened their grip on Iraq. A new era was dawning, however, which would see the end of the mandate and admission into the League of Nations as an independent nation. Under a newly elected Labour government, the British announced new treaty negotiations with Iraq in 1929, with a view to ending the mandate. On 16 November, the new treaty was passed by the Constituent Assembly and, in October 1932, Iraq took its place in the League of Nations as the first mandated state to gain its independence.

But British influence continued to remain in Iraq. The British-nominated Faisal was still the monarch, and presided over a state structure designed and instructed by British advisors. The British government also leased two bases for its military, and, as part of the treaty negotiations, retained a right to use all Iraqi facilities. British advisors and experts also remained in place in Iraq, located at key and sensitive points throughout Iraq's civil and military apparatus. Iraq was further tied to Britain by a series of military agreements, which meant that the training, equipping and development of Iraq's armed forces would be a British-managed affair. This tying of Iraq to Britain would last, according to the terms of the treaty, twenty-five years.

The British had therefore succeeded in holding Iraq together by introducing a system of government dependent upon the continued existence of a pliant monarch and his ability to garner support among Sunni Arab elites. Little had been done to contend with the most serious of problems facing the hastily cobbled together creation of Iraq, which principally revolved around the lack of any unifying consciousness and national identity (Eppel 2004: 21). The heterogeneity of Iraq's society had not been lost on the king. Shortly before his death in 1933, he provided an ominous and accurate analysis of the problem confronting Iraq. He lamented that 'In Iraq…there is still no Iraqi people, but unimaginable masses of human beings, devoid of any patriotic ideal…connected by no common tie, giving ear to evil, prone to anarchy, and perpetually ready to rise against any government whatsoever.' It is the nature of political mobilization among the people of Iraq that will be focused on next, in Chapter 3.

3 Conceptualizing Political Mobilization in Iraq

When considering Iraq in the early years of the twenty-first century, the prevalence of ethnic and sectarian-based identities is startling. Media reports focus almost wholly upon the 'ethnic and confessional' mosaic of Iraq. Regions have come into existence, such as 'Kurdistan' with its obvious ethnic connotation, and others with a particular Shiʿi bent are being mooted for the south of the country.[1] Perhaps most tellingly, Iraq's post-2003 political system is dominated by the politics of identity, with Shiʿi parties of religious orientation competing with Sunni Arab parties of Islamist, tribal and nationalist orientations, or, after 2014, the Islamic State, and with overtly Kurdish nationalist parties now more powerful than ever in the north.

In this chapter, the three principal means of conceptualizing Iraqi political life are outlined. These are: (i) the formation of nationalisms; (ii) the following of religious authorities; and (iii) association with ethnic origin. The discussion commences by considering the interplay between Arab and Iraqi nationalisms. It then continues with an assessment of the position of the Shiʿi, followed by charting the history of the Kurdish national movement. It concludes with an account of the position of the Assyrians and Turkmen in Iraq, communities which both have strong ethnic and religious identity markers. No attempt is made to present a separate assessment of a peculiarly 'Sunni Arab' dimension, the reason for this being that, as the 'dominant nation' in the modern history of Iraq, there was little need for communally based socio-political organizations existing in addition to those of the state (Wimmer 2004: 50).[2] The emergence of Sunni Arab organizations that occurred in the aftermath of Saddam's downfall is considered in Chapter 7.

Whether the emergence of communal politics and a potential ethno-sectarian civil war is a product of Iraq's socio-political history, or is in fact an anomaly caused by dictatorship followed by the effects of US actions (whether planned or accidental), Iraq's future now relies upon the seemingly quixotic task of balancing the demands of Iraq's principal communal groups, namely the Sunni Arabs, Shi'i Arabs and Kurds. While all those participating in Iraq's government vociferously claim to be ardent Iraqi nationalists, each group has a distinct idea of what it is to be an Iraqi, and, indeed, what Iraq should 'be' in the future. A communal, identity-based politics is therefore prevalent in Iraq at present. But has this been the case throughout its modern history, or is it a new feature on the political landscape of Iraq? This is the *identity debate* – in effect, what does it mean to 'be' Iraqi?

The Identity Debate

If the early history of the Iraqi state is considered, it is evident that issues relating to communal identity are not new phenomena. The Kurds rebelled in 1919, and then at regular intervals up to the present; the 1920 rebellion had a notable Shi'i clerical component to it; and the massacre of the Assyrians in 1933 came after their demanding of autonomy, based upon their previous status in the Ottoman Empire. But such problems in these earlier periods are not of the same type as those in evidence today. While I argue that there is now competition *between* (and often within) *groups* for power in the post-2003 period *over who controls the state*, the struggles at the beginning of the twentieth century can more accurately be described as conflict *between communal groups and the state*. Acting as the catalyst for these revolts in the early twentieth century, the state was 'a new centre from which power could be exercised and a new central focus for the segmental societies over which this new power was to be exercised' (Pool 1980: 331), with the new state causing 'people to rethink existing political identities, values and interests. Sometimes these were adapted to serve the state and its rulers; sometimes they were marginalised or suppressed' (Tripp 2000: 1). With the British empowering the Sunni Arabs as the pre-eminent office holders in the state, a 'pathological homogenization' of the state began in earnest (see Rae 2002: 2–5 for a definition of this term). The empowered political community became almost wholly Sunni Arab, and the government was perceived by outsiders to be the political embodiment of that community – a development which 'politicise[d] notions of ethnic belonging in a pervasive and divisive way leading to a compartmentalisation of the polity along ethnic lines' (Wimmer 2002: 173).

While it is difficult to argue against the occurrence of this 'homogenization' (it has become axiomatic to refer to pre-2003 Iraq as a 'Sunni Arab-dominated state' for good reason), a description and explanation of Iraqi political structure benefits from nuances provided by leftist analyses of power. From this viewpoint, it would be a mistake to consider that Iraq, upon its formation, was merely the coalescence of three communal groupings (Sunni Arabs, Shiʿi Arabs and Kurds), and two notable smaller communities (Assyrians and Turkmen). Instead, Hanna Batatu, in his epic analysis of Iraq's *Old Social Classes*, paints a vivid and complex picture of 'congeries of distinct, discordant, self-involved societies' (Batatu 1978: 13). He further comments on the nature of urban–rural differences, class structures, the intimate nature of tribal allegiance and the fact that social patterns in Iraq, as a 'new' state being exposed to modernity, were subject to extraordinary pressures that would transform structures and relationships within groups, whether ethnic, sectarian, class-based or tribal, as well as between them.

These two approaches to conceptualizing Iraqi society, with one considering vertical cleavages grouping defined communities together, and the other suggesting that the horizontal ordering of socio-economic class was more applicable to building an understanding of Iraqi political life, characterize the academic literature. The latter tends to be more prominent due to what was perceived as the expansion and consolidation of a secular, all-encompassing, Iraqi nationalism from the 1950s onwards. However, when the post-2003 situation is considered, with a resurrected or rediscovered communal political system dominating Iraqi political life, analyses of Iraq's political and social structures that place the emergence and consolidation of a cosmopolitan secular Iraqi nationalism above all other patterns of socio-political organization need to be critically reviewed.

In considering the historiography of Iraq from the mid-twentieth century onwards, it is possible to identify two interpretations of the character of the state. The first views the state and nation-building processes in Iraq as successful, with an Iraqi national identity emerging and becoming consolidated (dominated by an Arab nationalist discourse), and Iraq endowed with Western-styled state institutions (see Longrigg 1953 and Khadduri 1969 for examples of this interpretation). The alternative explanation is that 'from the start, post-1920 Iraq was a fraud' (Fieldhouse 2002: 22). Put more diplomatically, the notion of the existence of a unifying Iraqi identity has been questioned by some academics (see Kedourie 1970 for an example of this interpretation). The issue of Iraqi identities, following the removal of Saddam's regime, became a focal point of academic debate as experts struggled to account for what was seen as the evaporation of a secular, unifying civic nationalism and the rapid emergence and consolidation of communal identities. Postmodern conceptions of identity, and especially the understanding of identity as a social construction with individuals multiply positioned in society, were forwarded in contrast to others that conceptualized political mobilization in Iraq through ethnic and sectarian lenses.

Rather than subscribe directly to either of these approaches, a combination of them perhaps sheds more analytical light on the post-Saddam environment. This third trend in effect combines both approaches and recognizes the existence of overlapping vertical and horizontal cleavages within Iraqi society. In his seminal work on the Iraqi Shi'i community, Faleh Jabar modifies the linear conception of Iraqi society which envisages social structures as fluid and in constant change, moving from traditional (vertical) solidarities to modern (horizontal) ones as a result of modernity's impact, as described in Batatu's *Old Social Classes*, to one which accounts for the resurgence (or even resurrection) of these older associations, blaming this upon the effects of two Gulf wars and the legacy of dictatorship (Jabar 2003a: 36). By adding the profound catalytic influence of US actions in Iraq, this combined approach provides as comprehensive an understanding of Iraqi political mobilization as is possible. In order to make sense of this complex debate, the remainder of the chapter is divided into sections considering the interplay of Iraqi and Arab nationalisms in Iraq's history, and then considers the ethno-sectarian identities that currently characterize Iraq's political landscape.

Nationalism

One of the biggest tasks facing the British and empowered elites in the new state of Iraq was the building of an all-encompassing identity in which all components of society could subscribe, but which did not threaten the position of the elites themselves. 'Official' nationalism, as defined by the monarchy, accepted a dependency upon the imperial power along with the promotion of an 'Iraqi first' policy. Opponents to this position objected to the dependency upon the British, or were communists, or supported some form of ethnically based nationalism, namely, Arab and Kurdish (Natali 2001: 261).

This competition between Arab and Iraqi nationalism is important to understand as it presents a framework by which communal identities in Iraq can be understood in relation to the state. If media reports concerning today's Iraq are considered, Arab nationalism (*qawmiyya*) is commonly associated with a Sunni Arab position. However, for most of Iraq's modern history, those Shi'i Arabs who were secular in nature and feared the clerical establishment also openly supported a vision of Arab nationalism. In the early years of the Iraqi state (in the 1930s), Arab nationalism was a popular ideology among military officers who were exposed to and influenced by developments in the region as well as the emergence of fascism in Europe, and, conversely, leftist thinkers in the UK (Batatu 1978: 301).[3] Iraq also had its own exponents of the *qawmiyya* discourse. One of the leading pan-Arabists of the age, Sati al-Husri, was the Director of Education under King Faisal. In this influential position, Husri promoted a secular, ethnicized, Arab identity for Iraq, with little or no room in it for non-Arabs or the pious (see Baram 1994: 288). Such themes percolated into the school and wider education system, with history and language tuition becoming wholly Arabized.

The converse vision of Iraq was not as a distinctly Arab nation, but as a geographical defined area that was home to a range of communities linked by a common patriotism to the fatherland (*wataniyya*). An Iraqi nationalist discourse has traditionally recognized the social diversity of Iraq, and commonly made reference to Iraq being the descendant of the ancient Mesopotamian civilizations, thereby giving it some distinctiveness from the rest of the Arab world. Under governments that were of an Iraqi nationalist orientation (and particularly those of the monarchy and Qassem's regime from 1958 to 1961), a degree of acceptance could be witnessed among all of Iraq's communities towards the 'idea' of Iraq, and a notion of patriotism to the fatherland clearly developed, embracing the idea of Iraqis of different backgrounds being tied within the same geographical area (see Natali 2001: 263; Wimmer 2002: 176).

However, the existence of governments that have attempted to unify Iraq's peoples and promote an identity to which all groups could subscribe have been few and far between and, indeed, the ultimate manifestation of an Arab nationalist regime was that of Saddam. The result has been an inherent competition over who controls the institutions of state and what Charles Tripp refers to as the 'narrative' of the state (Tripp 2000). Indeed, the modern history of Iraq can be discussed in terms of communal groups attempting to either (a) dominate the institutions of the state, thereby controlling the narrative of the state (commonly between Sunni and Shiʿi Arabs), or (b) questioning whether a group should even be 'in' the state (commonly, the Kurds). The rise of Arab nationalist regimes also brought with it the Arabization of the army and the state apparatus and, under Saddam, the centralization of power in the hands of a relative few. Ethno-sectarian forces were held in place by a combination of judicious use of patronage with an overwhelming deployment of coercive force.

With Saddam's removal, these ethno-sectarian forces have been uncovered and, along with them, the problem of again creating an identity greater than the sum of its parts. The rebirth of the forces of the 'old Iraq' has been traumatic as different groups backed by, at times, opposing powers are thrust into the political arena. Post-Saddam Iraqi political development is now increasingly discussed with reference to two principal 'questions'. The first relates to religion and sectarianism; the second to ethnicity.

The Sunni–Shiʿi Divide

As we have seen in Chapter 2, Iraq's Islamic heritage is rich and complex. As well as being the centre of the grandest of the Islamic empires, it was also the theatre in which Islam's greatest formative events outside the Arabian peninsula occurred. The most important of these events was the competition over the leadership of the Islamic community following the death of the Prophet Mohammed. This competition caused a schism within the community between those who supported a hereditary line of succession (the Shiʿi) and those who did not (the Sunni). In subsequent centuries, this schism was mirrored in the political structure of the area, whether it was part of the Ottoman or Safavid empires or the Iraqi state. The Shiʿi, although in numerical terms a majority in the modern period only since the conversion of southern Arab tribes to Shiʿism in the nineteenth century, have traditionally been grossly under-represented within the organs of state. They have also been viewed with suspicion by successive Arab and Iraqi nationalist governments due to Iran being Shiʿi-dominated; for this reason, Iraq's Shiʿi have been considered to be influenced by their co-religionists in Iran by successive Iraqi governments and therefore suffered considerable discrimination.

The organization of the Shiʿi religious establishment has had a profound effect upon the manifestation of modern political structures within the community. From the formative period of Islam, the Shiʿi would only accept that the heirs of the fourth caliph, Ali (the Prophet's paternal cousin and son-in-law), could rightfully lead the Islamic community. In subsequent years, religious authority devolved to scholars known as *ulema* (doctors of religion) who were later renamed as *mujtahid*s. A few *mujtahid*s would succeed in gaining the acceptance of a large number of followers, allowing them to act as reference figures for how Shiʿis should live their lives. Such a figure is known as a *marja' al-taqlid*, or *marja'* for short, which translates as 'source of emulation' (Nakash 2006: 6). The most prominent *marja'* is now Grand Ayatollah Ali al-Sistani of Najaf, but there are also others in Iraq, Iran and Lebanon. One of the effects of having several different senior religious authorities in the Shiʿi world has been the emergence of a rich, varied and complex culture, resplendent in traditions, learning and instruction. It has also resulted in the Shiʿi, even when only considering those living in Iraq, becoming a politically fragmented community, with a range of parties and groupings, representing different trends within society and often following the teachings of a particular part of the religious establishment.

The focal points of the worldwide Shiʿi community are in Iraq, in the cities of Najaf, Karbala, Kazimayn and Samarra. However, the existence of a numerous, majority, Shiʿi community in Iraq is a phenomenon that has a relatively recent history, and cannot be traced directly back to the emergence of the original schism. Indeed, a majority Shiʿi population did not exist until the nineteenth century. Following the collapse of the Safavid state, Najaf and Karbala emerged as regional economic centres and Shiʿi strongholds in the mid-eighteenth century. Attacks by Sunni *wahhabi* forces against these two cities and their environs prompted many to convert to Shiʿism in order to benefit from the protection of the wider community. There were also environmental reasons as to why Najaf and Karbala grew and prospered, with changes in the water flow of the Euphrates forcing the migration of tribes to the cities. Finally, the enforcement of a policy of tribal resettlement in 1831 by the Ottomans created animosity towards the Ottoman government, prompting a protest-conversion to Shiʿism among many of those resettled around the holy cities (Nakash 1994: 443).

The combination of these factors saw tribal order disrupted, the urban population increase, sectarian identity strengthen and the reconstruction of identities to match the new environment. Following this conversion process, many tribes became divided into Sunni and Shiʿi branches, leading many observers to consider that the commonalities (of ethnicity, socio-economic characteristics) that exist between Sunni and Shiʿi communities may in fact be stronger than the often cited differences of religious dogma, and therefore more appropriate when discussing the nature of Iraqi identities.

The differences caused by religious dogma in today's Iraq are, however, deep and extensive. Wherever schisms within religions exist, it is possible to find deep-rooted divisions within societies which may have relatively little to do with the original problem, and Iraq is no exception. The continued empowerment of Arab and Turkmen Sunnis by the Ottomans certainly gave the schism a political and class-based edge, with Sunnis emerging as the designated ruling class, and Shiʿis not enjoying access to power to the same degree. But there also existed fundamental differences between the religious establishments of the Sunnis and Shiʿis. For the Shiʿis, the slaying of Hussein at the Battle of Karbala and the imposition of an unacceptable mechanism of succession remained as an emotively powerful force capable of mobilizing communities to act according to sectarian identity.

In addition to this continued memory of the formative moment of the schism, Faleh Jabar identifies five major issues that have played a pivotal role in the formation of an agitated Shi'i communit:y (2003b: 67–71). The first is political and focuses mainly on under-representation. At a political level, this under-representation allowed the 'narrative' of the Iraqi state to be dictated by groups which the Shi'i identified as being Sunni (whether these groups themselves did so openly or not). Unlike the Kurdish–Arab cleavage, which is considered later, the problem is not the legitimacy of Iraq as an entity, but the *identity* of the state itself (Anderson and Stansfield 2004: 119). An identity constructed around Arab nationalism and secularism, and perceived to be Sunni driven, never appealed to those Shi'i of a more spiritual orientation. It is this issue of political representation and control which promises to be the focus of attention in Iraq's future political development.

The second of Jabar's issues centres on economic grievances. Successive rounds of land reforms enacted by the Iraqi government were considered to be detrimental to Shi'i landholders. Under the Ba'th, Shi'i persons with business and industrial interests were deemed to be a 'menace to the nation', with many having their properties confiscated, and some being deported to Iran in the 1980s. The third issue is that of cultural encroachment. The emergence of a secular Arab nationalism in Iraq, replacing Islam as a political focus, was anathema to religiously minded Shi'i. The association of Arab and Iraqi nationalism with the glories of past empires also undermined the essence of Shi'i Islam with its legitimacy coming from the veneration of the family of Imam Ali. The fourth issue concerns citizenship rights. Shi'ism was, for the Iraqi government, equated with Iranian encroachment into Iraq's affairs, due to their shared religion and the extensive ties which continue to exist between the communities of southern Iraq and Iran. Vast numbers of 'Persians' (who were, in effect, Iraqi Shi'i) were deported on the eve of the Iraq–Iran War. The final issue was that of secularization. As the state modernized and grew, it assumed some of the functions that had previously been the responsibility of the religious establishment, including justice, education and tax collection. With its vast financial networks centred on different *mujtahids* and shrines, the encroachment of the secular state damaged the religious classes and weakened their position. Together, these issues sensitized the Shiʿi in Iraq, and galvanized the clerical class into taking actions to reassert their position in society.

Political Shiʿism has had a long history in Iraq, with the first attempts at state-building under the British having to contend with a Shiʿi-coloured rebellion in 1920. However, the emergence of contemporary organizations can be traced to the instability prevalent in the aftermath of the demise of the monarchy in 1958, with the oldest of contemporary Shiʿi political movements, *Hizb al-Daʿwa Islamiyya* (commonly referred to as Daʿwa), being established in the late 1950s in Najaf. Faced with the emergence of secular political powers capable of undermining religious authority (including the Iraqi Communist Party), the Shiʿi religious establishment, led by Grand Ayatollah Muhsin al-Hakim and later the inspirational Ayatollah Muhammad Baqir al-Sadr, was prompted into action and supported the establishment of a Shiʿi entity capable of confronting this secular encroachment. The organization that would translate the political concerns of the *hawza* into political action amongst the masses was Daʿwa (Aziz 1993: 208).

Whereas Daʿwa was a wholly 'Iraqi' creation, the next major force of political Shiʿism to emerge in contemporary Iraq, the Supreme Council for the Islamic Revolution in Iraq (SCIRI), has the imprint of Iran upon it. Now known as the Islamic Supreme Council of Iraq (ISCI), it was formed on 17 November 1982, in Tehran, as a result of efforts by the Iranian government to unite the fragmented Iraqi Islamist movements under an umbrella to coordinate Shiʿi groups fighting against Saddam's regime. With its public links to the Iranian clerical establishment, and the known involvement of Iranian *pasdaran* (Revolutionary Guards) with its military wing (the Badr Army), it is considered by many observers to be an Iranian proxy organization in Iraq. As such, it has been criticized by other Iraqi Shiʿi parties and groups, and most notably the Sadr Movement of Muqtada al-Sadr. ISCI is currently led by Sayyid Ammar al-Hakim, following the death of his father, Abd al-Aziz, in 2009 and the assassination in Najaf of his uncle Ayatollah Mohammed Baqir al-Hakim in August 2003.

During the 1990s, inside Iraq, the religiously based political parties were beginning to consolidate their position, as exemplified by the re-emergence of a new, more militant, organization under the leadership of the leading cleric in the late 1990s, Ayatollah Muhammad Sadiq al-Sadr. Another member of the al-Sadr family and cousin of the late Ayatollah Muhammad Baqir al-Sadr, Sadiq al-Sadr was a government-appointed cleric who initially appeared to act according to the wishes of the regime and was despised by other leading clerical families, and especially the Hakims, because of this. Forced into taking a more critical stance against the regime as it continued to assassinate more troublesome clerics, Sadiq al-Sadr rapidly developed into a charismatic and extremely influential figure, giving defiant sermons in his mosque at Kufa, with his representatives preaching to crowds of 2,000 in Baghdad, even though the government had banned such events (Cole 2003: 65). He even preached directly against Saddam Hussein, by comparing him to the Abbasid Caliph al-Mutawakkil – a figure despised by the Shiʿi. Recognizing the threat, Saddam acted in a characteristically brutal manner. Ayatollah Sadiq al-Sadr was assassinated in Najaf in February 1999, along with his two eldest sons, leaving his youngest son, Muqtada, as heir to the political legacy of what is now known as the Sadr Movement (see Chapter 7).

The final, and most important, Shiʿi actor is Grand Ayatollah Ali al-Sistani. Born in the early 1930s in Mashad (Iran), Sistani came to prominence in the 1990s. Since 1999, Sistani has been the supreme *marja* of the Shiʿi, not only in Iraq, but across the Shiʿi world. He is considered to be a moderate, in keeping with the Iraqi Shiʿi trend of 'quietism', which is best defined as the separation of spiritual duties from the affairs of state. However, in the inflamed political environment that has characterized Iraq since 2003, Sistani has become increasingly involved in influencing the direction of the political process by making timely announcements indicating how dutiful Shi'is should act. These pronouncements are perhaps the most powerful political tool in modern Iraq.

The Kurds

The second major cleavage in Iraqi society focuses upon ethnic identity. Whether the region was perceived as an imperial centre acting as a magnet attracting to it different communities, or as a border region between empires where a degree of isolation and freedom of action could be enjoyed, the result has been the accretion of peoples, cultures and ethnicities. The emergence of ethnicity as a politically relevant cleavage, however, is a relatively recent development. During the Ottoman period, ethnicity was not a recognizably contentious issue as Ottoman political life was structured around villages, tribes, confessional affiliation and even membership of craft corporations, rather than any perceived ethnic origin (Zubaida 2000: 364). What mattered, and what was noted on official documents, was whether an individual was Muslim, or Christian, or Jewish, and not whether a person happened to be Kurdish, or Arab, or Persian, for example. However, in the twentieth century, ethnicity assumed a prominent place as an identity marker not only in Iraq, but across the region. With the introduction of the Western concept of the nation-state, it now mattered which ethnic groups lived within the boundaries of the state, and nationalisms formed both because of the internal developments within groups, and the reactions of groups towards the policies of the new state.

In terms of 'ethnic groups', it is usual to subdivide Iraqi society into four groupings: Arab, Kurd, Turkmen and Chaldo-Assyrian. In understanding Iraq's modern history and future development, the situation of the Turkmen and Assyrians is important to note, but the characteristics and history of the second-largest ethnic group in Iraq, the Kurds, are what need to be addressed in a substantial manner in order to provide an understanding of the dynamics which may see Iraq restructured politically, if not actually fragmented into smaller states.

This is not to say that the Turkmen and Assyrians are not important politically – they certainly are. But the populations of these communities are not great enough to generate the critical mass of political influence necessary to effect large-scale change in Iraq. The Kurds, conversely, have this critical mass and are using it with increasing effect.

Commonly, Iraq is described as being divided into a majority Arab component, with a minority Kurdish population – the latter accounting for an estimated 20 per cent of the total population of the country. If the 'sectarian question' is one that is blurred and unclear, the 'ethnic question', with particular reference to the Kurds, is rather more straightforward to understand. Although many different ethnic groups are present within the boundaries of the Iraqi state, the principal debate has swirled around the position of the Kurds and their attempts to secure autonomy or even to secede from the state if presented with the opportunity. The debate has, in many ways, been quite different from that which concerns the Sunni and Shiʿi communities. Whereas most analyses of the Shiʿi recognize that they are content with the notion of being 'Iraqis', and secular Shiʿi can subscribe to notions of Arab nationalism as well, the same cannot be said for the Kurds as, quite simply, they are not of Arab ethnicity and have remained, at best, unwilling and at times unwelcome participants throughout Iraq's modern history.

The origins of the Kurds are unclear, but there is common consent within the academic literature that they are an Indo-European people descended from waves of migrations originating on the Indian subcontinent and spreading across the mountains of Turkey, Iraq and Iran, and into Europe, that occurred several thousand years ago. Kurds believe themselves to be direct descendants of the Medes, who secured their autonomy from the neo-Assyrian Empire and established their own Empire centred in the Zagros mountains. Some academics choose to delve even further into pre-history and claim that the Kurds are the direct descendants of the Hurrian and Hittite peoples (Izady 2004a) Such claims are difficult, if not impossible, to verify, but the important fact to note is simply that Kurds consider themselves to be different from those peoples around them, including the Arab population of Iraq. While their exact origins are blurred, what can be stated without fear of repudiation is that the peoples of the mountains of the Zagros enjoyed a similarity of culture, language and experience which resulted in the formation of a people defined by themselves and by others as being distinctive.

The Kurds now number perhaps as many as 25 million, spread across the border regions of Iran, Iraq, Turkey and Syria. Turkey is home to most Kurds, with as many as 12 million existing within its borders. Iraq has perhaps half as many, but constituting a greater percentage of the overall population of the country. As the fourth largest ethnic grouping in the Middle East (after Arabs, Turks and Iranians), the Kurds have continuously strived for at least heightened representation in the countries they reside, and occasionally outright independence. Any such development could obviously result in the loss of territory for any one of the states in which Kurds are found. Brendan O'Leary and Khaled Saleh note quite rightly that host states are therefore predictably opposed to the emergence of a meaningful Kurdistan, and display hostility even to the consolidation of Kurdish identity, as such a development may act to grow into something too potent to withstand (O'Leary and Saleh 2005: 9).

The evidential differences between the Kurds and their neighbours cannot be accounted for merely by reference to fabled ancestors in the very dim and distant past. Kurds are also a product of their environment, with Kurdish social and political structure being in many ways ideally matched to the necessity of living and existing in a mountainous region. Existing in a topographically fragmented region of high mountains and river valleys, the traditional structure of Kurdish social and political organization was inherently tribal, with a tribe being a socio-political unit with distinct territorial limits and membership based upon kinship (Van Bruinessen 1992: 51). Until recently, the main economic activity involved semi-nomadic pastoralism, with Kurdish society being predominantly rural and again influenced by local physical geography. The manifestation of these responses to environmental factors was a people inherently tied to the local environment and the rhythm of the seasons. But it also saw political and social discontinuities caused by the separation imposed by rugged topography, and promoted the consolidation of tribal organization and patrimonial leadership. Kurds were therefore not only isolated from the neighbours. They were also isolated from each other and it is this factor which is primarily responsible for the late appearance of an 'imagined community', as defined by Benedict Anderson, among the Kurds when compared with such developments among Arab, Persian or Turkish peoples (Anderson 1984).

Perhaps unsurprisingly when considering the mountain location of Kurdistan and the areas of relative isolation which exist there, Kurdish society displays a diverse range of religious beliefs. The majority of Kurds, perhaps as many as three-quarters, are Sunni Muslims, with 15 per cent being Shiʿi, and perhaps as many as 10 per cent adhering to ancient pre-Islamic religions, including Yezidism and other Zoroastrian-based faiths. Indeed, many Kurds believe their ancestors to be Zoroastrians, with many Kurdish customs and rituals perhaps being Zoroastrian in origin (Shourush 2002: 114). Kurdistan-Iraq is not only home to many Yezidi followers – it is one of *the* focal points for the worldwide Yezidi community, and especially the village of Lalish near Dohuk, where the most important of the Yezidi temples is located. While predominantly Sunni Muslim, Kurdish religious development has also been affected considerably by the prominence of Sufi orders, and particularly those of the Naqshabandiyya and Qadiri. Essentially a 'mystical' branch of Islam, Sufism promoted a much more personal sense of religious obligation among the Kurds that has, to a considerable extent, permeated through to modern Kurdish society. Although more orthodox Sunni practices are now becoming widespread in Kurdistan, the influence of Sufism still remains strong.

As with other communities in Iraq, it is clear that Kurdish society is heterogeneous in nature. With a rich tapestry of religions, tribes, and even dialects, Kurdish society is complex, and its political movements reflect this. However, for most Kurds, there remains one common grievance, which has a recent origin. This grievance was the creation of the state of Iraq itself. For many Kurds in Iraq (and, indeed, elsewhere), the problems they have faced in the twentieth century can be traced to the events surrounding the defeat of the Ottoman Empire in the First World War, and the redistribution of former Ottoman lands by the victorious Allied powers. Kurds believed, and expected, that they would be granted their independence, and, indeed, had good reason to expect this. Following the presentation of Kurdish claims at the Paris Peace Conference of 1919, the subsequent Treaty of Sèvres of August 1920 provided for the creation of a Kurdish state in areas of southern Turkey subsequent to a plebiscite to be held in August 1921, with the Kurdish-inhabited area of the Mosul *vilayet* also empowered to join the Kurdish state after August 1922 (Izady 2004b: 99–100). However, the treaty and its recommendation were reneged upon in the Treaty of Lausanne, in 1923, due to the pressures brought to bear by a newly resurgent Republic of Turkey, and the British desire to secure its grip upon the oil reserves of the Mosul *vilayet* (see Chapter 2).

Since then, the Kurds have been in a state of rebellion against the Iraqi government, which has varied in intensity throughout the twentieth century. The Kurdish population in Iraq was neither small enough to be wholly eradicated or assimilated, nor large enough to wrestle its freedom from the state. Instead, the Kurdish position in Iraq oscillated between periods of relative autonomy, through to periods of intense repression. Under the leadership of Mustafa Barzani, the Kurds succeeded in gaining autonomy for themselves in the north of Iraq between 1970 and 1974, but then found themselves caught between Iraq and Iran during the war of 1980–88. The alliance of Kurdish militias (*peshmerga*) with Iran was met with a brutal onslaught aimed at eradicating the Kurdish threat in the rural areas of northern Iraq once and for all – the infamous *Anfal* Campaign, followed by Saddam's use of chemical weapons against Kurdish civilian targets (most notably Halabja in 1988), in what was, by most formal definitions, an act of genocidal proportions (see Chapter 5).

Politically, the Kurds in Iraq have never been united even among those in pursuit of a common goal. The legacy of Kurdistan's tribal history continued into the twentieth century across rural areas, with some tribes often finding common cause with the Iraqi government against Kurds opposed to government policies, and others choosing to take up arms against other tribes for local reasons, or because of wider issues fuelled by a growing sense of Kurdish nationalism. The most important of the early political parties to ride the burgeoning sense of 'Kurdishness' (*Kurdayeti* in Kurdish) among the Kurds in Iraq was the Kurdistan Democratic Party (KDP). Founded in 1946, the KDP brought together two wholly different trends within Kurdish society – the tribal, rural Kurds, mainly from the Bahdinan region (around Dohuk and Barzan), and the leftist, urban Kurds from the cities of Suleimaniyya and Erbil. The former were led by the popular and charismatic figure of Mulla Mustafa Barzani – a famed guerrilla leader with a long history of fighting the Iraqi government, though initially because of tribal, rather than nationalist, reasons (Stansfield 2003). The latter were guided by Ibrahim Ahmed, a famed poet and lawyer from Suleimaniyya, and assisted by his young protégé Jalal Talabani. Due to the immense reputation of Barzani, it was natural that he headed the KDP, but the party remained heavily divided between the two wings. This division erupted into full-scale conflict between these wings in the 1960s, before Barzani managed to again assert his authority over the leftists. However, following the defeat of the KDP in 1975 and the permanent evacuation of Barzani from Kurdistan, Talabani announced the formation of a new umbrella organization named the Patriotic Union of Kurdistan (PUK), composed of several left-wing parties and organizations. The KDP quickly regrouped under the leadership of Mustafa's sons, Idris and Massoud, and again challenged for the accolade of being the undisputed leader of the Kurds of Iraq. This competition between the KDP and PUK, and between Massoud Barzani and Jalal Talabani, has been ongoing ever since.

The doggedness with which Kurdish parties have clung to their demand to have the distinctiveness of Kurds recognized formally and practically in Iraq undermines the arguments supporting the existence of a unifying Iraqi nationalism. At times, Kurdish parties have attempted to act as Iraqi nationalists (most notably in the post-Saddam period), but the association of Iraq with a Sunni Arab ideological agenda has always seen the Kurds return to a position which is inherently Kurdish nationalist in nature. The strengthening of Kurdish nationalist ideals has occurred throughout the twentieth century, often in reaction to chauvinistic Iraqi government policies, including military incursions into Kurdistan throughout the mid-twentieth century and, most strikingly, the attempt to eradicate the Kurds during the infamous *Anfal* campaign of the late 1980s and the use of chemical weapons against urban centres. None of these strategies succeeded in cowing the Kurds, but instead prompted an even stronger reaction against the construct of Iraq.

The emergence in 1991 of a region controlled by the Kurds in the north of Iraq, following Saddam's defeat in Kuwait, saw the consolidation of Kurdish nationalism and the widescale rejection of Iraq by Kurds.[4] The history of the de facto Kurdish state, which is considered in more depth in Chapter 7, is one characterized by survival against significant imposed and self-inflicted problems. The Kurds existed under double sanctions (from the UN imposed on Iraq, and from Saddam imposed against the Kurds), and witnessed the KDP and PUK embark on successive rounds of internecine fighting which saw the region dividing into two from 1994 onwards. Regional powers also were heavily involved in the affairs of the region, with the military forces of Turkey, Iraq and Iran all undertaking operations in Kurdistan-Iraq in the 1990s. But there were also developments which Kurds considered beneficial. From 1991, Kurds conducted their official affairs in Kurdish, taught in schools and universities in Kurdish, and existed independently from the rest of Iraq. Kurds represented themselves to the international community, and became leading members of the Iraqi opposition to Saddam. Although the details of the Kurdish de facto state are dealt with later in the book, in this discussion of the nature of identities in Iraq, it is essential to note that, from 1991, Kurds began to think of themselves as Kurds first, and then, only maybe, Iraqis second.

When the US began to seriously talk about forcibly removing Saddam Hussein from power, following September 11, 2001, the Kurdish parties expressed almost unqualified support for such an initiative. During the military operations to remove Saddam, Kurdish *peshmerga* from both parties operated alongside Coalition military forces, and Kurdish society at large openly supported the presence of Coalition forces and personnel in Iraq. For the first time in their history, the interests of the Kurds coincided with the interests of an 'imperial' power, and it has resulted in them assuming a position of prominence and influence in the affairs of Iraq. Over a decade after 'regime change' in Iraq, the KDP and PUK have managed to put their historic differences to one side and they succeeded in maintaining a peace between them as they negotiated Kurdistan's future in Baghdad. But they still remain vulnerable to their own internal differences, and the manner in which regional powers – and especially Iran and Turkey – can influence their actions to secure their own national interests.

The Assyrians and Turkmens

Often overlooked in assessments of Iraq's political development, the Assyrian and Turkmen communities are sizeable in terms of numbers, and politically important in terms of their influence in their ability to gain the support of powers outside Iraq. They are also useful case studies which can illustrate the complexities of identity politics in terms of determining the origins of groups, the diversity and even animosity that exists within groups, and the manner in which political boundaries and agendas are constructed according to the prevalent circumstances of the time.

The Turkmen community, as the name suggests, is tied to the wider Turkic family of peoples which trace their origin to Central Asian tribes who migrated into areas of the modern Middle East region and Turkey. There is a considerable divergence of views as to when Turkmen first came to Iraq.

Turkmen scholars claim that their people first came to Iraq in the seventh century, as soldiers recruited into the Muslim army (al-Hirmizi 2003: 16). Successive waves of immigration then occurred under the Seljuks, with Turkmens assuming positions of military and administrative responsibility in the empire. The consolidation of the Turkmen position in what was to become Iraq took place with the expansion of the Ottoman Empire. With the conquering of Iraq by Suleiman the Magnificent in AD 1535, followed by Sultan Murat's capturing of Baghdad in 1638, another influx of Turkmen settled in Iraq.

However, while the evidence that migrations occurred seems to be reasonably clear, it is not obvious how today's Turkmen community is descended from them. These communities did not live in isolation from those around, and often assimilated with the Arab communities of the region, with Arabic becoming their native language. The process could also work in reverse, with non-Turkmen employed within the Ottoman bureaucracy effectively becoming 'Turkified', and taking on Turkic customs and language as they undertook their work in the institutions of state, or in businesses in urban areas.

Today, the Turkmen people live predominantly in the north of Iraq, on a swathe of land stretching from the Syrian border in the north, to the Iranian border in central Iraq (Oğuzlu 2002: 142). As with any communal group in Iraq, no accurate statistics exist that indicate the size of the Turkmen community. Turkmen scholars estimate that they make up 10–15 per cent of Iraqi society, which would seem to be excessive, and Iraqi and Western sources believe the figure to be less than 5 per cent (Oğuzlu 2002: 143). There are several towns with notable Turkmen populations, including Talafar, Mosul, Erbil, Altun Kupri and Kirkuk, with a sizeable population also in Baghdad. There exists within the towns of the north (and especially Kirkuk) considerable ethnically based competition between Kurdish and Turkmen communities. Generally, the Turkmen consider themselves to be the original inhabitants of the major cities because they as a community were heavily involved in governmental and business activities, whereas Kurds were considered to inhabit the rural areas. In Erbil and Mosul, where the populations are either heavily mixed (in the case of Mosul, but still with a dominant Arab population), or obviously almost wholly Kurdish, as in Erbil, such claims do not raise political tempers. However, in the case of Kirkuk, the Turkmen claim that the city was originally founded by them, and that the policies of 'Arabization' by Saddam (with non-Arab peoples being removed) and then 'Kurdification' by the KDP and PUK after 2003 (with non-Kurds being pressured to remove) have prompted serious inter-ethnic problems between the Turkmen and Kurdish communities and parties. These problems also have a regional dimension, with the Turkish government keen to protect the rights of their Turkic cousins, while also working to prevent the continued rise of a Kurdish entity. The location of Kirkuk on top of Iraq's second largest reserves of oil obviously is a factor in making the city such a focal point of political competition, and it is interesting to ask whether Kurds would want Kirkuk if the oil was not there, and if the Turkmens would be so determined to deny Kurdish claims if the geological strata of the area were not so well endowed.

The position of the Turkmen in the Iraqi state has changed over time. Following the establishment of the Republic of Turkey in 1923, they wished to see Turkey annex the Mosul *vilayet* and for them to become part of an expanded state. Under the monarchy, the Turkmens benefited as the old administrative and business classes of the Ottoman Empire, and enjoyed a relatively trouble-free existence. However, with the demise of the monarchy, they found themselves increasingly discriminated against by the policies of successive regimes that focused upon communal differences within society. The Kirkuk Massacre of 1959, which resulted from the Iraqi government allowing the Iraqi Communist Party (which, in Kirkuk, was largely Kurdish) to foment problems between Kurds and Turkmen, saw numerous deaths. Under the Baʿth Party, the discrimination against Turkmen increased, with several leaders being executed in 1979, and many Shiʿi Turkmen killed for their affiliation with the clandestine Daʿwa Party. Perhaps the most telling indicator of the deterioration of the Turkmen position in Iraq can be viewed in the wording of successive Iraqi Constitutions. From being recognized as a constitutive entity of Iraq in the Constitution of 1925, the Turkmen were later denied this status alongside the Arabs and Kurds.

In many ways, the position of the Assyrian Christians in Iraq bears some similarities with that of the Turkmen. Both are 'minority' populations when compared with their Arab and Kurdish neighbours, with the Christians in Iraq perhaps numbering no more than 1 million persons (O'Mahony 2004: 123), and with no major population concentration existing beyond the presence of some Christian quarters in major towns in the north of the country, and particularly in Erbil, Dohuk and Mosul, but with the majority living in Baghdad. The Christian community is again characteristically diverse. The majority are Catholics of a wide range of denominations. There then exist Eastern Arab Orthodox Christians, and smaller numbers of Protestants and Anglicans. In practice, the Chaldean Catholic Church is by far the largest and most influential in the Christian community with perhaps as many as 70 per cent of Iraq's Christians belonging to it.[5]

Assyrians are keen to associate themselves with the glories of the ancient Assyrian Empire, and describe themselves as being the 'original' inhabitants of Iraq. However, as with the Kurdish claim of descent from the Medes, it is virtually impossible to prove these contentions. Indeed, the presence of Assyrians in modern Iraq is a relatively recent phenomenon. Originally from the Hakkari region of south-west Turkey, the British army settled some 20,000 of them in Iraq, and particularly in the north, following their occupation of the former *vilayet*s of the Ottoman Empire. Enjoying positions of responsibility within the British army, the Assyrians were deeply resented both by Muslims on religious grounds, and by Kurds as they were settled in Kurdish population centres.

The position of the Assyrians in Iraq is now very difficult. Facing a rise in Islamic sentiment in society on the one hand, and the appearance of a Kurdish de facto state on the other, they consider that their future in Iraq looks bleak indeed.

Relations between the principal Assyrian political party, the Assyrian Democratic Movement (ADM), and the Kurdish parties have become so poor following the elections of December 2005 that the ADM chose to join forces with the Shi'i United Iraqi Alliance (UIA), rather than remain under the wing of the Kurds. Fearing the potential Islamization of the state, or its break-up with a Kurdish entity appearing in the north, the Assyrians have embraced a communal agenda which has even managed to broach the often difficult relations that have characterized Chaldo–Assyrian interaction. In so doing, they propose the creation of a small 'Assyrian Administrative Region', with its centre being the town of Bekhdeda, east of Mosul, as being the only guarantor of their freedoms in the future.[6]

Identity and the State

Conceptualizing Iraqi society is a task that is dependent upon the period being discussed, and the specific condition of state–society relations that prevail in particular areas. It is possible to show examples of a secular civic nationalism existing at one time and place, only then to see the most rampant examples of ethnically based nationalism occurring in another. Similarly, the efficacy of religion as a force of socio-political mobilization has varied across time and space. While identities have therefore been in a seeming permanent state of flux in Iraq, one aspect has remained constant, and that is the role of the state in striving to create, or impose, an identity upon Iraqi society. From being initially relatively willing to attempt to build an inclusive Iraqi identity, the Iraqi state became dominated increasingly by a particularly exclusive Arab nationalist agenda which, under the Ba'th Regime, saw the state revert to the deployment of unparalleled force and societal coercion as it sought to impose an order deemed in its interests over the different segments of Iraq's society. Next, in Chapter 4, the main focus is on tracing the growth of authoritarian Iraq.

4 From Authoritarian to Totalitarian State, 1933–1979

For many observers, Iraq is synonymous with dictatorship. Indeed, Iraq's association with authoritarian and totalitarian methods of governance is so strong that it has been considered, by some commentators, that there exists some inherent trait within Iraqi society predisposing it to be managed by a 'strong man' heading an all-pervasive, controlling, state. In supporting this line of argument, evidence from Iraq's history and pre-history is often deployed, with notable examples of authoritarian leaders and seemingly aggressive peoples being used to contextualize modern Iraq as being not unusual when the wider sweep of Iraqi and Mesopotamian history is considered. The strictures placed upon Babylonian society by Hammurabi, the martial expertise of the Assyrians and the cruelty of the Mongols have all been referred to in order to illustrate that manifestations of authoritarianism in Iraq are, in fact, the norm.

Iraq is also not unusual in being described as such. If the wider regional context is considered, popular (mis)conceptions of Middle East politics abound, particularly in the post-September 11 environment. Jill Crystal succinctly describes these misconceptions: 'all of Middle Eastern politics is authoritarian and violent and... these features spring from deep within society – from Islam (where everything Arab originates) or from the same dark source from which Islam itself sprang' (Crystal 1994: 263). According to this line of thinking, something 'primordial' exists in Arab and Islamic culture, which predisposes modern Middle Eastern societies to be governed by authoritarian regimes (Ayubi 1995: 258).

Such arguments are problematic for many reasons, not least that they essentialize Arab, Islamic and Iraqi societies to an unacceptable degree. They also fail to make valid comparisons between Middle Eastern societies and those in the West, conveniently ignoring the violent periods in the histories of European states, which often occurred concomitantly with the emergence of more urbane polities in Arabian and Islamic lands. Consider, for example, the situations afflicting northern Europe in the period between the eighth and thirteenth centuries. At a time when the Abbasid Caliphate ruled the Arab and Islamic world, Europe was far from peaceful, and few cities, if any, could compare to the splendour that was Baghdad.

The Dictator Debate

These comparisons suggest the existence of a double standard, at least in terms of popular understandings, but they do beg a serious question when Iraq's modern history is considered. Put simply, why has the modern history of Iraq been dogged by a succession of authoritarian military regimes, with the latter half of the twentieth century being characterized by the emergence of the Ba'th Party and the hardening of an already extensive authoritarian state into one of the most infamous examples of a totalitarian state in history? If the argument that such characteristics are merely the product of Arab culture and Islam is dismissed (which I choose to do), then how can Iraq's modern experience of authoritarianism and totalitarianism be explained?

The neo-conservative influenced administration of George W. Bush thought it had a simple answer to what it perceived to be a simple question, and the answer could be found in the personage of Saddam Hussein. Demonized during the run-up to the invasion of Iraq in 2003, Saddam and members of his immediate circle were identified as being the primary, indeed, the only, obstacle preventing Iraqis from throwing off the shackles of dictatorship and embracing democratic ideals. Attractive in its simplicity, but brutally flawed because of it, events in Iraq since Saddam's downfall suggest that the removal of a totalitarian regime may result in democratic development taking place, but with results far removed from those expected by policy-planners in Washington, DC. Indeed, while it is possible to make the argument that democratic development was taking place in Iraq after 2003, particularly if the elections of the post-Saddam period are recognized as democratic (which is contentious), it is perhaps more accurate to say that democratic development was taking place in *regions* of Iraq – areas that were islands of stability, such as the Kurdistan Region. But the resurrection of communal identities, empowered by democratic procedures, threatened the very existence of the Iraqi state, with a Kurdistan region already established, and the chances of a southern Shi'i region emerging becoming very high. Democracy, far from being alien to Arab (and, indeed, other ethnicities present in Iraq) and Islamic society, had in fact proved to flourish in the absence of Saddam's dictatorship. The problem instead seemed to be that the structure of the Iraqi state itself struggled to accommodate the democratic demands that were emerging from within Iraq's varied communities. In other words, it is not Iraqis who are alien to democratic ideals, but the construct of Iraq itself acts as a catalyst in the formation of non-democratic regimes.

I argue that the *predisposition* of Iraq to succumb to authoritarian methods of government is a product of the bringing together of disparate communities following the downfall of the Ottoman Empire and the empowerment of one group over all others. As we have seen in Chapters 2 and 3, the making of Iraq by the British in the 1920s endowed it with patterns of state–society relations which were, by all accounts, unstable. However, merely because the *predisposition* exists does not mean that Iraq's authoritarian future was *predetermined*, and therefore other developments have to be identified. The continued presence of an imperial power (Britain) acted as a catalyst in the formation of anti-colonialist, Arab and Iraqi, national movements. These national movements were mainly found within the elites empowered by the British, and to a significant extent within the 'new middle classes' of urbanized Sunni Arabs. For the latter group in particular, the officer corps of the army became the vehicle by which they would achieve societal and political advancement and, as a result, promote the nationalist cause. The Iraqi army would soon be called upon to protect the state not from the designs of foreign powers, but from threats emanating from within Iraq itself that were perceived to challenge the edifice of the Arab nationalist state. Assyrians, Kurds, Turkmens and Shiʿi would all suffer the attention of the military in the years following Iraq's independence in 1932, but the civilian government itself would quickly fall foul of the army as it continued to try and balance increasingly prevalent nationalist aspirations with satisfying the desires of Britain. It is therefore of no surprise that Iraq was the first 'post-First World War' Middle Eastern state in which a military coup occurred in 1936, with the military forcing seven cabinet changes between 1936 and 1941, and later removing the monarchy itself in 1958. The *emergence* of authoritarianism in Iraq can therefore be traced to three interrelated factors, these being:

1 The rise of the military in the political life of Iraq.
2 The continued communalization of Iraqi political life.
3 The growth of Arab nationalism in reaction to the continued involvement of Britain in Iraq's affairs.

These three factors are addressed in the forthcoming analysis and together illustrate the emergence and consolidation of authoritarianism in Iraq over a fifty-year period between the 1920s and the 1970s. From the 1970s, I argue, changes began to occur that moved Iraq from being authoritarian to totalitarian. However, this metamorphosis is not permanent and, next, in Chapter 5, a situation is described in which Iraq's government returns to being authoritarian in the 1990s, due to its relatively enfeebled position following Saddam's unsuccessful venture into Kuwait.

As I am distinguishing between authoritarian and totalitarian systems, it is useful at this point to quickly define these terms. In his classic analysis of authoritarianism, Juan Linz defines authoritarian regimes as being 'political systems with limited, not responsible, political pluralism: without elaborate and guiding ideology (but with distinctive mentalities); without intensive nor extensive political mobilization (except some points in their development): and in which a leader (or occasionally small group) exercises power within formally ill-defined limits but actually quite predictable ones' (Linz 1964/1970: 255). Such elements, it will be argued, were present in Iraq until at least 1968 and the second Baʿthist coup. Totalitarian systems, however, display quite different characteristics. In her classic work *The Origins of Totalitarianism* (1951), Hannah Arendt defined totalitarianism as being 'the permanent domination of each single individual in each and every sphere of life' (1962: 326; Brooker 2000: 9). Developing upon Arendt's definition, Schapiro identifies five characteristic features of totalitarianism, and three distinctive 'pillars' supporting a totalitarian state – all of which can be applied to Saddam's Iraq from the late 1970s until the beginning of the 1990s. These 'five features of totalitarianism' are:

1 Personalized rule by a leader.
2 The subjugation of the legal order.
3 Control over private morality.
4 Continuous mobilization.
5 Legitimacy based upon mass support.

As will be seen, it is a relatively straightforward task to apply these five features to Saddam's Iraq. In addition, the applicability of Schapiro's (1972) three 'pillars' are even more striking. According to him, the three pillars on which such regimes are built are:

1 Ideology.
2 Party.
3 Administrative machinery of state.

I contend that characteristics of political control in Iraq display qualitative differences between the period of Ba'th Party domination (particularly from the 1980s onwards), and previous periods of military and/or monarchical control. To understand why and how Iraq moved from being an authoritarian state up until the 1970s, then emerged as a totalitarian state under Saddam from the 1980s onwards, two further developments have to be factored into the analysis. The Ba'th regime was undoubtedly a product, and a reaction, of the regimes it succeeded. Indeed, the patterns of authoritarianism had already been well established in Iraq before Saddam and the Ba'th gained prominence, and these patterns conditioned the post-1968 Ba'thist regime. However, to explain how the Ba'th regime moved Iraq's political system from being authoritarian to totalitarian, with personalized rule emerging and all segments of political life subordinated by the regime, other dynamics have to be factored into the equation. Rather than merely using the coercive force of the military, a far more effective method of strengthening a hold over society is by co-opting individuals into depending upon the continued existence of the status quo for their own well-being, and this co-optation was facilitated by the exponential rise in oil revenues from the 1970s onwards. Rather than economic development promoting democratic ideals and structures, as early modernization literature suggests, in Iraq the inverse effect can be seen, with rentierism (the overwhelming dependence of the state upon revenue from a particular source, allowing it to reduce the need to depend upon society in general while simultaneously increasing society's dependence on the state itself) consolidating the authoritarian state in Iraq and providing the resources necessary to transform authoritarian Iraq into the totalitarian state headed by Saddam (al-Naqeeb 1990: 91; Crystal 1994: 263). The impact of the rentier economy therefore constitutes the fourth theme explaining the rise of the totalitarian state.

The final theme considers the role of institutions of repression in sustaining state violence. In addition to identifying the building of an expansive and all-pervasive security network in Iraq, the role of Saddam Hussein himself has to be acknowledged. While undeniably *the* most influential figure in the building of the totalitarian state, Saddam, it is argued, should still not be considered as the singular evil genius who stood in the way of Iraq being a democratic state. Indeed, rather than inventing the institutions of totalitarianism with which Iraqi society would be subjugated for nearly three decades, it is argued that Saddam merely refined institutions and practices already put in place by previous regimes. As such, Saddam was not an aberration in the history of Iraq (as the administration of George W. Bush would tend to argue). Instead, he should be more accurately seen as a logical product of a construct (Iraq) characterized with inbuilt instabilities since its inception, which predisposes (but not predetermines) the rise of non-democratic regimes.

The Military in Political Life

The rise of authoritarianism in Iraq can be traced to the tensions caused by the legacies of British colonial involvement in the formation of civilian governments that were more often than not perceived to be corrupt and inefficient. A further formative factor, underlying the first, is that the decision-makers within the new state were almost wholly Sunni Arabs. However, rather than being a cohesive body of people, the Sunni Arab elite were quite heterogeneous. Some had been of high social status under the Ottomans and opposed those who deserted the empire to fight alongside the British. Others, including the core of the military, the Sharifians, were seen as 'penniless parvenus and opportunists' by the old social elites (Hemphill 1979: 88) and relied upon their association with the monarch for their elevated position within society (Marr 2004: 33). The struggle for political power in the early years of the Iraqi state was therefore not held between different communal groupings, but instead *within* the one empowered by the British to control the levers of power – that of the Sunni Arabs.

For both the British and for Faisal, the creation of an Iraqi army was deemed to be of paramount importance. As we have seen in Chapter 2, the most important issue for Winston Churchill, chairing the Cairo Conference, was to ensure that Iraq could be made a secure territory within the British sphere of influence, but at as little cost to the British as possible. However, the Iraqi state of the early 1920s was inherently weak, without either an indigenous central authority or any institutions capable of projecting power (Tarbush 1982: 73). For Faisal, political survival meant building consensus and unity within Iraq, effectively bringing together diverse peoples with little history of political community into a national project. But, until the lengthy process of institution-building and social engineering could achieve this, the monarchy itself would remain at risk from internal forces. To maintain internal order, to protect the monarchy and to allow the British to draw down their forces, an indigenous Iraqi army was needed by the British and by Faisal, in equal measure. As such, the army was designed from the very outset as an internal security force, to be used against those who threatened the state (Hashim 2003a: 31).

The Iraqi army was established in 1921, with Sharifians placed in positions of leadership – Jaʿfar Pasha al-Askari was made Iraq's first Minister of Defence, and Nuri al-Saʿid (his brother-in-law) was made Chief of General Staff (Hazelton 1989: 9).[1] Once in position, Askari employed those officers who had served in the Ottoman army and in the Arab Revolt and who were overwhelmingly Sunni Arabs, and Arab nationalists. Following the Cairo Conference, the army was expanded and developed under British guidance. The intention was that it would develop to such an extent that the British could down their own forces – the logic being very similar to that seen in post-2003 Iraq – but leave behind an Iraqi army capable of quelling the levels of dissent seen in the 1920 revolt. Faisal certainly needed an army. A resurgent Turkey in the north continued to press for its claim to the Mosul *vilayet* to be recognized. Also in the north, Kurdish tribes remained in a state of perpetual revolt, and political authority in the south and west of the country remained in the hands of prominent tribes. Perhaps most worrying was the ongoing hostility of the Shiʿi population towards the newly appointed king, with Shi'i *mujtahid*s continuing to agitate against the monarch. Both Faisal and the British therefore needed to expand the army, and quickly.

But the expansion did not proceed with initial haste. In the first three months of its existence, the army only recruited some 2,000 men, mainly due to the fact that most recruits were attracted by the higher salaries paid by the British to serve in their own indigenous forces, the Levies (Tarbush 1982: 84). Following increases in pay, however, recruitment improved and, by 1925, supply was in excess of demand. By 1935, the army stood at 15,300 and was organized into three cavalry regiments, six field and five mountain batteries of artillery, and seven infantry brigades. The Royal Iraqi Air Force had also grown from a few planes, to three squadrons (Marr 2004: 44). While the overall figures begin to look impressive from the 1930s onwards, the imbalance of Sunnis to non-Sunnis continued to remain. Just as the army of post-2003 Iraq is dominated by particular groupings (and most notably the Shi'i and Kurds), the same dynamic characterized the post-1920 Iraqi army, except this time, while the majority of recruits were from the Shi'i community, the officer corps remained almost wholly Sunni Arab (Hashim 2003a: 31). On its creation, the army absorbed 640 returning ex-Ottoman and Sharifian officers into its ranks, quickly establishing the core of the officer elite, and additional officer cadets were quickly recruited. Again, these were overwhelmingly Sunni Arabs, with only a quarter coming from other backgrounds (Tarbush 1982: 78). The pattern is even starker ten years later. Considering the backgrounds of a sample of sixty-one officers, Tarbush found that only one was a Shi'i and two were Christian, with the remainder being Sunni (1982: 79).

The military quickly became seen by those Sunni Arabs not part of the old established social classes of the Ottoman era as the primary means of social mobilization and political progression in the new Iraq (Tripp 2000: 47). A 'new middle class' of non-propertied individuals and groups had emerged that challenged the traditional landed classes for political influence in the new state. In Iraq, as in other Middle Eastern states, they penetrated the institutions of the newly formed military, securing through it prestige and influence, and making it the vanguard of their nationalist cause (Halpern 1962: 278–9; Stansfield 2005a: 359). This emergent new middle class of Sunni Arabs, greatly influenced by prevailing Arab nationalist thought, and exposed to the actions of nationalist groups such as *al-Ahd*, would soon begin to question the legitimacy of the monarch as he struggled to balance nationalist concerns with the requirement of satisfying his British advisors.

The emergence of the military as a serious actor in the politics of Iraq took place throughout the 1930s, with the army quadrupling in size. Along with this increased size came an equally notable change in political outlook. Still overwhelmingly Arab nationalist, the officer corps of the army began to see themselves as the most organized body within the Iraqi state, modern in outlook and aspirations and not tied to the customs and traditions of a bygone age, as they considered many of their countrymen to be. They also viewed with dismay the political and economic development of Iraq during the 1920s, seeing a succession of governments come and go, with the king seemingly unable, or unwilling, to wrestle Iraq free from the fetters of the British. The military elite also viewed regional developments with interest, and none more so than the example provided by Kemalist Turkey. Resurgent following the defeat of the Ottoman Empire in the First World War, and proving to be more than a match for European imperial powers, the Turkish model was viewed with admiration among Iraq's officer corps. The application of this model to Iraq, they believed, would see the emergence of a strong, centrally organized, Arab nationalist state capable of eradicating the involvement of the British in the affairs of state, and pursuing policies that would modernize and develop the country. Those that opposed these ideas – whether because they considered the British to be vital to Iraq's development (which included many among the king's entourage), or because they objected to the manner in which political power in Iraq was organized, such as the Kurds and the Shiʿi *mujtahid*s – would soon come into contact with the rising force of the military, inculcated with a Sunni Arab vision of nationalism, and increasingly intolerant of imperial involvement.

The Role of the Military and the Communalization of Political Life

The first to suffer at the hands of the army in Iraq were neither the Kurds (who remained in a state of semi-permanent rebellion in the mountain fastnesses of the north), nor the Shi'i, who continued to remain troublesome in the holy cities and across the south. Instead, it was the small Assyrian community which paid the price for being perceived to be threatening Iraq's integrity, and for also being seen as willing collaborators with the British. The massacre of the Assyrians in 1933 illustrates perhaps better than any other event the Arab nationalist orientation of the military in Iraq, and its willingness to eradicate any threat to Iraq's Arab nationalist identity.

Unlike the Chaldeans, the (modern) Assyrians are not indigenous Iraqis. Instead, their homeland was in the Hakkari region of south-eastern Turkey. During the First World War, the Assyrians rebelled against the Turks and joined forces with advancing Russian troops. Following the end of the war and the reinvigoration of Turkey under Ataturk, the Assyrians fled to Persia and then, under British sponsorship, 35,000 Assyrians were settled in Iraq (Tarbush 1982: 96). Displaying open loyalty to the British, large numbers of Assyrians were recruited to serve as 'Levies' and, after the war, were settled in areas of northern Iraq on land expropriated from rebellious Kurds, where they enjoyed British protection from both Arabs and Kurds alike.

The Assyrians were both feared and fearful. As a military force, the Levies were, at first, superior to the fledgling Iraqi army. But, as a minority within a newly independent Iraq, the Assyrians were all too aware of the overwhelming weakness of their position. While their British protectors remained in Iraq, the Assyrians had little to fear. But, with Iraq applying for membership of the League of Nations in 1930, leading to its independence from Britain in 1932, the Assyrians began to fear what the future held for them. As is the case in post-2003 Iraq, the Assyrians considered that their best option lay in establishing an autonomous enclave in the north of Iraq (Husry 1974: 167–8). However, when negotiations collapsed, fighting quickly broke out and, considering the Assyrians to pose a threat to Iraq's integrity and identity as an Arab nationalist state, the northern-based units of the Iraqi army (and some opportunistic Kurdish tribes) under the command of Colonel Bakr Sidqi marched against the Assyrians.

After skirmishes occurred between Assyrians and Iraqi soldiers, Bakr Sidqi's troops entered the town of Sumail on 11 August 1933, massacring some 300 men and killing several women and children. As many as forty Assyrian villages were then targeted and looted, mainly by Kurds, with as many as 600 Assyrians being killed (Stafford 1935: 244; Tejirian 1972: 150). Long despised for their association with the British and their unwillingness to acquire Iraqi citizenship and learn Arabic, little sympathy existed for the plight of the Assyrians, and the elimination of the Assyrian 'threat' was applauded throughout Iraq. Most importantly, the crushing of the Assyrians also marked the arrival of the army as a domestic force in Iraqi politics. Instead of protecting Iraq from external threats, the army would be increasingly deployed by the Iraqi government to subdue those groups that opposed it, and to enforce its authority over Iraq.

The second notable example of the military beginning to play an increasingly prominent role in the defence of an Arab-nationalist defined Iraq was in the further subjugation of Shiʿi tribes. Unrest erupted in the mid-Euphrates region in January 1935. The causes of it were wide-ranging, but mainly related to the overall lack of representation of the Shiʿi in the Iraqi government, while still accepting the legitimacy of the Iraqi state (Tripp 2000: 82). When the government refused to acknowledge the grievances of the Shiʿi, as expressed in a document called the *Mithaq al-Sha'b* (People's Pact), sporadic revolts broke out across the south from May 1935, continuing into the following year. Again, under Sidqi, the army was used to quash Shiʿi tribal revolts with heightened levels of brutality, including summary executions and the imposition of martial law (Marr 2004: 43).

In the north, the Kurds had remained in a perennial state of chaotic insurrection. Following the rebellions of Sheikh Mahmoud in the 1920s, the Kurds had continued to rebel against their inclusion in the state of Iraq. However, they would more often than not take up arms against each other in a series of inter-tribal squabbles and, while the instability created by this fighting caused concern in Baghdad as it impeded attempts to extend the dominion of the state over the still-disputed Mosul *vilayet*, the various localized Kurdish insurrections could still be managed by the Royal Air Force bombing particularly troublesome villages, and by the empowering of various tribal leaders at the expense of others. Starting in the 1940s, a new, Kurdish nationalist agenda began to appear among the Kurds, which brought them into direct confrontation with Arab nationalists in a battle that would continue unabated for the rest of the century. The emergence of Kurdish nationalism in Iraq came about because of two formative influences. The first was the emergence of a charismatic leader in the figure of Mulla Mustafa Barzani. After rebelling throughout the 1930s, Barzani was sent into exile from Kurdistan to Nasiriyya, and then kept under house arrest in the Kurdish city of Suleimaniyya. The second influence was the appearance of Kurdish nationalist parties of leftist orientation across Kurdistan (see Jwaideh 1960: 794). One of these, *Hiwa*, would rescue Barzani from Suleimaniyah and return him to Barzan. From there, he organized the Barzani Revolt of 1943, calling for the establishment of a Kurdish autonomous province. It would take the might of the Iraqi army to again quell the rebellion, forcing Barzani to flee to Iran along with 3,000 of his fighters. Following his involvement with the short-lived Kurdish Republic of Mahabad in 1946, Barzani was forced into exile in the USSR, where he would remain until the deposal of the monarchy. But Barzani's exile did not weaken the newly found nationalism of the Kurds. Before his leaving, Barzani had been instrumental in the creation of the Kurdish Democratic Party (KDP), along with other prominent figures, including Ibrahim Ahmed and, a few years later, the future President of Iraq, Jalal Talabani (Stansfield 2003: 63–6).

By the 1950s, the Iraqi army had become the principal means by which Iraq's integrity would be maintained and by which Iraq's Arab nationalist identity would be protected from the danger posed by the Shiʿi religious establishment, Kurdish nationalists and other threats. Even so, it is important to stress that the military were not acting on their own initiative. Instead, they were used in a calculated and ruthless way by civilian politicians, who more often than not had their own rivalries in mind, rather than any provincial problem that threatened the state. However, from being a tool of the Iraqi government, the increasingly confident army would soon turn its attention towards its civilian masters, who were still perceived to be acting in the interests of Britain.

The Intensification of Anti-Imperialist Sentiment

The sensitivity of the military establishment to the continuing presence of the British in the affairs of Iraq was heightened by several events. The first of these was the awarding of the Iraq mandate to Britain. As the new king, Faisal would have to find a way by which he could maintain at least cordial relations with Britain, while satisfying the demands of the increasingly vociferous Arab nationalists who had served under him in the Arab Revolt, and who were now placed in commanding positions in the Iraqi army. This was not an easy task to perform and, from the outset, Faisal's attempts to maximize his autonomy brought him into direct conflict with the British High Commissioner, Percy Cox (Dodge 2003: 20). The attempts by the British to rein in the errant Faisal only served to heighten nationalist sentiment further, while also undermining the legitimacy of the monarchy itself.

The second event was the negotiating of the Treaty of 1922, and its subsequent renegotiating in 1930. Rather than being seen as evidence of Britain lessening its grip on Iraq, the Treaty of 1922, with its specified British advisors and provision for a British military presence, was taken by nationalists as proof that British motives were actually the opposite – that they would remain in Iraq, at least for the twenty years duration of the treaty, if not longer. Even though the Treaty of 1930 would ultimately lead to Iraq's accession to the League of Nations in 1932, it was viewed by nationalists as protecting British interests in Iraq, particularly as the development, training and equipping of Iraq's military remained very much in British hands.

The third event was the death of Faisal. Often unfairly criticized as being a weak ruler, Faisal was painfully aware of the political and social currents that existed within Iraq, and the need to ensure that the British involvement remained at a level that would satisfy her, but not so high as to incur the wrath of the nationalists. With his death in 1933, Iraq lost a steadying influence and gained, at least from the perspective of the British, a hugely destabilizing one in the form of Faisal's son, Ghazi. While undoubtedly less skilled than his father in balancing Iraq's political forces, the contempt with which Ghazi held the British meant that, from his viewpoint, such skills were simply not needed. Instead, Ghazi played to an Arab nationalist agenda, openly displaying his distaste of the British, and even being involved to some degree with the later Bakr Sidqi coup which would remove from the cabinet those deemed to be pro-British in their outlook.

The Bakr Sidqi coup of 1936 reflected the growing discontent of the military with a civilian government considered to be corrupt and still too heavily controlled by the British. Where the inspiration for the plotters came from, however, is debatable. Most observers point to the influence of authoritarian ideas originating in the rising fascist dictatorships of Europe. Nazi Germany in particular is often cited as being influential, as an example that could be applied to Iraq by showing that a monolithic, militaristic, government was able to unify fragmented countries and modernize backward societies (Marr 2004: 45). The evidence for this far-right association is, however, unconvincing and an equally possible 'left-wing' influence could be advanced. The English academic Harold Laski (professor of political science at the London School of Economics from 1926 until 1950) was a controversial figure who influenced significantly members of the *Ahali* group in Iraq, some of whom encouraged Sidqi's venture.

Whatever its cause, the coup, which came about at a moment when the army began to emerge as a prominent political force in Iraqi politics following the Assyrian massacre and the putting-down of Shiʿi rebellions in the early 1930s, aimed to replace the government rather than remove the king, who was perceived to be very much an anti-British Arab nationalist. In so doing, it effectively swept away the old ruling elite of Iraq, replacing it with those deemed more acceptable from the perspective of the army. But, rather than follow a distinctly Arab nationalist programme, the new government's promotion of an 'Iraqi First' policy quickly mobilized opposition against it, leading to Sidqi's assassination by Arab nationalist officers in Mosul in August 1937. Over the next four years, the military would involve itself in the affairs of state at an unprecedented level, with Arab nationalist officers consolidating their position in the military establishment and beginning to exercise considerable influence in the affairs of the government (Tripp 2000: 94). The death of Ghazi in suspicious circumstances in 1939 stoked further anti-British sentiment as popular opinion believed the British to have been directly involved in his killing/assassination (Anderson and Stansfield 2004: 18). With the reoccupation of Iraq by British forces in 1941, removing from power the government of Rashid Ali that had refused to accept British demands for Iraq to cease diplomatic relations with axis powers, Arab nationalists became more determined than ever to gain meaningful, no-strings, independence for Iraq. They viewed civilian governments as being inherently pro-British, particularly as the anglophile Nuri al-Saʿid enjoyed a period of prominence as the figure to whom the king and the British would turn when problems arose.[2]

Following Ghazi's demise, Iraq was headed by an infant monarch, Faisal II, with Prince Abd al-Illah appointed to govern as regent until the young Faisal came of age. Immensely unpopular due to his pro-British leanings, nationalist sentiment in Iraq continued to grow, and exploded when the treaty of 1930 came to be renegotiated with the British in 1947. Always a symbol of British imperialism, for Arab nationalists the only successful outcome to the treaty negotiations would be the termination of the British presence from Iraq and the ending of Britain's meddling in Iraq's affairs. Therefore, the signing of what became known as the Portsmouth Treaty in January 1948, which removed British troops from Iraq but still militarily tied Iraq to Britain until 1973, was met with uproar on the streets of Iraq and culminated in the *wathba* (literally, 'leap', but in effect, an uprising) of early 1948. Different from previous outbursts of public dissatisfaction due to the mass nature of the event, the *wathba* illustrated the growing power of political parties capable of mobilizing the masses, and especially that of the Iraqi Communist Party (ICP). Socio-economic problems afflicting Iraq in the post-war period served to strengthen the parties of the left considerably, which also remained opposed to the intervention of imperial powers in the affairs of Iraq. The most notable example of such intervention was the continued private (largely British) ownership of the Iraqi Petroleum Company (IPC) and, when the nationalization of Iranian oil interests by the new nationalist government of Mossadeq coincided with large-scale industrial action among port workers in Basra, ICP-inspired riots broke out across Iraq in 1952 and, as with the *wathba*, were coloured by strong anti-imperialist sentiment (Marr 2004: 71–2).

The signing, in 1955, by Prime Minister Nuri al-Saʿid of a security agreement with Turkey, Iran and Pakistan, known as the Baghdad Pact, would spell the beginning of the end for the monarchy and witness the taking of power by an Arab nationalist military. While undoubtedly alleviating Iraq's fragile security problems by building stronger relationships with Turkey and Iran (which also weakened the ability of the Kurds to trouble Baghdad), it also split the Arab world in two, with Egypt and Iraq competing with each other for effective leadership of the Arab world (Kerr 1971: 4–5). Prime Minister Nuri's problem was that Nasser not only had strong public support in Egypt, but that he also enjoyed strong public support in Iraq as well. Benefiting from the already vocal anti-imperialist sentiment apparent in Iraq, which was consolidated by propaganda emanating from Cairo's 'Voice of the Arabs' radio station, opposition to the regime in Iraq began to grow. Iraq's continued alliance with Britain during the Suez Crisis of 1956 further consolidated this opposition against the monarchy. Politically, the opposition was becoming very well organized and disparate groups began to coalesce under an anti-imperialist, and anti-monarchy, banner. The emergence of a new political front, the United National Front, uniting the National Democratic Party, the Istiqlal, the ICP and the recently formed Ba'th Party, was itself a significant threat to the continued existence of the monarchy and its pro-British supporters. However, it was dissension in the armed forces that would ultimately remove the regime. Several conspiracies had already been uncovered by the repressive Nuri and dealt with harshly. But it would take only one conspiracy to succeed and bring an end to nearly four decades of monarchical rule in Iraq.

Towards Totalitarianism

The monarchy came to a bloody end on 14 July 1958 when forces loyal to Abd al-Karim Qasim and Abd al-Salam Arif marched on Baghdad, taking control of key government buildings and executing the king and the royal family in the grounds of the royal palace. Nuri al-Sa'id initially escaped, but was then found trying to flee Baghdad in a woman's cloak and killed on the spot. The events leading to the coup can be traced to the establishment of the 'Free Officers' Movement' in 1952, which hoped to emulate the success of Nasser in Egypt. By 1957, the movement had established several cells within the army under the leadership of Qasim. The movement's aims included: (i) a struggle against imperialism and an end to foreign bases; (ii) the removal of feudalism; (iii) an end to the monarchy; (iv) the introduction of democracy; (v) recognition of the rights of the Kurds; (vi) cooperation with Arab countries; (vii) promotion of Arab unity; and (vii) the return of Palestine (Marr 2004: 83–4). While the movement had specific aims, however, it had little idea how to enact even the general policies that would achieve them and, far from promoting democracy and recognizing the rights of the Kurds, for example, the military government of Qasim would be the first of several that would see Iraq move from being authoritarian to totalitarian.

The revolution of 1958 finally removed the last vestiges of British colonial involvement from Iraq (but still stayed clear of nationalizing the IPC for fear of upsetting its predominantly British stakeholders), and established the army as the principal arbiter of power. However, the coup leaders were far from united in their visions for Iraq's future. Arif led one group, best described as 'Arab nationalist', and advocating union with Egypt and Syria as part of the United Arab Republic (UAR). The 'Iraqi nationalist' group (inheriting the mantle from the Sidqi government of the 1930s) was headed by Qasim and included the ICP. The latter group won out after a tense few weeks of jockeying for political position following the coup. However, a cleavage had opened in Iraqi politics between the Arab nationalists on the one hand (and especially the Baʿth Party), and Iraqi nationalists on the other (and most notably the ICP), with the Baʿth Party growing significantly following the revolution of 1958 and becoming the natural home to those who opposed Qasim and the ICP. The rise of the Baʿth Party saw some of its members become increasingly confident and aggressive. Illustrating this is the attempt made upon Qasim's life in October 1959. The attempt ultimately failed – by all accounts it was badly botched – but it was the first moment that the name of Saddam Hussein was heard. It would not be the last.[3]

Qasim's government came to an end as bloody and violent as that of the monarchy. Viewed as being increasingly weak and ineffective following a string of events that exasperated Arab nationalists, including the emergence of a vibrant new Shiʿi religious movement, *hizb al-Daʿwa*, and Qasim's allowing of the exiled Mulla Mustafa to return to Iraq, only to see him and the KDP commence a fully fledged war in 1961 that achieved notable successes against the Iraqi army, Qasim's opponents in the armed forces and in the Baʿth began to plot his downfall. On 8 February 1963, Ba'thist and Arab nationalist military figures overthrew Qasim's government after heavy fighting in Baghdad. Qasim was killed the day after, and his body displayed on public TV for all to see.

The first Ba'th government was duly formed, but it would be the military figure of Abd al-Salam Arif that would head it, with Ba'thists holding important positions within the government – Ahmed Hassan al-Bakr was made Prime Minister and Ali Salih al-Sa'di was appointed as his deputy, for example. The Ba'thists immediately showed the ruthlessness with which they would later be so closely associated, rooting out Qasim supporters and ferociously persecuting members of the ICP. However, while particularly adept at removing opponents operating outside the regime, they proved less able at identifying adversaries closer to home. Proving as inept as Qasim in weakening what had now turned into a Kurdish insurgency, and falling foul of the Arab nationalist hero Egyptian President Nasser, who openly encouraged a change of government in Iraq, the days of the first Ba'thist government were numbered. On 18 November 1963 – less than a year from coming to power – Arif announced that the military would take control of the country and dismissed the Ba'thists from their posts. Iraq remained under military rule for the next five years, first under Abd al-Salam Arif, and then his brother Abd al-Rahman. Although unceremoniously dumped out of office, the Ba'thists were not to retire graciously into history. Instead, they would learn the painful lessons inflicted upon them by Arif's smooth seizing of power. Hassan al-Bakr and his young deputy Saddam Hussein learnt primarily that, while they needed the military to come to power, it was a mistake to trust the military once in power. It would also not take a genius to realize that the rapid turnover of governments in Iraq suggested that extraordinary measures should be taken in order to secure a new regime from the attentions of the military, the street, the Shi'i and the Kurds. The manifestations of such thinking would become readily apparent following the second Ba'thist coup of 1968.

Successful coups in Iraq have always been collaborative ventures. From the alliance between the Free Officers and the

Iraqi Communist Party in 1958, through to the allying of the military with the Ba'th Party in 1963, two or more groupings were always involved, but it would always be the military, as the most organized and effective partner, that would ultimately commandeer power in the state. The coup of 17 July 1968 was, in its execution, little different from its predecessors. It was again a cooperative venture, this time between a diverse group of military officers and the Ba'th Party, with the military taking a leading role in its execution. This time, however, the Ba'th had learned their lessons of working with the military in the coup of 1963, and, instead of being cast aside once the revolution had taken place, the newly appointed President, Ahmad Hassan al-Bakr (a military figure, but also a Ba'thist), and his two colleagues, Salih Mahdi Ammash and Hardan al-Tikriti, quickly purged the coup coalition of the most important military figures, and then turned on the communists and Kurdish nationalists to remove any internal threats to the regime (Mufti 1996: 198). Later, Saddam Hussein would act to remove internal threats to his ascendancy from within the Ba'th Party itself. Both Ammash and Hardan al-Tikriti were targeted by him and his already expanding security apparatus in 1971, with the latter coming to a suspiciously untimely end in Kuwait, and Ammash made ambassador to Moscow – an appointment made in such a way that he apparently could not refuse. By 1974, Saddam was second only to Bakr. As vice-chairman of the pre-eminent decision-making body in the state – the Revolution's Command Council – and heading the rapidly expanding security services, it would not be long before Saddam emerged from the shadow of his elder kinsman and became the undisputed ruler of Iraq.

Still essentially authoritarian rather than totalitarian in nature, the Ba'thist state would be transformed from the mid-1970s onwards by changes occurring in the world oil market. Benefiting from the nationalization of the oil industry in June 1972, Iraq would see its oil revenue increase exponentially following the rise in oil prices ordered by the Organization of Petroleum Exporting Countries (OPEC) in the aftermath of the oil embargo caused by the 1973 Arab–Israeli War. Iraq's oil export revenue had already seen a 100 per cent rise in the decade following Qasim's coup, from $244 million i 1958 to $488 million in 1968, but this was dwarfed by th increase that occurred in the next ten years, which saw re enues rocket to $21.4 billion (Stork 1982: 32). The windfa provided the Baʿth government with an ability to insula itself from society at large, and to protect itself through mea sures ranging from expanding the state sector, and associate job creation, through to the building of an expansive an sophisticated internal security apparatus (see Dodge 200 68). With regard to the Baʿth government of the 1970s *nc* having to depend upon raising taxes to fund governmer activities, the figures make clear reading. For the perio 1927–31, 81 per cent of government revenues came fror taxation. This steadily decreased to 27 per cent in the 1950 and 23.5 per cent in the 1960s. With the windfall from o rent accumulating in government coffers, the figure collapse to 11.5 per cent in 1974 (Mufti 1996: 201). While the Irac state was taxing its citizens less, it was also employin more of them than ever before. Between 1968 and 1978, th number of government employees more than doubled fror 276,605 to 662,856, while the number of armed forces pe sonnel increased from 100,000 in 1970 to 250,000 in 198(with a further 175,000 serving in the Popular Army (a Baʿthis militia), and 260,000 working in the police force (all figure from Mufti 1996: 201). What is essential to realize is tha by 1990, an estimated 21 per cent of the workforce and 4 per cent of households were directly dependent upon the stat for their well-being (Dodge 2003: 68–9, quoting al-Khafa 2000: 68). This overwhelming dependence upon the state wa complemented by an immense expansion of the securit apparatus. By 1980, the year that Iraq went to war with Iran a fifth of Iraq's economically active labour force (about 3. million people) were institutionally charged, in peace time with one form or another of violence (Makiya 1998: 39).

The Totalitarian State

By the late 1970s, Iraq was rapidly becoming a totalitaria state, closely matching the definitions presented earlier in th chapter. By the end of the decade, the 'cult of the leader' was already established in Iraq, with Saddam clearly the most important figure in the regime, having succeeded Ahmad Hassan al-Bakr in 1979 following his encouraged retirement. Ba'thism had also been developing into a mass movement, with membership of the party being the principal mechanism by which individuals could secure social advancement, and benefit from the vast patronage structure controlled by the state and funded by Iraq's immense oil wealth. By 1976, Ba'th Party membership is estimated to have reached half a million – an exponential increase on previous decades' membership (Makiya 1998: 39). By the mid-1980s that figure had perhaps risen to an astonishing 1.5 million (Moss Helms 1984: 87). Whatever the true figure, it is clear that Ba'thism had become a 'mass' political movement. Meaningful political opposition also did not exist, apart from in the Kurdish mountains and within the Shi'i south – both opposed to the Arab nationalist narrative emanating from Ba'thist Iraq, and both increasingly mobilized to promote their own visions of Iraqi nationalism in clear competition with the Sunni-Arab dominated vision held by the Ba'th.

The impact of this grandiose rentier system on Iraq was devastating for the development of a civil society or democratic system of government in Iraq. With Saddam in charge of a patronage system effectively administered by the Ba'th Party, there was little incentive for individuals to subscribe to political groups that challenged the status quo. State patronage, however, was only one method of limiting political opposition, and Saddam remained wholeheartedly committed to the more violent attributes of state control and created a sophisticated network of security and intelligence organizations. Five primary agencies constituted the Iraqi security apparatus: *Jihaz al-Amn al-Khas* (Special Security); *al-Amn al-'Amm* (General Security); *al-Mukhabarat* (General Intelligence); *al-Istikhbarat* (Military Intelligence); and *al-Amn al-'Askari* (Army Intelligence). In addition to these organizations, there also existed a number of party security agencies, police forces, paramilitaries and special units, all armed to protect the regime from any actual, perceived or threatened form of opposition (Boyne 1997, 1998; Marashi 2003). These organizations formed an Orwellian web of mistrust, fear and coercion which comprehensively permeated every aspect of Iraqi life, and few formations of civil or political life could exist in such an environment, least of all the fragile institutions necessary for representative democracy to emerge (Stansfield 2005b). In such an environment, Kanan Makiya despondently opined, 'opposition can no longer arise except in people's mind, and then it is not really an opposition at all' (1998: 37–8).[4]

The effect of this dual strategy of patronage and coercion was to 'atomize' Iraqi society – in effect weaken bonds within society and link each individual vertically to the patron-state (al-Khafaji 2003: 77–92). Political affiliation to any party other than the Baʿth was prohibited and often, as in the case of *Daʿwa*, punishable by death. Class-based political organizations struggled to survive due to the invidious nature of the rentier system, and the targeting of horizontal linkages in society by the regime. The result was the consolidation of power in the hands of the totalitarian state, with the institutions of civil society necessary for the initial emergence of democracy failing to emerge beyond anything but a superficial, and controlled, measure.

By 1980, Saddam had succeeded where other regimes and individuals had failed. He had freed his regime from the instability of Iraqi political life by placing Iraq under the tyranny of a totalitarian system of government. He also ensured that revenue was used to improve Iraq's infrastructure, embarking upon extensive road-building projects, and building hundreds of schools and hospitals. Indeed, Saddam's Iraq displayed advanced socio-economic indicators, and new economic wealth and rapid modernization all assisted in further blunting opposition to the regime (Marr 2004: 176). Of course, this was assisted greatly by the availability of spectacularly high oil revenues, but it was also down to his actions and 'special' abilities as a leader who was prepared to take extreme actions and measures. In taking such actions, however, he was not unique in Iraq's history. The blueprints of political violence had all been established in previous decades. Saddam merely took these blueprints to extremes never before witnessed.

5 Iraq at War, 1979–1989

By 1979, Saddam Hussein was the undisputed ruler of Iraq. Through his own innate political sense, charismatic appeal (which is often forgotten), and ability and willingness to threaten and to use disproportionate violence, he had succeeded where his predecessors had failed, by controlling the military and vigorously attacking any threat, potential or otherwise, to his regime. He had also invested heavily in Iraq's infrastructure and succeeded in transforming Iraq's public services. But serious problems still remained. The Kurds were as troublesome as ever, but had largely been subdued following the demise of Mulla Mustafa Barzani. Kurdish *peshmerga* brigades were still roaming the mountains, but were more concerned with fighting each other than turning their attention to the Iraqi military. The Shiʿi too were largely subdued due to the efforts of the expanding Iraqi security services. However, Saddam was well aware that Iranian influence could quite easily aggravate either of these problems, and he, along with his predecessors, remained fearful of Iranian meddling and interference. Iraq also had other ongoing disputes with Iran. Chief among these was the status of the Shatt al-Arab waterway in the south of the country. Providing Iraq's only access to the high seas, the Shatt was a geopolitical chokepoint that could strangle Iraq's economy if controlled by Iran.

History of Iran–Iraq Relations

The contestation over the border lands between Iran and Iraq has an old history, as has competition between powers in Iran and Iraq in general. At various moments in the distant past, Iraq fell under the sway of Persian powers, including the Achaemenids and later the Sasanids, and the opposite also occurred, with Iran being part of the Abbasid Empire governed from Baghdad. These historical facts would be used by both Baʿthist Iraq and the Islamic Republic as a rationale and justification for territorial claims in the present (Bakhash 2004: 12). In more modern times, Iraq itself was contested territory between the mighty Ottoman and Safavid empires. It was during this struggle that sectarian differences between the Sunni Ottomans and the Shiʿi Safavids became important, and the sixteenth and seventeenth centuries were characterized by a series of conflicts between the two. The Persian–Ottoman 'Treaty of Peace and Frontiers' signed at Zohab in 1639 brought an end to the fighting, but, following the collapse of the Safavids in 1722, the Ottomans used the opportunity to invade Iran and claim large swathes of territory. In what, at least superficially, mirrors the war between Iran and Iraq 250 years later, Iranian forces counterattacked, forcing the signing of a treaty in 1746 basically agreeing that the boundary would remain as it had been designated in 1639 (Schofield 2004: 31; Bakhash 2004: 13).

Following a further brief two-year conflict starting in 1821, Qajar Iran signed a new treaty in 1823 with the Ottomans, again confirming the boundary identified by earlier treaties. Further conflict attracted the interest of Britain and Russia and, with their assistance, a new agreement on the boundary was reached, enshrined in the Treaty of Erzurum of 1847. Before this treaty, the definition of the boundary between Iran and Ottoman Iraq had remained vague and ambiguous, and particularly in the south towards the head of the Gulf. In an attempt to resolve this, the Treaty of Erzurum defined the boundary in this area as being the low-water mark on the Iranian side of the Shatt al-Arab (the confluence of the Tigris and Euphrates before it empties into the Gulf), effectively granting all of the river to the Ottomans and beginning what would be a long-lasting competition between Iran and Iraq in the twentieth century for control over the waterway (Hünseler 1984: 11).[1] A complex agreement, slightly modifying the Shatt boundary, occurred in 1937 and granted the waters around the Iranian city of Abadan to Iran in order that ships loading at its ports would be doing so in Iranian waters. A second agreement that would have seen authority in the waterway shared between the two powers was never signed.

A brief rapprochement occurred between Iraq and Iran following the signing of the Baghdad Pact in 1955. However, it was short-lived with tensions between the two countries becoming yet again strained following the revolution of 1958. The emergence of a revolutionary, seemingly pro-Nasserite regime in Iraq, willing to deal with the Soviets, was deeply unsettling for the pro-Western shah, who was fearful of possible Soviet expansionism threatening Iran from the north (Bakhash 2004: 15). Qasim himself proved to be uncooperative when Iran attempted to reopen the possibility of sharing the administration of the Shatt al-Arab, and even went further by claiming the entirety of the Shatt, and a three-mile area around the Iranian port-city of Abadan. Tensions between the two countries escalated, with Iraq expelling many thousands of Iranian nationals, and placing its military forces on alert. This time, however, the tension would come to nothing. Iraq continued to control the Basra Port Authority, while Abadan remained resolutely Iranian.

But, for Tehran, the friction caused by Iraq's tenure of the Shatt would not subside and was now seen as a matter of national pride. Qasim too was not shirking from confronting Iran and proceeded to follow a range of actions, none of which would encourage the development of neighbourly cooperation between the two powers. First, Qasim claimed Iran's oil rich province of Khuzistan (the centre of Iran's oil industry) as being part of Iraq due to it being populated by Arabs. This was not, by all accounts, a new claim and can be first traced to Ottoman dissatisfaction regarding the 1639 treaty (Hünseler 1984: 10). His naming it 'Arabistan' was then mirrored by the Iraqi government renaming the Persian Gulf as the 'Arabian' Gulf, in a move clearly designed to mobilize Arab popular support behind the military regime and challenge Iran's predominance in the Gulf.

By now, the issue of control over the Shatt had become one of national security and also pride for both states. For Iraq, Basra was its only deep-water seaport and no threat to its access to the sea could be entertained. Therefore, Iran's attempt to have the boundary between it and Iraq redesignated as the *thalweg* (a line following the deepest water in the river) of the Shatt fell upon deaf ears in Baghdad. Already tense, Iran's relations with Iraq would deteriorate even further following the second Baʿthist coup of 1968. Overtly Arab nationalist, and keen to shore up popular support in Iraq by adopting an aggressive foreign policy and an anti-Western stance, the new Baʿthist government was viewed with alarm in Tehran.

The rising oil prices of the 1970s saw Iraq and Iran engage in large-scale development of economic infrastructure, including the port facilities and the oil industry. For Iraq, this indicated that maintaining control of the Shatt was more important than ever before. For Iran, the area around the Shatt became of increased strategic importance as well, with the city of Khorramshahr being critical to Iran's economic well-being, as its port was the main gateway into Iran for imports. The oil industry of Khuzistan too was expanding, with Iran investing heavily to transform it into a major industrial centre (Bakhash 2004: 18). The confluence of interests that had emerged at the head of the Gulf had reached a critical mass by the beginning of the 1970s. National interests coincided with economic investments and regional politics, with the historical memory of previous centuries being evoked by both sides to prove the legitimacy of their claims. The Shatt al-Arab was therefore central in understanding the causative factors underpinning Iraq's invasion of Iran. However, while it was perhaps the most important *reason* why Iraq invaded Iran in 1980, it was not the *trigger*. The spark that ignited the Iran–Iraq War was, in fact, several hundreds of miles away in the mountains of the north.

The Kurdish War

The Iraq army, as we have seen, was conceived primarily as a means to combat internal security threats to the regime, rather than potential enemies emanating from abroad. As such, it had spent considerable time and effort putting down a variety of rebellions and insurrections among recalcitrant tribes, fervent followers of indignant Shiʿi *mujtahid*s and other ethnic groups, including the Assyrians and the Turkmen. The deepest internal security problem facing Iraqi governments, however, was the threat posed by the Kurds. Ever since the invention of Iraq in the 1920s, the Kurds had remained perennial thorns in the side of Arab-nationalist dominated governments and it would be uncommon for years, or even months, to go by without there being an uprising taking place somewhere in Kurdistan. At first, these uprisings tended to be localized in nature, and often focused upon particularly tribal grievances rather than anything overtly 'Kurdish'. However, the consolidation of a Kurdish nationalist movement occurred from the 1940s onwards, with 'tribal' Kurds under the leadership of the charismatic Mulla Mustafa Barzani finding common (if uneasy) cause with the urban leftist intelligentsia of cities such as Suleimaniyya under the common banner of the Kurdistan Democratic Party (KDP). The demands of the KDP and Barzani focused almost always upon demanding an autonomous province for the Kurds, covering the northern governorates of Iraq (Erbil, Suleimaniyya and Dohuk) and, following Barzani's return from exile in 1958, the Kurds again began rebelling in 1961 due to Qasim's attempts to weaken Kurdish influence in Iraq, and opposition emerged in Kurdistan to the Iraqi government's Agrarian Reform Law (Jawad 1982: 48).

The Kurds constituted a real threat to Iraq's territorial integrity, while also symbolically challenging the notion of Iraq's dominant Arabness. During the 1960s, the Kurds moved from being insurgents, hitting Iraqi garrisons and outposts and then vanishing into the hills, to holding a great swathe of territory and even establishing judicial and administrative institutions. Barzani and the KDP also controlled Iraq's borders with Turkey and Iran, with the latter increasingly seeing the Kurds as potential proxies to be empowered as Tehran's relations with Baghdad deteriorated throughout the decade. Between 1961 and 1970, the situation in Kurdistan closely mirrored political developments in Baghdad.[2] With each new government in this period, the Kurds would be offered a truce, only for negotiations to fail and for the Kurdish rebellion to continue as before (Jawad 1982: 49). The most notable of these negotiations were those headed by Prime Minster Abd al-Rahman al-Bazzaz. The 'Bazzaz Declaration' went further than ever before in meeting most of the Kurdish demands for autonomy, language rights and representation in the institutions of state (Bakhash 2004: 20). However, with the deposing of the military government and the emergence of the Baʿth regime in 1968, the agreement was never implemented. Instead, the new government moved quickly to attempt to defeat the rebels once and for all. In what was, by all accounts, a full-scale war, the Kurds inflicted heavy losses upon Iraqi forces, and caused significant damage to the oil infrastructure in the north of the country. Embroilment in a draining and destabilizing war with the Kurds was exactly what the new Baʿthist government did not need. Such a conflict would destabilize and discredit the government, while allowing the military to maintain its influence in the affairs of state. Recognizing the need to regroup in order to strengthen the regime, weaken the military as a potential source of a coup and to then strengthen it to defeat the Kurds, the Iraqi government desperately needed time. The seriousness of the situation was amply illustrated by the despatching of Saddam himself to negotiate the March Agreement of 1970.

For the Kurds, the March Agreement was the beginning of the first 'golden era', with the second occurring in the 1990s. The agreement promised the Kurds full recognition of their nationality and autonomy within four years. Kurdish was to be made the primary language in Kurdish areas, and an official language of Iraq. Kurdish governors were appointed in the major cities, and Kurdish ministers sat in Baghdad. There remained, however, one point on which neither the Kurds nor the Iraqi government could agree. The inclusion of the city of Kirkuk, with its mixed population of Kurds, Arabs and Turkmen, and sitting on top of one of Iraq's largest oilfields, into the Kurdish autonomous region was a non-negotiable demand of the Kurds. For the Iraqi government, Kirkuk was central to the economic well-being of the state, and would also give the Kurds the economic wherewithal to expand their autonomy to actual independence, thereby destroying Iraq's territorial integrity. The two sides therefore agreed to resolve the situation by holding a plebiscite sometime in the future. Even with the fate of Kirkuk hanging over the March Agreement, there still existed considerable optimism for the future. However, it was not to last. As the Baʿth government regrouped its strength throughout the early 1970s, it would soon show that it had little intention of honouring the far-reaching Articles of the March Agreement, and particularly with regard to deciding Kirkuk's future by holding a plebiscite, as Barzani demanded. Following the collapse of negotiations in March 1974, the government unilaterally announced the Autonomy Law for Iraqi Kurdistan on 11 March. The KDP rejected it and, on the following day, the Kurds resumed their offensive.

The fighting of the mid-1970s was some of the most serious yet to have occurred in the northern mountains. By sheer weight of numbers, the Iraqi army won back territory but it was a piecemeal process and tremendously costly in terms of casualties and resources. Also, progress against the Kurds slowed to a halt as they were pushed further into the mountains – terrain in which they operated with heightened effectiveness. It was at this moment that Iran became involved. Any instability in Iraq was welcomed by the shah, and none seemed to be more capable of causing problems than the Kurds. From 1975, Iran increased its supply of weapons to the *peshmerga*, and it was estimated that some 1,000 Iranian military personnel were also sent to operate the more technically advanced equipment (Jawad 1982: 56).

The Iraqi government needed to act quickly. It could not entertain the prospect of a full-scale war with Iran, and desperately needed to end the threat posed to the stability of the regime by the Kurds. The end of the Kurdish rebellion would therefore be tied by Iran to the resolution of the Shatt al-Arab dispute. Meeting in Algiers in March 1975 during an OPEC summit, the shah and Saddam (now vice-president) came to an understanding that would have far-reaching consequences. The Iranian government agreed 'to establish confidence and security all along the frontiers and to have a strict and efficient control of all subversive infiltration', effectively ending aid to the *peshmerga* of Kurdistan-Iraq (Jawad 1982: 57). The Kurdish rebellion collapsed, with Barzani leaving Kurdistan-Iraq, never to return.[3] The KDP split in the aftermath of the collapse, with Mustafa Barzani's sons, Idris and Massoud, leading what continued to be called the KDP, and Jalal Talabani emerging to lead a new union of leftist parties, known as the Patriotic Union of Kurdistan (PUK). The price for Iraq was not inconsiderable. The boundary between the countries, with reference to the Shatt al-Arab, would now be delimited along the *thalweg*, but it was a boundary that Iraq had consistently refused to allow in the past, and it would not be long before Baghdad would seize upon an opportunity to claw back full possession of the waterway.

The Decline into War with Iran

Considering the simmering tension that existed between Iraq and Iran over such geopolitical flashpoints as the Shatt al-Arab and Khuzistan (not to mention Kurdistan), it is surprising that war between the two neighbours did not break out before 1980. However, while Iran remained continuously exercised about not having some form of control over the Shatt (until 1975), the position of a long coastline and the establishing of military bases along it, thereby lessening the importance of the Shatt to Iran's national security, meant that continued Iraqi predominance in the waterway would not necessarily result in Iranian military action. The same could not be said for Iraq, however. Even with full control of the Shatt al-Arab, Iraq's outlet to the sea-lanes was tenuous, and dependent upon Iranian goodwill – something that could not always be guaranteed. With the boundary now running down the *thalweg* of the waterway, Iraq now faced a serious problem.

Whether or not Iraq would have invaded Iran merely to regain control of the Shatt al-Arab is a debatable point. However, what is clearer is that the decline into war was for several reasons, of which the Shatt al-Arab was one, which were interrelated and tied with Iraq's regional relations and domestic politics (Sirriyeh 1985: 483). The clearest example of such a reason was the Islamic revolution in 1979 which overthrew the shah. The emergence of not only an Islamist government in Iran, but a Shiʿi Islamist government, was profoundly worrying for Baʿthist Iraq. The possibility of the revolution spilling over from Iran into Iraq was something which Baghdad feared, and with good reason. The new regime in Iran was not at all alien to the Iraqi Shiʿi. Iran's new revolutionary leader, Ayatollah Ruhollah Khomeini, had resided in the Iraqi holy city of Najaf for several years, where the Iraqi government allowed him to preach against the shah. In so doing, Khomeini had come into contact with prominent Iraqi Shiʿi *mujtahid*s and had developed a considerable support base among the more radically minded in Najaf and the other shrine cities. It was not as if Iraq's Shiʿi needed much encouragement to revolt against the Baʿth regime either. For several years, Saddam had been struggling to deal with the prominent Iraqi *mujtahid* Ayatollah Mohammad Bakr al-Sadr and, failing to muzzle him, executed him and his sister in 1980. In addition to the damage caused to the regime by such individuals, the Daʿwa Party, now existing underground due to membership of it being punishable by death, succeeded in mounting a series of high-profile attacks against the regime, and very nearly assassinated Tariq Aziz (then of the RCC) in April 1980.

Iran was also supporting the efforts of the regrouping Kurdish parties in the north, with the KDP recommencing operations against the Iraqi military. Iraq followed suit by supporting Iranian Kurdish parties to take up arms against the Islamic Republic. In geopolitical terms, the change of regime in Iran did not alter the same strategic challenge faced by the shah – for Iran, Iraq remained as the major obstacle to the Iranian quest for regional hegemony (Karsh 1989b: 29). But fundamental changes had occurred in how the governing regimes of both Iran and Iraq now viewed each other. Between the shah and Saddam, there had existed deep-rooted suspicion, certainly, but this was of a geopolitical and security-related nature. Between Saddam's Iraq and the Iran of the Ayatollahs, the concerns had now taken on a deeply ideological meaning which would make war, if not inevitable, dangerously likely (Chubin 1989: 13).

With the shah's army replaced by a seemingly inchoate revolutionary rabble, Saddam sensed an opportunity. Perhaps realizing from his own experience just how weak revolutionary regimes tended to be in the first months in power, Saddam prepared his forces to launch a pre-emptive attack against Iran. He had good reason to feel confident that he could deal the Islamic Republic a crippling blow. It was clear that the Iranian military was not in a position to defend Iran's borders due to executions, purges and dismissals taking place since the shah's removal (Bakhash 2004: 21), and the most able military units were tied down fighting Kurdish rebels in Iranian Kurdistan. There had also been an attempted military coup, the 'Nuzhih plot', with which the Iraqi government were involved (Gasiorowski 2002: 645–6). Its failure resulted in the military being purged and the Iranian air force (by its close association with the plotters) being critically weakened, and the regime itself looked far from being unified. Indeed, Iraqi military intelligence consistently reported upon the deterioration of the Iranian military and the fractured political system (Marr 2004: 183). In addition, Iran had found itself internationally isolated, at least from the West, and managed to immediately alienate the US after seizing its embassy and diplomats in November 1979. From Saddam's perspective, Iran was an easy target. The defeat of the revolutionary regime would enhance his standing in the Arab world, restore full control of the Shatt al-Arab and perhaps even allow him to place in Tehran a government of his liking (Bakhash 2004: 22). Iraq formally denounced the Algiers Agreement on 17 September 1980, with Saddam tearing up the agreement in front of the Iraqi parliament, broadcast on Iraqi television.

Iraq Advances

By late August 1980, tensions had erupted into skirmishes. In September, Iranian forces shelled the Iraqi towns of Khanaqin and Mandali, with Iraq responding by occupying the district in which the Iranian artillery had been based. The decline into full-scale conflict became readily apparent when Saddam officially abrogated the Algiers Agreement on 17 September, with Iran responding by bombarding the Iraqi side of the Shatt al-Arab two days later. At this, Saddam responded with what may be considered to be a pre-emptive strike, launching a bombing mission into Iran aimed at air bases and associated facilities. The first phase of the land war then commenced on 23 September; the Iraqi army invaded Iran and made rapid advances. The towns of Qasr-e Shirin, Mahran and Musiyan were all captured and, in the south, Khorramshahr fell to Iraqi forces on 24 October (Marr 2004: 184). For Saddam, the invasion was very much a 'demonstrative war' (Chubin and Tripp 1991: 54), that is, its aim was to impress upon Iran (and also the Arab world) the supreme power of the Iraqi military, and to force them to accept his terms rather than the further devastation such a military could inflict upon the weak, post-revolutionary Islamic republic. Saddam announced cease-fire terms, almost certainly expecting Tehran to accept them in order to at least ensure that the regime would not collapse. These terms focused quite predictably upon ending Iran's involvement in the domestic affairs of Iraq (and with particular reference to logistically supporting the Kurds, and agitating the Shiʿi), and accepting Iraqi demands to control the Shatt. Iran, however, had been bloodied but not cowed. While the Iraqi army had achieved notable successes and managed to occupy the land in proximity to the boundary, the holding of the key supply nodes of Dizful and Abadan allowed the Iranian military to replenish their supplies and to plan their counterattack (Marr 2004: 185). Within weeks, it became clear that Iran was far from being in awe of the supposed superiority of the Iraqi army. Even Saddam Hussein, in a rare moment of frankness, admitted as such in a speech to the Iraqi national assembly (Tripp 2000: 233). This second phase of the war, which was in effect a stalemate, would last for one year.

With hindsight, it is obvious that Iran had several advantages over Iraq. Perhaps most importantly, the simple demographic differences between them benefited Iran. Although the Iraqi military was better equipped and its organization was more coherent, the Iranians could still withstand more casualties than Iraq, and the loss of territory was not of pressing strategic concern to a country so expansive. After the initial gains were made by Iraq in 1980, a stand-off effectively ensued throughout 1981. Saddam, concerned about the loyalty of his largely Shiʿi army, and its effectiveness in general, was unwilling to mount further attacks and instead expected, and hoped, that the Iranian government would succumb to his ceasefire demands. The Iranian leadership, however, had no such intention and instead countered the Iraqi army at the front and began an extensive regrouping and re-equipping of its military forces. Key to this was the rapid expansion of the Revolutionary Guards (the *pasdaran*), who were deployed to urban centres and were more trusted than the army itself, with its presumed pro-monarchy feelings (Ansari 2003: 232). In addition, Iran also benefited from an upsurge in the activities of radical Shiʿi movements in Iraq, and from the reinvigoration of the KDP as a prominent guerrilla force in the Kurdish mountains.

The sensitizing of the Shiʿi in Iraq was as much Saddam's fault as it was the product of Iranian machinations. Still fearful of any signs of organized resistance emerging against the regime from within the Shiʿi, any possible threats were dealt with harshly by the security forces, and Saddam would attempt to weaken the links enjoyed by Iraq's Shiʿi with those of Iran by encouraging Iraqis to divorce 'Iranian' wives, and appealing to myths supporting the superior nature of Arab identity (Tripp 2000: 234). Iran, however, was not innocent of encouraging the activities of anti-regime Shi'i movements. New groups emerged with Iranian backing, their *raison d'être* being the establishment of an Islamic state in Iraq. Most notable of these groups was the *Jama'at al-'Ulama al-Mujahidin* led by Mohammad Bakr al-Hakim. In 1982, Hakim's group and others came together under Iranian sponsorship to form the Supreme Council for Islamic Revolution in Iraq (SCIRI), which, in post-2003 Iraq, would become one of the most important participants in the Iraqi government.

Iran Counterattacks

By 1982, the Iranian military was ready to launch its counterattack, marking the third phase of the war, which would start in March 1982 and end in the autumn of the following year. Iraqi forces suffered high losses and were pushed out of all the areas they had captured only two years previously. The recapturing of Khurramshahr – highly important for both tactical and symbolic reasons – was achieved in May. The speed of the Iranian advance, and the high economic cost of the war, forced Saddam to offer a ceasefire which would return all border issues back to the *status quo ante* of 1980. However, the Iranian government, buoyed by the success of its counterattack and deeply hostile to the continued existence of the Ba'thist regime in Iraq, rejected the proposal – in effect committing Iran to the invasion of Iraq and the replacing of the regime with one deemed acceptable to Tehran. But, by rejecting the proposal and by continuing with the attack, the Iranian leadership had made several critical mistakes. First, the ceasefire proposed by Saddam would have been so damaging for himself personally, in terms of questions being asked about his judgement and leadership abilities, that it is unlikely he could have remained for long as president without finding himself sent into exile, or worse. Second, Iran made the same mistake as Iraq did in invading Iran in the first place. Rather than an invasion being the spark which triggers the downfall of a weak regime, it became the catalyst by which support for the regime began to consolidate, and especially within leadership circles.

The Iraq army, now fighting on their own soil against a foreign invader, managed to hold their defensive positions and inflict heavy losses upon the Iranian army. The front stretched from the south, across the centre and into the north, but the defences held, withholding repeated Iranian offensives. Both combatants had now painted themselves into geopolitical corners. Ceasefires had been rejected, and the conflict had taken on a distinct ideological edge. These factors pushed both countries into adopting increasingly extreme methods in an attempt to secure a breakthrough. From 1983, the growing revolutionary fervour saw the numbers of Revolutionary Guards increase, and a popular mobilization (*basij*) was also undertaken, recruiting men and boys into a popular army (Ansari 2003: 234). With manpower being plentiful, but equipment still in short supply, Iran would resort to a method of attack destined to instil fear into their Iraqi adversaries and Western observers alike. Human waves of poorly armed, modestly trained, but highly motivated and zealous volunteers were sent to overrun heavily defended Iraqi positions. Apart from minor victories, which would be quickly countered, these attacks failed, but the notion of revolutionary Iran as being a fanatical opponent that would stop at nothing to sweep the Ba'th regime from power served to encourage Saddam to utilize all means at his disposal to ensure Iraq would not be defeated. Following Iran's capture in 1984 of the strategically positioned Majnoon – an artificial island situated on the major oilfield of Qurna – Iraqi forces responded by deploying chemical weapons during the operation to retake it. Far from being a unique occurrence, the Iraqi military would come to depend upon chemical weapons throughout the duration of the war, and the use of them would become integrated into the way the Iraqi army would fight. It would be Iraqis themselves, however, in the form of Kurds, that would suffer most as Saddam used chemical weapons to counter the threat posed by the alliance of the Kurdish parties with Iran, and to teach them a lesson they would never forget.

The Kurdish Threat

The impact of the war on the Kurds was double-edged. On the one hand, they suffered alongside the rest of Iraq's population, perhaps disproportionately so with many of their settlements in the proximity of the Iran–Iraq boundary being destroyed, as Kurdistan was also a theatre of battle. But the war also presented several benefits to the beleaguered Kurds. Perhaps most importantly, it provided a much-needed respite from the hardships of asymmetrical warfare which they had been forced into by the end of the 1970s (Stansfield and Resool 2006). The Iraqi army units based in the north and tasked with fighting the Kurds were withdrawn from their bases around Kurdistan in the early years of the war and confined to barracks in the major cities. This move allowed the *peshmerga* to consolidate their hold in the Kurdish mountains, and even to establish a presence in the environs of Erbil and Suleimaniyya.

Even so, the leaderships of both the KDP and PUK realized the inherent danger of choosing sides, particularly when it was far from clear in the early days of the war which combatant would be victorious. This question was also complicated by the fact that the Kurds did not have a favoured victor in mind. While both Kurdish parties were relieved to see the Iraqi military weakened and Saddam's attention forced away from the Kurdish rebels, they realized that the choice they were presented with was far from being ideal. If Iraq won, Saddam would be even stronger and be seen as the defender of the Arab world against the Persians. The position of the Kurds in such a scenario would be even worse than that endured to date. If Iran won, however, rather than dealing with an Arab nationalist government (which was at least secular, from their perspective), they could be faced with an Iranian-style theocracy, and the treatment meted out to the Iranian Kurds in the days following the overthrow of the shah raised serious concerns among the Iraqi Kurds.

But, being located on the border between Iraq and Iraq, neutrality was never going to be a realistic option. When the fighting moved north throughout 1982 and 1983, the Kurds soon found themselves having to pick sides (Van Bruinessen 1986: 19). The initial fighting saw the KDP and PUK divided and fighting as proxies on behalf of Iran and Iraq respectively. In 1982, Iranian forces allied with KDP *peshmerga* to attack the KDP of Iran (KDP-I), based inside Iran, to prepare for an assault upon Iraqi positions over the border. The KDP-I appealed to the PUK for assistance, which it duly provided, effectively bringing them into a de facto alliance with the Iraqi government. These alignments continued into the next year, with Iran and the KDP attacking Iraqi positions at the strategic town of Haji Omran, and capturing large swathes of territory along the border. The threat posed by the Kurds to the Baʿth regime saw Saddam resort to previously unseen levels of violence which would prove to be harbinger of events to come. In July 1983, following the successful Iran-KDP attacks, Iraqi security forces surrounded the camp of Qushtapa, south of Erbil, which was home to several thousand members of the Barzani tribe relocated from their home areas. Some 8,000 men and boys were removed from the camp, never to be seen again. Their mass graves in the Anbar province of Iraq would only be found following Saddam's removal.[4]

It would not be long before the PUK too was firmly in the Iranian camp. Following the collapse of PUK negotiations with the Iraqi government in 1984, which failed again because of disagreement over the status of Kirkuk, the army launched a wave of attacks against Iraqi Kurdish settlements throughout 1985. The PUK found itself then the de facto ally of Iran, and Tehran quickly sponsored negotiations that led to a strategic agreement between the KDP, PUK and Iran. The military successes of the Kurds in alliance with Iran awoke Saddam to the fact that a very real threat had emerged in the north that threatened the survival of his regime.

Following the continued advance of the Kurds throughout 1987, Saddam despatched his cousin, Ali Hassan al-Majid, to Kurdistan as the secretary-general of the northern bureau of the Baʿth Party, with absolute authority over the military and security apparatus (Resool 2003: 67). His response to the Kurdish threat was swift and devastating. Following the capture of positions in the Dokan valley in April by *peshmerga*, chemical weapons were used to attack the PUK's regional command and surrounding villages, killing perhaps as many as 400 civilians (Human Rights Watch 1993 47). Worse was to come, as the attack of April did not prove to be an isolated use of chemical weapons. Indeed, a strategy was formulated which would see chemical weapons deployed against Kurdish population centres, alongside a process of depopulating the entire rural area of Kurdistan.

Kurdish military successes achieved with the support of Iran would see the Iraqi government move from pursuing policies of forced assimilation and political marginalization, to one which was undoubtedly genocidal in nature and intention (Wimmer 2002: 12). Recognizing that the mountains of Kurdistan were safe havens for *peshmerga* fighters, al-Majid divided the rural areas of the region into eight 'prohibited areas' in which the military was cleared to kill 'any human being or animal present within these areas' (Human Rights Watch 1993: 79–84). Villages in these areas (which covered virtually the entirety of the rural areas outside the major cities) were systematically destroyed, and civilians arbitrarily executed. Indiscriminate bombardment of civilian areas, the internment of all males and the usage of chemical weapons were all features of the *Anfal* Campaign. At least 180,000 people lost their lives, with countless numbers deported and resettled. Kurdistan's villages were not merely razed, either: they were made permanently uninhabitable, with water supplies destroyed and fields mined.[5]

Although the *Anfal* affected all of Kurdistan, it would be the town of Halabja, located east of the Darbandikhan Dam, which would become its infamous symbol. On 16 March 1988, PUK and Iranian forces captured the town. Although nothing in Halabja itself was of particular value to Iran or Iraq, it had intrinsic strategic value due to its proximity to Suleimaniyya, Darbandikhan and Kirkuk. Al-Majid's response was swift and terrible. Halabja was subjected to an aerial and artillery bombardment with chemical and neurological weapons, in which approximately 5,000 civilians were killed.

Even today, nearly twenty years later, the town remains haunted by the legacy of these weapons. Congenital defects are common among newborns, and the town still bears the scars inflicted on the day of the bombardment. Halabja was also not an isolated incident, but the assault on the town remains the single most emotive memory of how the Kurds have suffered at the hands of the Iraqi government. It would be this memory that would drive the Kurds to pursue heightened degrees of autonomy as soon as the opportunity presented itself.

The Tanker War

Following the failure to defeat Iran in the early years of the war, and then Iraq's managing to withstand the onslaught of the Iranian counterattack, both sides had, since 1983, been facing each other from well-defended positions, but with little movement of the front line occurring from one year to the next. The war had therefore changed from being of a fast-moving nature, with rapidly advancing armies and quick victories, to being a war of attrition of a type not seen since the horrors of trench warfare of the First World War. For Iraq in particular, this was a type of war that it had least expected, and certainly did not want to fight, as such conflicts were extremely costly to fund and would inflict proportionally higher casualties upon the smaller population of Iraq than it would on Iran.

The beginning of the end of the war can be traced to Iran's capture of the Fao peninsula in February 1986. Now in a position to threaten the northern Gulf and cut Iraq's access to it, Iran turned its attention once again to capturing Basra. With the offensive beginning in earnest in January 1987, Iranian forces launched their 'final offensive', but met stiff resistance from Iraqi Republican Guard units that had benefited from a rapid expansion and reorganization of their command structure following the loss of Fao. By March, it was clear that Iraq had again fought Iran to a standstill. This failure, followed by the destruction of their Kurdish allies by the *Anfal* Campaign in the north, would prove to be a turning point in the war, emphasizing to Iran, for the first time, that it would be virtually impossible to defeat the Iraqi military inside Iraq.

The endgame of the war was also coming about because of the attention it was receiving from the international community. Ever since Iraq had failed to secure an Iranian surrender in the early 1980s, Saddam had been seeking to internationalize the conflict in a bid to have a brokered ceasefire imposed and thereby save face. Iraq had done rather well at making itself out to be, if not the 'good guy' of the conflict, then the slightly better option to support. Gulf Arab countries had contributed significant amounts to Iraq's coffers, and the US had little option but to support Saddam following the Iranian embassy debacle. The US's favouring of Iraq was proved in the late summer of 1983 when US Special Middle East Envoy Donald Rumsfeld visited Saddam. By the mid-1980s, the US had accepted that an Iranian victory and Iraqi collapse would not be in its interests and, in a policy known as Operation Staunch, pressurized its allies to not provide support to Iran (Marr 2004: 188). Apart from the 'Irangate' affair which saw some US equipment covertly find its way to Iran, US actions would continue to target Iran's ability to fight the war effectively.

The end of the war came about when the tanker war escalated to a point that triggered international involvement in the dispute. The Gulf itself had become a theatre of war as far back as 1984 when Iraqi aircraft attacked shipping bound for Iran. In retaliation, Iran destroyed tankers heading for Iraq and its allies in the Gulf, including Kuwait and Saudi Arabia. The conflict escalated to the point that the US offered to reflag Kuwaiti vessels as its own, and also to offer them protection against Iranian attack (Gross Stein 1988: 148).[6] However, the first US casualty following its taking of sides in the conflict was not inflicted by Iran but, ironically by Iraq. On 17 May 1987, the warship USS *Stark* was hit by two Iraqi Exocet missiles. The attack was possibly in response to the Iran-Contra affair, or merely an accident (which seems unlikely).[7] However, the effect was to ensure that the US would remain in the Gulf, and seek to bring an end to the conflict. Further events occurred which threatened to bring the US into direct confrontation with Iran: these included the hitting of US-flagged ships by Iranian Silkworm missiles, the damaging of US ships by Iranian mines, the sinking of two Iranian frigates by the US (thereby destroying half of the Iranian navy) and, tragically, the destroying of an Iranian civilian airliner by the US air-defence cruiser *Vincennes* (Marr 2004: 190).

By 1987, it was clear to Iran that the war must come to an end. Both Iraq and Iran had been devastated by nearly a decade of brutal war, but now Iran was faced with a conflict against a vastly more effective and dangerous enemy in the form of the US. The Secretary-General of the United Nations, Perez de Cuellar, put forward UN Security Council Resolution 598, which was adopted in July 1987. The resolution called for a ceasefire, a withdrawal to internationally recognized frontiers, an exchange of prisoners and an investigation into the reasons why the war was fought. Even in 1987, however, Tehran could not accept that it had not defeated the Baʿthist regime, and it did not immediately accept the resolution, thus giving Saddam one final opportunity to inflict bruising damage upon Iran and salvage at least a little prestige from the calamity inflicted upon Iraq by his opportunistic war. By 1988, Iraq's military was looking in good shape. Benefiting from foreign support and an increase in oil revenues, Iraq's military had increased to 1.3 million troops. On 22 February, Iraq launched a missile bombardment of Iran using Scud missiles, with attacks on Tehran, Esfahan and Qom that lasted until April. An Iranian attack in the north of Iraq, at Halabja, on 16 March, was also met with a ferocious chemical assault as we have seen, introducing a fear that Tehran itself could be bombarded with chemical and nerve agents at any moment. This never happened, but the threat was enough for civilians to leave Tehran in droves. The Iraqi military then turned its attention to Fao and, again deploying chemical weapons, captured the peninsula by the end of April. Iran, with its military forces in disarray and facing international isolation, accepted Resolution 598 on 17

July 1988. Iraq claimed a victory but, in effect, both Iran and Iraq had lost.

The Political and Economic Impact on Iraq

After fighting for eight years, Iraq had gained no territory and had not removed the Islamic regime from power in Iran. In addition to the fact that the war had ultimately been a futile exercise, Iraq had suffered perhaps as many as 100,000 killed, with many more wounded (Hiro 1989: 213–15). Iraq's infrastructure was also badly damaged, and its oversized military was draining the country's already heavily depleted treasury. Iraq had run up debts to foreign countries, mainly the Arab Gulf states, to the value of an estimated US$80 billion (Khadduri and Ghareeb 1997: 80). With associated interest rates, this figure was probably closer to $100 billion. Of this, Kuwait and Saudi Arabia were owed about $50–60 billion, with a further $24 billion owed to the states of the OECD, $10 billion to the Soviet Union and $9 billion to private banks (Farouk-Sluglett and Sluglett 1990b: 21). If the damage to the infrastructure (estimated to be $200 billion) along with foreign debt, estimated oil revenue losses and estimated GNP losses are combined, the cost of the war to Iraq comes to a staggering $452.6 billion (Mofid 1990: 127–8). This debt, accumulated over a mere eight years, was 254 per cent of all the oil revenue Iraq had received in the fifty-seven years that it had been an oil producer (Alnasrawi 1994: 100). Although Iraq's oil exports had recovered due to the constructing of pipelines south into Saudi Arabia and north into Turkey, the value of oil had declined considerably since the heady days of the 1970s and, in 1988, Iraq's oil revenues amounted to only $11 billion, which was only half of the revenue generated in 1980 (Tripp 2000: 248).

The problem was compounded by the fact that the war had ended, and, very soon, the swollen Iraqi army would soon be demobilized, unless another venture could be identified to keep it occupied. Hundreds of thousands of soldiers were returning to their homes but to no jobs, and Saddam knew all too well that bored and dissatisfied armed men could present a serious threat to his regime if not adequately provided for. But demobilization of the military threatened to create social instability which Saddam would find almost impossible to manage, as the Iraqi army had increased in size from 110,000 in 1974 to 1,000,000 in 1988.

In addition to having to plan what to do with a million-strong army while being in a position of almost economic ruin, Saddam also had to contend with serious challenges to his authority emanating from the officer corps as the details of the war were being increasingly dissected in the aftermath of the UN resolution. For many, Saddam was not above being blamed for the war and its conduct. He could also not claim to be all that stood in the way of Iraq being invaded by Iran and turned into an Islamic republic, as he had done. With the danger of the external enemy removed, Saddam's stature was diminished and potential challengers could almost certainly be expected to emerge (Tripp 2000: 248).

Towards Kuwait

Saddam's regime therefore had to deal with an existential threat from disgruntled elites that no longer blindly supported him, while also finding a solution to the dire economic position inflicted upon Iraq by eight years of war at the same time as Iraq's labour force was expanding as the soldiers returned. The problems were intrinsically related. His normal *modus operandi* in such circumstances would have been to use Iraq's wealth to ensure that threats to the regime did not emerge. However, in the years following the war, he simply could not do this. He therefore had to revisit the tactics which he had used so effectively when he last had to consolidate his hold on power, in the late 1970s. The greatest threat to his continued hold on power promised to emerge from within the ranks of the officer corps. Following the Iranian advances of the mid-1980s, Saddam had been forced to relinquish more authority to military commanders themselves, and to entrust them with reorganizing the army in order to counter the Iranian threat. This they ably did, as is evident by the successful defence of Basra. However, the emergence of a new, confident cadre of military officers commanding an army of vastly increased size and capability was seen by Saddam as an existential threat to his own longevity.

Saddam therefore focused his efforts upon the officer corps of the armed forces. Never one to miss an opportunity to purge potential opponents, he set about breaking any resemblance of cohesion within the officer corps, favouring some and dismissing others. In some cases potentially influential officers were eliminated, others retired. When attempted coups did occur, as happened towards the end of 1988 and in early 1989, Saddam took advantage of the opportunity to purge the officer corps of any potential threat that had not been removed by his previous, slightly more nuanced methods. The highly influential General Abd al-Rashid was killed, and purges of the military followed in the aftermath of the uncovered coup attempts. The eliminating of military figures who could pose a threat to the continued existence of Saddam culminated with the 'unfortunate' helicopter crash which killed Saddam's cousin Adnan Khairallah Tulfah, but curiously left the pilot alive, in May 1989 (Tripp 2000: 249–50). With the military leadership diluted, Saddam then set about a programme of extensive patronage through limited political reform and extensive economic liberalization. However, the economic plans in particular were hamstrung by the servicing of the debt accrued during the war.

While successful in maintaining his position, the fact that coups had been even planned forced Saddam to consider the staffing of key positions within the government, the party and the military even more carefully and with a greater degree of suspicion. Now, even Saddam's kinsmen who had been empowered by him throughout the 1980s were viewed with wariness, forcing him to rely on an even more focused grouping of relatives. Increasingly, governing Iraq was becoming a family business, with Saddam's sons Uday and Qusay appointed to prominent positions, along with other members of the al-Majid clan of the al-Bu Nasir tribe.

As usual, Saddam proved himself to be a master of manipulating Iraq's domestic political life. Threats certainly existed, but this time from within the regime and the military, and he proved more than able at diluting them and preserving his leadership. Threats from the Kurds and the Shiʿi remained subdued, with the leaderships of the KDP and PUK forced to operate from the town of Nawzang on the Iranian side of the boundary, and the Shiʿi parties suppressed by the seemingly omnipotent security services. However, to survive and to keep the wheels of Iraq's extensive patronage system turning, Saddam needed funds. After the war, Iraq's annual food imports bill stood at $3 billion at least, with the cost of imports for civilian, military and reconstruction purposes estimated to be $11 billion in the early 1990s. Of this, some $4 billion was allocated to the military. At war's end in 1988, Iraq was generating some $0.7 billion in non-oil foreign exchange, and $13.16 billion from oil (all figures from Farouk-Sluglett and Sluglett 1990b: 20–2). If the military component had not been pursued so adamantly, then Iraq's economic situation, while not strong, would certainly have been manageable. But, with Saddam continuing to expand the security services and police in the late 1980s into 1990, and with the military remaining as large as ever, a quick and easy fix was needed to improve Iraq's precarious economic position.[8] That fix would be Kuwait.

6 The Pariah State, 1989–2003

The Iran–Iraq War inflicted a grotesque level of destruction and human misery on both sets of combatants. For Saddam, the culmination of the war brought perverse and detrimental political and economic problems, even though the war towards its end was characterized by Iraqi military successes. The legacy of the so-called victory over Iran was a large, well-equipped and buoyant army with no external escapade to keep it diverted, combined with an economy crippled with foreign debt and with little ability to repay it. Saddam's mechanisms of patronage would soon run out of the essential funds which had kept Iraqi society behind the regime in the past, and the newly found confidence of the army presented Saddam with a potential threat to his own domestic survival. Saddam had achieved, at best, a pyrrhic victory, and its negative effects needed to be rectified swiftly.

For Saddam, the post-Iran–Iraq War period presented him with threats to the continued existence of the regime. These threats ultimately led him into Kuwait and the commencement of a series of actions that would culminate in the violent removal of Saddam himself from power a decade later. Of the problems Saddam faced, by far the most significant were those associated with the economy and the immense debt Iraq had accrued which enabled it to defeat Iran. Indeed, the crippling of the economy was perhaps only slightly less worrying than an actual Iranian victory would have been.

Even as early as 1988, one country was consistently placing itself as the ideal solution for Saddam's economic and social problems. Kuwait was rapidly being perceived in Baghdad as the ungrateful smaller neighbour which was in need of being taught a decisive lesson. It was indeed the case that Iran had been defeated with Iraqi blood and foreign money. But much to the disgust of Saddam, the foreign money had to be repaid. During the course of the war, Baghdad had borrowed perhaps as much as $100 billion, with half of this coming from the Gulf states, and mainly from Kuwait and Saudi Arabia. Saddam had openly referred to his actions against Iran as being part of a broader struggle between Arabs and Persians, with funds provided by Arab states (and particularly Kuwait, which would have struggled to survive an Iraqi defeat by Iran) being considered by him to be more donations than loans. Kuwait, however, did not agree and was in no mood to assist Saddam by reducing debt repayment quotas or assisting in the rising of oil prices. Indeed, the Kuwaiti emir had identified the economic vulnerability of Saddam as being a weakness which could be used to enhance Kuwait's security by forcing Iraq into settling their long-standing border dispute. The emir must have been either supremely confident or totally lacking in any understanding as to how Saddam would react (Hiro 2001: 20–7).

Towards War

The fact that Kuwait, a state which Saddam believed had benefited from the Iran–Iraq War, decided to raise its oil production, taking up the unused Iraqi quota set by OPEC, added a considerable insult to a grievous injury. In addition to this Kuwaiti accumulation of wealth, there was to be no arrangement to reduce Iraqi debt repayments. As far as Kuwait was concerned, Iraq had borrowed and the debt must be repaid (Mohamedou 1997: 123).

Saddam was never one to take insults lightly, and Kuwait's actions were in danger of rapidly attracting his wrath. The situation reached a crisis point in 1990 when the oil price fell below the OPEC-agreed level of $18 a barrel, with Kuwait largely to blame for exceeding its agreed quota. The effect upon Iraq would be to further weaken the economy, with Saddam himself noting that, with every dollar lost on a barrel of oil, Iraq would lose $1 billion annually. However, intransigent as ever, Kuwait continued to exceed the OPEC quota. To make matters even worse, the oil was primarily being obtained from the Rumaila field, which straddled the Iraq–Kuwait boundary. By June the oil price fell to $11 a barrel, leaving the Iraqi economy in a state of siege, with no funds available to service foreign national debt, of which a great proportion was owed to the country perceived, with good reason, to be causing the collapse in oil prices in the first instance – Kuwait.

Increasingly exasperated, the Iraqis continued to try and appeal to the Arab nationalist sensitivities of the Gulf states. Tariq Aziz eloquently tried to tie the debt of Iraq to the payment made by 'the rivers of blood of its youth in defense of the [Arab] nation's soil', and more threateningly, associated economic weakening with military action by stating that 'the Kuwaiti government's deliberate attempts to bring down the Iraqi economy is an aggression no smaller in its consequences than a military aggression'. But Kuwait still remained impervious to the pressure (Mohamedou 1997: 128; Hiro 2001: 28).[1]

The involvement of the US did little to calm Iraqi tempers. By 21 July, the US was getting clear evidence from satellites that Saddam had positioned a force upwards of 30,000 men on the border with Kuwait, yet still US representatives seemed to be turning a blind eye. Margaret Tutwiler, the US State Department's spokeswoman, declared on 24 July that '[the US does] not have any defense treaties with Kuwait and there are no special defense or security commitments to Kuwait' (Mohamedou 1997: 129). If Saddam needed it spelling out, then surely his meeting with the US ambassador to Iraq, April Glaspie, on 25 July, could not have made the US position seemingly any clearer, with Glaspie telling Saddam that the US had 'no opinion on the Arab–Arab conflicts, like your border disagreement with Kuwait' (Mohamedou 1997: 129).

By 31 July, the tension was palpable as Kuwaiti and Iraqi representatives met in Jeddah, Saudi Arabia. Iraq's delegation was led by Izzat Ibrahim al-Douri (deputy chairman of the RCC), Sa'doun Hamadi (deputy prime minister) and Ali Hassan al-Majid (aka Chemical Ali after his gassing of the Kurds). The meeting ended in failure, and Iraq was now committed to embarking upon a foreign military excursion to secure Saddam's regime. Whatever the intentions of the US were in presenting such an ambiguous position regarding Iraqi aggression, and they have been questioned, the result was that Saddam believed that the US would not be hostile towards an Iraqi occupation of Kuwait. Just after 2 a.m. local time on 2 August 1990, Iraqi troops invaded.

The Invasion of Kuwait

The occupation of Kuwait was achieved in less than a day and, for a jubilant Saddam, victory could be claimed at a variety of levels. He had removed the constraints imposed by imperial map-makers upon Iraq by improving Iraq's much-needed access to the sea and by reintegrating Kuwait back into its rightful position as part of Iraq. But, more importantly, while Saddam overtly claimed that he had acted in the interests of Iraqi nationalism, the real motives were instead related to the survival of his regime. The invasion of Kuwait had at its very core the weakened state of the Iraqi economy. The fact that Kuwait had also acted in a manner which provoked the personal sensibilities of the regime only served to foster the belief that the occupation of Kuwait was morally a totally defensible act.

It did not take long for the war-ravaged Iraqi military and security services to inflict their unique brand of viciousness upon the Kuwaiti population. In a scene perhaps unrepeated since the worst days of the Second World War, Iraq plundered Kuwait in a manner which was truly awesome in its scale and obscene in its nature. Under the guidance of the now infamous Ali Hassan al-Majid, the Iraqi security services routinely kidnapped Kuwaiti men, subjected Kuwaiti women and girls to sexual assault and looted Kuwait of anything of value.

The US was swift to condemn the Iraqi assault, acutely aware that the fourth-largest army in the world was on the verge of securing the largest oil reserves in the world in Saudi Arabia. After attempts by King Hussein of Jordan to deal with the invasion through an Arab framework faltered, the UN Security Council condemned Iraq on 6 August and passed Resolution 661, imposing economic sanctions on Iraq and occupied Kuwait (Malone 2006: 61). King Fahd of Saudi Arabia simultaneously requested the support of the US in defending his country. Seemingly oblivious to the gathering pace of international condemnation, Saddam still refused to take advantage of possible olive branches and pursued a policy of increasingly aggressive posturing. The announcement on 7 August that the US was deploying the 82nd Airborne Division to Saudi Arabia was countered on 8 August by the RCC officially announcing the occupation of Kuwait, to be followed by its full annexation as the nineteenth province of Iraq on 28 August. Saddam's strategy was now making it very difficult for even his closest regional friends to support him (Coughlin 2002: 255–6).

By mid-August, the battle lines were drawn. European forces joined the US contingent in Saudi Arabia, along with the Arab armies of Syria and Egypt. A foreign force of 600,000 soldiers was deployed to Saudi Arabia over a six-month period, and President Bush and Prime Minister Thatcher compared Saddam's invasion of Kuwait with Hitler's annexation of the Sudetenland, ominously noting that 'appeasement does not work'. Thatcher in particular was in no mood to be conciliatory towards Saddam. UK–Iraqi relations had been deteriorating at a rapid rate, especially since Saddam ordered the execution of the *Observer* journalist Farzad Bazoft on charges of espionage, and the huge scale of Iraq's non-conventional weapons programme was being realized. Saddam now tried to dig himself out of what had become a very dangerous hole by seeking to link his occupation of Kuwait with the plight of the Palestinians, deploying the feeble argument that both were products of imperial meddling which needed to be resolved.

Such strategies were ultimately doomed. Yet, whilst he could see the scale of the forces against him, he had little option but to continue on the path of near-destruction. The domestic conditions which led him to invade Kuwait – a huge underemployed military and dire economic realities – still remained as potent agents of instability. With the invasion of Kuwait, these serious issues were now merged with Ba'thist political ideology supporting fully the removal of colonial boundaries. Saddam could also not afford to be seen to be backing down, considering his weakened domestic political situation. To ensure that his eastern flank remained secure, Saddam concluded a humiliating peace deal with the Iranian president Rafsanjani. However, he could not afford to lose any more face. No matter if he thought it was a good idea, Saddam had to stay in Kuwait and could not withdraw voluntarily without seriously exposing his regime to a coup d'état from within either the Ba'th Party or the military, or both. The UN Security Council passed Resolution 678 on 29 November 1990, authorizing member states to use 'all necessary means' to evict Iraq from Kuwait if a withdrawal was not completed before 15 January 1991 (Malone 2006: 68–9). However, domestic issues were of a much greater concern for the Iraqi leadership than was the presence of an overwhelming opposing armed force in Saudi Arabia. For the Iraqi leadership to comply with the deadline would have meant losing face to such an extent in Iraq that their survival after any withdrawal from Kuwait would be seriously doubtful. The scene was set for war.

Operation Desert Storm

The Coalition forces commenced their attack on Iraq on 17 January 1991 at 2.38 a.m. local time, under the name Operation Desert Storm. It was to be the most intensive aerial bombardment ever seen. Unlike the Iran–Iraq War, the Coalition forces had the technology to overcome Saddam's impressive aerial defence network, and could strike the infrastructure of the regime at any moment. The air assault continued for six weeks and attempted to degrade Saddam's institutions of domestic and military control. But still Saddam remained defiant. Institutions of government had been badly damaged, yet he attempted to rally Iraqis by proclaiming that the 'mother of all battles' had commenced.

In an attempt to internationalize the conflict, Saddam ordered the launching of ballistic missiles against Israel, in a move similar to that which had seen Scuds launched against Tehran only a few years before, and on 18 January missiles hit Tel Aviv and Haifa. Saddam desperately needed an Israeli response as only a Zionist attack against an Arab state could weaken the Coalition against him. However, against serious odds, Western diplomats were successful in preventing an Israeli counterattack. After this, Saddam then turned to environmental terrorism and began pumping oil from captured Kuwaiti terminals into the northern Gulf, obtaining a place in the record books for the ignominious honour of being responsible for the world's largest-ever oil slick at an estimated 240 square miles.

A final 'last chance' was given to Iraq, with President Bush serving notice that the immediate and unconditional withdrawal from Kuwait must be under way by 23 February. For Saddam, submitting to this demand was simply not an option. The withdrawal of the army from Kuwait before any fighting had taken place would seriously have threatened his own survival. Instead, he wanted the army to fight the Coalition, not necessarily to hold Kuwait, but to be seen as defending Iraq against insurmountable odds, and thereby gain a small degree of honour from the situation. The army would then be withdrawn and Iraq forced to accept ceasefire terms. It was simply unacceptable to have these troops return to Baghdad after preparing them for war over the last six months. In addition, the forces in Iraq (which perhaps didn't number any more than 200,000) were units which had little value for Saddam. Units which were useful for Saddam (i.e., Republican Guard divisions) were mainly held in reserve, and were used with devastating effect in a highly orderly manner to put down the uprisings which took place after Saddam's eviction from Kuwait.

The much-vaunted land invasion aimed at removing the Iraqi army from Kuwait inflicted a rout of embarrassing proportions. Fighting was over within forty-eight hours, and Kuwait was liberated. Again, still concerned about the legitimacy of his regime, Saddam continued to call his adventure into Kuwait a victory, but was not overly concerned about whether his forces in the Kuwaiti theatre survived or not. Indeed, when the Coalition forces continued to slaughter Iraqi military formations which were retreating but carrying arms, such spectacles were probably being greeted with relief by the Iraqi leader. The most dangerous sight Saddam could imagine would have been armed Iraqi soldiers returning en masse from Kuwait, as he would have been the natural focus of their anger. For the Coalition, the devastation being wrought upon the Iraqi military was becoming a serious public relations problem, particularly after Coalition forces butchered a defenceless Iraqi convoy on the Mutla Ridge running out of Kuwait. With Iraqi forces expelled from Kuwait, President Bush called a ceasefire on 25 February 1991.

Should the Coalition have entered Iraq, thereby forcing Saddam into early retirement? It is a question often asked. However, at the time, public unease about the war was growing in the West, and the scenarios for what would happen in Iraq if Saddam's iron grip were removed had not been adequately considered (and one would suggest that they still had not been in 2003). Therefore, the war officially ended with the liberation of Kuwait, yet, because of his survival, Saddam still claimed victory. In a sense, he was partly correct to do so, in domestic terms at least. If it is accepted that Saddam's primary aim was to ensure the survival of his regime, and the greatest threat against his regime was the military and the economic difficulties Iraq faced, he achieved a partial result. He managed to get the US to weaken his own army for him, thereby strengthening his position within Iraq. The future systematic destruction of the Iraqi economy under sanctions also perversely strengthened his regime by weakening greatly those who could have previously opposed him, yet allowed him to blame the suffering of the Iraqi people upon the machinations of the West. Iraqi society became focused upon issues of day-to-day survival rather than on notions of political betterment. When Saddam asked his military intelligence commander General Wafiq al-Samarraʿi what his evaluation of the preceding months of the war was, Samarraʿi , 'I think this is the biggest defeat in history.' Saddam's reply, perhaps referring more to his domestic position rather than his vastly denuded regional standing, was simply 'that's your opinion' (Coughlin 2002: 274–5). Arguably, the great survivor had lived to tell the tale by paying a sacrifice in Iraqi blood.

The Uprisings

Saddam's days following his expulsion from Kuwait looked to be seriously numbered, and President Bush's calling on the people of Iraq to 'take matters into their own hands' on 15 February 2005 suggested that regime change was a serious possibility (Malone 2006: 84). However, the lack of organized political forces meant that any opposition to Saddam would have to emanate from within society and be spontaneous in nature. When the uprisings did break out, they were widespread but disorganized due to the lack of political direction. For Saddam, if he were to face a popular rebellion against his rule, there was rarely a better time than 1991. The earliest signs of unrest could be seen developing in the south of Iraq in February 1991 as anti-Baʿth demonstrations broke out in and around Basra, resulting in the killing of a number of Baʿth Party officials (Bengio 1992: 7–8). Saddam's marginalization of the Shiʿi and the harsh suppression of their political movements had created resentment which could only be controlled by the all-pervasive Iraqi security apparatus. However, with the south now effectively a war zone, Saddam's grip was lessened. As his military forces fled Kuwait, only to be slaughtered by allied forces at such atrocities as the Mutla Ridge, dissent reared its head first in the ravaged, once-proud army. Interestingly, the uprising in the south did not commence in Shiʿi towns. It started in the Sunni towns of Abu'l Khasib and Zubair, 70 kilometres south of Basra on 28 February 1991, before spreading to the Shiʿi strongholds of Basra, Najaf and Karbala.

In Kurdistan, the uprising commenced on 4 March in the small mountain town of Raniyah, and from there spread to the major Kurdish population centres. As the *rapareen* ('uprising' in Kurdish) gained momentum, forces from the KDP and PUK (ostensibly under the unifying banner of the Iraqi Kurdistan Front – IKF), assumed control of the insurgency. By 19 March, Kurdistan was in Kurdish hands. The appropriation of Kurdistan by the *peshmerga* of the KDP and PUK sensitized regional capitals and the Coalition alike to the distinct possibility that Iraq was on the verge of collapse. The belief that this possibility might in fact become a reality was reinforced by how the uprising in the south was developing during the Kurds' rebellion.

Back in the south, the uprising had developed a new political colouring that made it distinctly unattractive to the governments of the Coalition. Initially, the uprising was unified in its antipathy towards Saddam, yet remained distinctly 'Iraqi' due to the fact that the forces involved during its inception had been mainly from the retreating army, with little involvement from Shiʿi religious parties. This was to change as Shiʿi Islamist parties returned from their imposed exile in Iran to join the fray, with the intention of exerting control over the direction of the uprising and promoting their own distinctive agenda.

SCIRI military units joined the rebellion, under banners openly proclaiming an agenda to bring Iraq under Shiʿi rule. The use of any religious slogan in what was essentially a secular state was a questionable tactic, but SCIRI's slogans also inferred Iranian expansionism and anti-Iraqi nationalist sentiment. The sudden prevalence of posters depicting a stern-looking Ayatollah Khomeini and Ayatollah al-Hakim, combined with the arrogance which characterized SCIRI actions as its forces attempted to seize control of the leadership of the rebellion, only served to introduce concerns among the insurgents. Indeed, SCIRI's announcements at this time resembled more the oppressive regime the rebellion was opposing, rather than the voices of those seeking freedom from authoritarianism. Ayatollah al-Hakim's commanders, for example, issued directives stating that 'all Iraqi armed forces should submit to and obey SCIRI orders' and 'no idea except the rightful Islamic ones should be disseminated' (Bengio 1992: 10). Such proclamations were not well received, particularly as the uprising was far from homogeneous in character, with participants including military figures, ex-government officials, communists and people unattached to any particular political or organizational framework. The attempt by SCIRI to introduce a narrowly defined religious direction only served to fragment the forces in the south that were opposed to Saddam's regime. In 1991, an Iraqi nationalist movement could probably have removed Saddam from power. A Shiʿi theocratic agenda tinged with Iranian colouring certainly could not.

With what looked like Kurdish nationalist and Shiʿi religious uprisings now in place, the situation was perhaps met with greater fear in Washington and London than it was in Baghdad. No contingency plans had been made for the eventuality of Saddam's regime falling, and Saddam's downfall brought about by uprisings that had taken on a distinctly communal tone was certainly not an acceptable outcome to the situation. The West preferred a return to the 'old days', a pre-1991 status quo, and certainly not a new political order. The triumph of the Kurds and Shiʿi would therefore be short-lived as the expected allied support failed to appear.

Even though President Bush had called upon the Iraqi people to overthrow the regime of Saddam, it was obvious that the US would not support any Shiʿi uprising against him, and the Kurds in the north would similarly fall foul of Turkish lobbying in Washington. Without external support, neither of these uprisings could spread to the centre of the country and to Baghdad in particular. Threatened by rebellion in the north and south, the regime consolidated its support-base in the central governorates and became galvanized in the face of a significant collection of disparate threats to its existence. The regime had certainly been weakened by the onslaught of the Coalition, yet the most important factor was that it remained stronger and more unified than its opponents. Saddam empowered his immediate family and supporters, with Ali Hassan al-Majid being made minister of the interior,

Izzat Ibrahim al-Douri dispatched to the south to quell the rebellion and Saddam's son-in-law, Hussein Kamel, appointed minister of defence. Another cousin was made governor of Kirkuk and other regime favourites were drafted in. Saddam recognized that the most significant threat to the regime came from the southern uprising; the Kurds as always were more concerned about securing autonomy rather than controlling Iraq, whereas the Shiʿi threat was much more significant in that it directly threatened to overthrow the regime. The return of forces loyal to Saddam to the south saw the rebels targeted with the most repressive measures yet deployed by Saddam against Iraqis. The Republican Guard, reasonably intact after the Coalition bombardment, set about repressing the Shiʿi rebels with great ferocity and, by mid-March, the uprising had been crushed.

The Kurds were next on the list. Moving his forces from south to north, Saddam sent the Republican Guard into the rebel Kurdish areas and, from 28 March onwards, the Kurds were forced out of the major cities and into the mountains bordering Iran and Turkey. Fearing a chemical bombardment to match those seen in the late 1980s, Kurdish civilians also fled and, by the beginning of April, news channels were broadcasting scenes of deprivation and human suffering on an immense scale in the Zagros Mountains. Men, women and children were shown huddled together, freezing to their deaths as Turkish soldiers looked on and the US seemed impotent to assist. On 5 April, the UN Security Council passed Resolution 688 demanding an end to the repression of citizens in Iraq, but, on the ground, the numbers of refugees continued to swell. The allies attempted to resolve the problem by establishing a small 'safe haven' near Dohuk on 28 April. However, it was a month too late. Approximately a million Kurds had reached the Turkish border by the end of April, with more on the way.

The UN Security Council's Resolution 688 authorized humanitarian assistance to the Kurds, and the US and UK imposed 'no-fly zones' to prevent Iraqi aircraft from flying north of the 36th parallel (Malone 2006: 86). However, for the Kurds this was not enough as they had to deal with the practical realities on the ground, which meant negotiating with Baghdad. Even though Saddam had been devastated by his defeat in Kuwait and had lost control of sixteen out of Iraq's eighteen provinces by the spring of 1991, the Kurdish leadership had no alternative but to seek an accommodation with him in order to curtail the humanitarian catastrophe occurring in the mountains.

The Kurds were lucky. Saddam, content that the Kurds had been stopped from threatening to secede from the state and aware that the international community at large, and Turkey and the US in particular, had no desire to see them independent of Iraq, withdrew his forces from Kurdistan. His motives were pragmatic as he recognized that his forces would be needed to ensure that his regime remained well defended in Baghdad in the critical months to come, and he also needed to have them available in case the Shi'i rebelled again. He placed the Kurdistan region under an economic embargo, meaning that it existed under UN and internal constraints, isolated from the rest of the world due to the UN sanctions regime and also denied economic interaction with Arab Iraq. However, even if the conditions were far from perfect, the Kurds, at last, had their autonomy. The extent of the Kurdistan Region in the 1990s can be seen in Map 2 (page xx), along with the area of territory that the Kurds declared as being historically part of Kurdistan, but occupied by Saddam's regime. These 'disputed territories' included the city of Kirkuk and would remain a fixation of the Kurds that they would take into the post-2003 period.

Elections were held for the Kurdistan National Assembly (KNA) in May 1992, with presidential elections taking place simultaneously. The result was predictable. The KNA's 105 seats were divided equally between the KDP and PUK, with five seats allocated for the Christian minority. The presidential vote proved to be inconclusive, as both Barzani and Talabani received similar votes (perhaps with Barzani getting slightly more). However, after a tense military stand-off between PUK and KDP forces, both agreed to put the question of who should be president on hold, but power in Kurdistan became divided evenly between the KDP and PUK in a system known as '50–50': if a minister came from one party, his deputy would be from the other. While certainly a way to ensure parity in terms of elite representation, the division resulted in a stagnated government, with no decisions being made, and with both the KDP and PUK viewing each other with suspicion (Stansfield 2003: 146). The situation deteriorated into violence, with skirmishes between KDP and PUK forces in 1994 developing into full-scale conflict between the two and the expulsion of the KDP from Erbil.

The Coalescing of Opposition Movements

As has been seen, opposition movements in Iraq have been a feature of the political landscape since its foundation. The KDP and PUK were but two of several Kurdish political parties opposed to Saddam. With a pan-Iraq agenda, the ICP continued to oppose the regime, and the more religiously minded Shiʿi gathered around the Daʿwa Party and SCIRI. However, the opposition, before 1990, was not unified. Even following the invasion of Kuwait, opposition forces could not find a common position as a first step to mounting a serious challenge to the regime. The KDP and ICP remained cautious, the PUK seemed to be pro-US and SCIRI and the Islamic Movement of Kurdistan (IMK) appeared to bear more animosity towards the 'Great Satan' of the US than they did against the despot resident in Baghdad.

Parties opposed to Saddam's regime were influenced by neighbouring powers, particularly as Iraq's security services had made it virtually impossible for activists to stay safely inside Iraq, let alone organize meaningful actions against the regime, and each neighbour would use opposition forces to forward its own agenda. Syria and Iran in particular were heavily involved with Iraqi opposition movements in the 1970s and 1980s. Damascus had the allegiance of the pro-Syrian Baʿathists, the ICP and various military groups. But Tehran had the powerful Islamist groups including SCIRI and Daʿwa. Each had also been dealing with the Kurdish parties for several years, with Talabani even being resident in

Damascus in the late 1960s. Other important and powerful nations also began to realize that perhaps Iraq was on the verge of significant change. Saudi Arabia, left behind in the game of collecting Iraqi opposition parties due to the Kurdish conflict being rather distant from its borders, and having little interest in supporting the Shiʿi, now sought to form pro-Saudi groups. As such, the Free Iraqi Council (FIC) was formed under the leadership of Saʿad Jabr in February 1991. A further force was still not represented – that of dissident ex-Baʿathis and Iraqi military. As there was no one particular opposition group with which they felt comfortable, they formed their own party under British and American sponsorship and guidance known as the Iraqi National Accord (INA) under the leadership of Dr Iyad Allawi. All of these groups met under the banner of the Joint Action Committee in Beirut in March 1991.

The US, however, had a problem as the majority of Iraqi opposition movements had stronger links with Iran and Syria than they did with the US. Indeed, some of these groups, including SCIRI, were perceived to be in opposition to US interests, never mind those of Saddam, and the Kurds, with their mercurial propensity to switch sides, were viewed with suspicion by the US. The US needed to gain influence over the opposition movements quickly, and it identified Dr Ahmed Chalabi as being the tool by which to achieve this. Having come to the attention of the CIA as an educated and persuasive individual (albeit with allegations of serious fraud committed in Jordan blackening his reputation), Chalabi was deemed to be ideal as an organizing figure capable of bringing together the fractious forces of the Iraqi opposition, particularly as he had no constituency in Iraq by which he could threaten either US policy, or other groups in the opposition. In short, he was supposed to play the role of the puppet coordinator who was to break the hold of Damascus and Tehran on the Iraqi opposition.

Chalabi convened a meeting of the Iraqi National Congress (INC) in Vienna in June 1992. With generous US backing, he secured the support of the established political parties, including the PUK and KDP, and also other powerful entities such as the INA. However, even from this first meeting, which occurred in the aftermath of the uprisings and the near-defeat of Saddam, the opposition was divided. Indeed, winning points against opposition partners seemed to be as important as removing Saddam's regime for many opposition players and, later in the 1990s, components of the opposition would choose to ally with Saddam himself in order to alleviate the threat posed by their opposition competitors – a strange state of affairs indeed, and one which Saddam joyously embraced.

The divides were immediate and apparent for all to see. The division of the Kurds into their two fiefdoms within Iraqi Kurdistan, and the mutual antipathy they had for each other, permeated the opposition in general and polarized political activity. Chalabi established the headquarters of the INC in Salahadin – a small mountain town 20 kilometres north of Erbil, and also home to the headquarters of Barzani's KDP. Relations between Chalabi and Barzani were cordial but far from warm, particularly as the INC had been set up with US money and had limited popular support. The fact that Chalabi also seemed to have closer ties with Barzani's rival, Talabani, only served to create further distrust and suspicion. Antipathy between the KDP and INC was therefore apparent from the outset. Furthermore, the INA of Allawi did not take kindly to the newly acquired US-inspired influence enjoyed by the INC, particularly as the INA again was an older organization and one which was seen by many of its members as representing the Sunni ruling minority (even though Allawi himself is a secular Shi'i). The competition between Allawi and Chalabi was therefore understandably severe and was made undoubtedly worse due to the INA, in addition to the KDP and INC, also establishing its headquarters in the small and increasingly claustrophobic town of Salahadin.

Sanctions on Iraq

Various reasons are put forward as to why the US did not enter Baghdad to remove Saddam. However, it would appear to be the case that a combination of regional sensitivities, the unwillingness to embark upon a military campaign which had unknown political consequences and the lack of a UN mandate to overthrow the regime were responsible for reining in the more ambitious components of the Coalition (Abu Galal 2002: 4–5). With Saddam still in power, other measures were needed to ensure that his regime would not endanger neighbours again. To achieve this, an elaborate sanctions regime was constructed which, while achieving the aim of ensuring that Saddam's ability to threaten regional security was markedly constrained, also subjected the people of Iraq to a further deterioration of socio-economic standards and conditions.

The initial resolution against Iraq was SCR 661 of 6 August 1991, calling on member states to stop financial activities with Iraq and Kuwait. The UN established the Sanctions Committee to monitor the implementation of this resolution (Niblock 2001: 99–100). Such actions fitted neatly within norms deemed acceptable when dealing with situations which broke UN agreements, as Iraq's invasion of Kuwait clearly had. However, the continued survival of Saddam after his expulsion from Kuwait came as a distinct embarrassment and cause of concern for the US and its allies. It was clear that Saddam remained firmly in control of Iraq, and internal dissidents (hopefully, from the perspective of the US and UK, emerging from within the military rather than from the Shiʿi religious establishment and the Kurdish nationalist movement) had virtually no opportunity to overthrow him. It was also clear that Saddam was, in many ways, down but not out and was still driven by the same internal problems of regime legitimacy and economic weakness which were the reasons why he invaded Kuwait in the first place. Therefore, as far as the US was concerned, sanctions would not end merely with the liberation of Kuwait. Rather, they would continue to be imposed in an attempt to weaken the Iraqi regime by making it vulnerable to internal dissent and unable to exert any kind of military influence in the wider region (Abu Galal 2002: 69).

The aims were clear, but simplistic, and lacked an understanding of the mechanisms by which Saddam's regime operated in the Iraqi state. Over the next decade, Saddam would use sanctions to strengthen himself in relation to his people, and to use the devastation caused by sanctions to Iraq as an immensely effective propaganda tool which mobilized the forces of Iraqi nationalism behind him (at least in the centre of the country), and left the reputation of the US and its allies in the Middle East in ruins as they continued to impose what was increasingly seen as a morally bankrupt policy.

The cessation of the Gulf War saw the Security Council passing Resolution 687 on 3 April 1991. This resolution would create the framework within which Iraq had to operate. The sanctions of 661 were maintained, but provision was allowed for the import of foodstuffs and items of 'essential civilian need'. The resolution attempted to strait-jacket Saddam, both domestically and financially. The Iraq–Kuwait border was to be protected by a UN observer unit (UNIKOM), and Iraq also had to accept clauses aimed at removing its chemical and biological weapons programme and its ballistic missile programme (for missiles with a range of over 150 km). In order to achieve these tasks, the UN Special Commission (UNSCOM) was established with an extensive mandate to inspect Iraq's non-conventional weapon's programme and to supervise the destruction of Iraq's missile capabilities. Nuclear weapons research was also prohibited, and the International Atomic Energy Agency (IAEA) was tasked with ensuring Iraq's compliance, alongside UNSCOM. Resolution 687 also held Iraq responsible for all damages inflicted on Kuwait, and a compensation fund was established to pay reparations for Kuwaiti losses – a policy which surely must have infuriated Saddam as such funds would come directly from Iraq's oil exports (Niblock 2001: 102–3). Despite clauses which indicated that the duration of the stringent controls placed upon the Iraqi economy would be relaxed, there was in effect no short-term reduction of the comprehensive sanctions regime. The only oil exported was small amounts to Jordan and, by not permitting Iraq to export its only item of value, the sanctions meant that Baghdad had no means of raising foreign currency with which to purchase the necessary food and medicines of which Iraqi society was in such desperate need. Before the invasion of Kuwait, revenues from oil sales accounted for an estimated 60 per cent of Iraq's GDP. By 1991, Iraq's GDP had fallen by 75 per cent, with its GDP being roughly equal to what it was in the 1940s – before oil revenue dominated the Iraqi economy (Center for Economic and Social Rights 1996). The effect of this collapse was a phenomenal rise in prices of basic foodstuffs and medicines, but with salaries remaining stagnant for those lucky enough to be receiving them. Reflecting on the situation in 1995, the UN estimated that some 4 million people – 20 per cent of the population – were living in conditions of extreme poverty.[2] This debilitating state of affairs was to remain in force until December 1996.[3]

The Arrival of the Inspectors

UNSCOM and IAEA inspectors began arriving in Iraq in June 1991 under the leadership of executive chairman Rolf Ekeus (Aburish 2000: 316). The inspectors were a cause of grave concern for Saddam. The acceptance of their activities in Iraq was a reflection of Iraqi weakness in the days after the end of the Gulf War, and to Saddam, consistently aware of the legitimacy of his regime being undermined, they were a serious threat. Furthermore, and from Saddam's point of view quite understandable, a great deal of time and resources had been invested over a thirty-year period in developing the WMD programme. He may have had no option but to let the inspectors in, but he was in no mood to allow them to disarm Iraq without a struggle. The pattern of cooperation and obstruction with the UN was set from the moment UNSCOM arrived, and the relationship between Saddam and the UN would for the next eight years be characterized by an elaborate game of hide-and-seek, with the Iraqi leader resorting to ever higher levels of brinkmanship with his UN counterparts.

If the technical and political task of disarming Iraq was not complex and difficult enough, the UN also faced a serious practical problem. As part of the chastisement of Iraq, it was planned that funds derived from the sale of Iraqi oil would be used for the wholescale funding of UN operations in the country, including the activities of UNSCOM (Niblock 2001: 100). The rationale behind such a strategy was straightforward, yet it was perceived in Baghdad as being yet another attempt to undermine the legitimacy of the regime. It was an understandable concern. Saddam was, in effect, paying the forces tasked with ensuring his own enfeeblement. The Iraqi government clearly saw the basic paradox which had entrapped the UN: under sanctions, no oil could be exported, yet oil had to be exported in order to fund UNSCOM, UNIKOM, the Compensation Commission and the extensive humanitarian aid programmes of the UN agencies – all of whom were assembling with unashamed eagerness to operate in Iraq with Iraqi money.

The Iraqi government therefore possessed a modicum of room in which to manoeuvre and to influence UN actions in a manner that would support the Iraqi aims of: (i) protecting the regime in the aftermath of the Gulf War and the uprisings; (ii) protecting the sovereignty of Iraq by limiting the effectiveness of external bodies such as UNSCOM; and (iii) seeking the lifting of sanctions on imports and exports, and particularly on oil (Niblock 2001). With the UN dependent upon Iraq funding its operations on its soil, Saddam could influence the actions of the UN in Iraq to a considerable degree. For the UN, permission to export oil had to depend upon Iraqi acceptance of its involvement in its affairs, including UNSCOM activities. For the Iraqis, exporting oil was not worthwhile if it ultimately eroded Iraqi sovereignty and the legitimacy of the regime.

The first attempt to break this stalemate came on 15 August when the UN Security Council passed Resolution 706 authorizing Iraq to export $1.6 billion in oil over a six-month period, with 30 per cent allocated to the Compensation Fund, payments to UNSCOM and the IAEA, and payments for the purchase of food and medicine, to be cleared by the Sanctions Committee. Saddam rejected the offer, claiming with a certain degree of justification that the deal infringed upon Iraqi sovereignty. Saddam then continued to hinder the operations of UNSCOM until the UN itself ordered him, through Resolution 707, to afford UNSCOM 'unconditional and unrestricted access to all areas' (Aburish 2000: 218). This, interestingly, he did and UNSCOM started to show impressive results. But, still, Saddam's policy of concealment and obstruction continued unabated throughout the period of UNSCOM inspections. In addition, Saddam clearly had recognized that his unwillingness to export oil was creating a serious predicament for the UN, and limited the efficacy of its organizations and agencies. Concomitantly, the continuing deterioration of the Iraqi economy under sanctions could be blamed on the UN and the openly antagonistic US and UK governments. If anyone was to blame for the deaths of Iraqi children, the Iraqi government ensured that it would be Washington and London, and not Baghdad, which would ultimately benefit from the rapidly rising discontent growing within society.

Defection

UNSCOM received a boost in August 1995 with the defection of Saddam's close confidants and sons-in-law, Hussein and Saddam Kamel, in what was perhaps the most damaging blow Saddam had suffered since becoming president. Hussein Kamel's desertion was a particular embarrassment as he was the head of Iraq's weapons programme. As such, he provided Western intelligence services and UNSCOM with a comprehensive account of Saddam's WMD programme, including a startling revelation that Iraq had been within three months of testing an atomic weapon before the commencement of Desert Storm (Coughlin 2002). The information certainly reinvigorated the embattled UNSCOM, but the two brothers would find that Western intelligence services could be as calculating as Iraq's were brutal. After passing over considerable amounts of evidence, they were disregarded by Western intelligence services. Living in Amman and despondent at the treatment they had received, they surprisingly accepted an invitation from Saddam to return to Baghdad in February 1992. They were met by what must have been a rather terrifying reception committee at the Iraqi border with Jordan, led by Uday Saddam. Within days they were dead, killed by their own kinsmen after Saddam threateningly decreed that the dishonour brought about by their treachery reflected upon their wider family.

The Failed Coups

Fighting between the KDP and PUK broke out in 1994 due to the intractable historical problems which coloured the relationship of the two parties. Power-sharing mechanisms within the Kurdish administration, the domination of decision-making by the political bureaus of the KDP and PUK, all combined with the animosity caused by twenty-five years of fighting culminating in internecine Kurdish bloodletting on a ferocious scale. For the Iraqi opposition, this fighting was highly destabilizing. However, divisions within the US administration were just as destructive to opposition unity, as differences in strategies began to show between those who advocated the seizing of territory by the Iraqi opposition (and usually some combination of the Kurds and the INC) and those who supported a coup d'état. Until 1994, US advocates of a war of liberation under the umbrella of the Iraqi opposition had failed to succeed in attracting the ear of the president and the policymaking community. However, with the defection of a high-ranking Iraqi military intelligence chief, General Wafiq al-Samarra'i, the advocates of a military coup now had a figure who could powerfully influence the direction of the debate.

The CIA, ostensibly supporting the INC, had become increasingly alarmed at the entrenchment of the supposedly weak Saddam in Baghdad and the embarrassment caused to the unity of the Iraqi opposition by the intra-Kurdish fighting. This, combined with the difficulty of coercing Chalabi into acting according to the CIA agenda, promoted the position of the exponents of the military coup. It was during this period that the CIA covertly began to strengthen its ties with the INA, while still publicly keeping its links with the INC. In an environment of intra-Kurdish fighting and of internal apathy between the INC, KDP and INA, together with the subterfuge of the CIA, the components of the Iraqi opposition became far more adept at spying on each other rather than worrying about Saddam.

The INC and INA now began to pursue different plans, each with support from different sectors of the US administration, but with the CIA being involved with each. Chalabi worked with the newly defected al-Samarra'i and developed a plan which combined a popular uprising with a military insurrection (Hiro 2001: 84). However, at the same time, the CIA was also working out the details of a military putsch with the INA, all being planned in the Kurdish town of Salahadin. Both sides knew of the plans of the other, and it would be unlikely that Saddam's security services were not following events closely either. With the plans for their military assault nearing completion, the INC believed that US support was guaranteed, and the plan was ready for implementation by early March. However, the INA had since convinced the CIA that an attack by the INC and its Kurdish allies would be met by a devastating Iraqi counterattack, and support for Chalabi was withdrawn at the eleventh hour. With the pulling out of the US, Barzani similarly refused to become embroiled in an escapade which, if successful, would see the strengthening of Chalabi and, if unsuccessful, would more than likely see Iraqi Republican Guards entering KDP territory. For Barzani, it was a lose–lose situation.

Still confident that the US would ultimately come to their aid if the early stages of the plan proved to be successful, the INC and the PUK opened their assault upon Iraqi troops on 4 March 1995. While the Iraqi V Corps folded in the face of their advance, the failure of popular uprisings to occur in Kirkuk and Mosul, combined with the lack of air support from the US, meant that the INC-PUK venture inevitably stalled. Al-Samarra'i's promised defections of officers did not occur, and, seeing the PUK commit itself against Saddam, Barzani used the opportunity to claw back some of the areas lost to the PUK in the intra-Kurdish fighting, heightening tensions with his old foe. For the Iraqi opposition, the divisions were now apparent for all to see. PUK and KDP rivalry was at an all-time high; the KDP and INC remained inherently suspicious of each other; and the INC-PUK attack, while not resulting in Saddam's downfall, had sensitized the Iraqi leader to the dangers of having an organized, capable opposition force resident in Iraqi Kurdistan. Furthermore, the US was discredited in the eyes of the Iraqi people and opposition.

If the INC was having a bad time of it in 1995, its arch-rival, the INA, was not faring much better. The INA had brought the possibility of an anti-Saddam coup to the attention of the CIA in the summer of 1994 (Hiro 2001: 102). Benefiting from contacts with the Republican Guard through the intermediary services of retired Brigadier General Muhammad al-Shahwani, the INA leader Dr Iyad Allawi approached the UK Secret Intelligence Service (MI6) and the CIA with the plan. By March 1995, the CIA viewed it more favourably than it did the INC-PUK initiative, with King Hussein of Jordan won over by the US administration allowing Amman to become the centre of operations for the attempted coup against Saddam.

By early 1996, the coup attempt was gathering momentum. Sporadic attacks coordinated by the INA had created an atmosphere of fear and instability in Baghdad; the CIA and INA were steadily transmitting propaganda into Iraq; and King Hussein had increased the diplomatic pressure by convening a conference of the Iraqi opposition and limiting access into and out of Iraq from Jordan. However, with the involvement of so many groups, it was a relatively easy task for the Iraqi *mukhabarat* to follow the progress of the plotters, and Amman in particular was an easy environment for Iraq's counter-terrorist units to operate in. Chalabi, aware of the fact that Saddam's security services had full knowledge of the INA plan, went to the CIA with what must have been a certain amount of joyous indignation to inform them that their plan was in danger of becoming a bloodbath. However, CIA Director John Deutsch chose to identify Chalabi's stance as being a still-smarting reaction to the failure of the US to support the INC in 1995. His reading of the situation was understandable, particularly as the INA had attempted to blow up Chalabi's Salahadin office the previous October.

By mid-June, Saddam had begun to round up the plotters and by the end of the month over 100 officers were imprisoned from across the spectrum of the Iraqi military and security services. Of those officers implicated in the planned coup, the vast majority were Sunnis from the families commonly associated with the regime. Few survived, and Saddam had secured a major victory against what was perhaps the most serious challenge to his survival. The success of the coup had been prevented only by the pervasiveness of Saddam's intelligence network and the inability of the CIA to coordinate the Iraqi opposition. Still, one problem continued to linger. The INA was destroyed as an immediate concern but the INC still remained in sovereign Iraq, in Kurdistan, and was buoyed by the partial success of its 1995 outing against Saddam's northern forces. With the INA threat removed, the INC and the PUK were about to feel the wrath of the bloodied but undefeated heavyweight.

The Opposition Defeated and Kurdistan Divided

By 1994, Iraqi Kurdistan had been torn into two separate administrative zones. Talabani's PUK had removed Barzani's KDP from the majority of the Kurdish-held regions, though Barzani still retained control over the lucrative border crossings with Turkey. Recognizing his weak position, Barzani maintained strong links with Baghdad, while still ostensibly supporting the US-backed INC. The situation between the KDP and PUK deteriorated, as each possessed what the other wanted. Barzani wanted to be identified as the leader of the Kurdistan national movement in Iraq. However, this was difficult to achieve when his adversary, Talabani, controlled the majority of the region and held the regional capital Erbil. Similarly, Talabani wanted what Barzani had: access to revenue. He controlled the most significant population centres of Kurdistan, but did not have the resources to administer them adequately in addition to developing his militia. The situation was therefore dangerous and unstable.

Both sides had regionalized their predicament years earlier, and both had followed the paths determined by their geopolitical locations. Barzani, with his border and economic relationship with Turkey, had strong links with the Turkish military and assisted it in its targeting of Kurdistan Workers' Party (PKK) bases. Links were also strong, if covert, with Baghdad. The PUK, conversely, had a decent relationship with Iran, which perhaps could be seen as surprising since the Islamic Republic wouldn't necessarily make an ideal bedfellow with committed socialists. However, Talabani needed support, and Iran was ready to give it.

With Iranian support, the PUK attacked the strategic Haji Omran region in August 1996. The KDP was furious and appealed to the US to end the PUK-Iran offensives. Barzani was desperate and would seek whatever support was necessary to remove Talabani once and for all, appealing directly to Saddam for assistance to 'ease the foreign threat' posed by Iran. Saddam saw an opportunity not only to attack the PUK, but to remove the INC presence once and for all. Saddam would also benefit in other ways: the PUK would be severely weakened, Chalabi would be destroyed, the Americans would be embarrassed and the reputation of Barzani would be soiled among Kurdish nationalists for allying with Saddam – all this to be achieved in one clean and relatively simple military outing.

On the morning of 31 August 1996, 30,000 Republican Guards entered Erbil. The PUK in the city, commanded by Kosrat Rasoul, ordered an evacuation, but the INC lost at least 200 soldiers and intelligence operatives in the ensuing rout. The CIA had evacuated days before, and Chalabi had no choice but to flee. The KDP chased the retreating PUK out of Kurdistan and, for a brief period, Barzani was in control of the entire region. However, Talabani mounted his counterattack with Iranian weapons and by the end of October had recaptured all of his lost territory apart from the city of Erbil itself.

Saddam was victorious. The INA and INC had been removed as serious threats to his regime. Talabani had been grievously hurt by the ravaging of his forces by the Iraqi-backed KDP. The US had been forced to acknowledge the pre-eminence of Saddam over Iraq, and their intelligence operations had been decimated. Barzani, now in control of Erbil and the border with Turkey, was more powerful, but tainted with his collusion with Baghdad. In effect, the Iraqi opposition to Saddam was at its lowest ebb; the Kurdish movement was in turmoil and Saddam had proved to the world that Iraq still belonged to him.

Oil for Food

Meanwhile, the Iraqi economy remained in a dreadful state and Saddam was forced to fund a system of patronage from rapidly diminishing resources. It seemed that his policy of maintaining the suffering of the Iraqi people, creating a propaganda card of the most illustrative proportions, had now reached the point of being unsustainable to the regime (Baram 1998: 65). Furthermore, Saddam's technique of subduing political forces within Iraq with a balance of terror and patronage was now threatened, as the economic situation had declined to a point where Saddam had to resort to unsustainable tactics to maintain his position as patron. Throughout the early years of sanctions, Saddam had the necessary resources to import food (the basis of his patronage) by printing currency, with the result that the value of the dinar plummeted as inflationary pressures impacted upon the economy. By the mid-1990s, the US dollar exchanged at approximately 3,000 dinar (it had previously been three dinar to the dollar), and the rate would rise or fall drastically with rumours regarding the lifting of sanctions or the acceptance of the oil-for-food programme (Baram 1998: 67–9).[4] With the Iraqi population's purchasing power at an all-time low, Saddam had to make a choice. He could either use his final reserves of hard currency to flood the market with food, or accept an oil-for-food initiative. He chose the latter.

The Iraqi government accepted what was to become known as the oil-for-food deal (SCR 986) on 20 May 1996. The deal allowed the Iraqi government to export $2 billion in petroleum and petroleum products over a six-month period, with $200–300 million being allocated for the Kurdish north (Niblock 2001: 117–18). The oil-for-food programme was continued at regular six-monthly intervals, with all renewals occurring within the framework of SCR 986, but with later renewals increasing the amount of oil allowed to be exported to $5.2 billion every six months and, in December 1999, the ceiling on Iraqi exports was lifted by the UN Secretary-General.

The total figures give an idea of the scale of this programme. Over all phases (I–XIII) Iraq had exported oil to the value of $64.231 billion. Of this, 25 per cent (app. $16 billion) went to the Compensation Fund for Kuwait, 2.2 per cent (approximately $1.5 billion) went to UN agency operations, and 0.8 per cent (approximately $0.5 billion) was allocated to the weapons inspection programme. The oil-for-food deal was in its thirteenth phase under the provisions of Resolution 1447 of 4 December 2002 when Coalition forces invaded Iraq in the spring of 2003. By this time, according to the UN Office of the Iraq Programme (OIP), some $26.8 billion-worth of humanitarian supplies had been delivered to Iraq, with an additional $10.1 billion-worth of supplies awaiting delivery.[5]

While the oil-for-food programme allowed Iraq to export oil, Saddam was particularly concerned that his acceptance of SCR 986 would enable the US to maintain sanctions as a tool aimed directly at his regime, and also reduce international pressure for sanctions to be lifted. However, his fears were perhaps unwarranted. Saddam's acceptance of the resolution allowed him again to strengthen his position within Iraqi society, while improving the socio-economic conditions of the Iraqi people. For Saddam, the oil-for-food deal gave him many powerful propaganda possibilities. First, when Iraq was well provided for, the regime would take the credit; when there were failings, the UN would bear the brunt of the criticism with accusations of inefficiency and corruption. Second, the deal almost certainly averted a humanitarian catastrophe in Iraq – a situation which could have threatened the existence of the regime. Third, and perhaps most importantly for

Saddam, the deal effectively removed Saddam's obligation to provide for the Iraqi people. Funds the regime had allocated for foodstuffs and essential supplies could now be redirected to consolidating the patronage structure within the political elites, re-equipping and restructuring selected military units, and financing the smuggling of weapons and associated technology (Baram 1998: 72–3).

Sanctions Busting

Not only did the oil-for-food programme make available a great amount of cash, but the regime would turn the provisions of the programme into a revenue generator for itself. In a first phase of manipulation, Iraq awarded oil-buying contracts (which it was mandated to do under UN provisions) to companies which had a long history of dealing with Iraq and companies which were considered 'friendly' to the regime. The regime also implemented a series of 'kickbacks' by which the Iraqi government would receive a 5 or 10 per cent commission from companies in order to clinch the deal. Needless to say, the practice was kept highly secret, but it seems that procedure was kept in place for the duration of the programme. It is unknown exactly how much Saddam generated by this method, but the *Wall Street Journal* speculated that *every* barrel of Iraqi oil had been subject to this manipulation, and in a one-year period (winter 2000 to fall 2001) the regime would have generated $175 million.[6] The regime also accrued large amounts of hard currency through exporting oil outside the remit of the oil-for-food programme. Operating through a variety of companies headed by Uday Saddam, the regime earned an estimated $8.3 billion between 1996 and 2002 in oil trade with Turkey.[7] It is further estimated that the regime received anywhere between $200 and $450 million per annum between 1994 and 2001 in goods derived from trade with Jordan and perhaps as much as $2 billion generated from trade with Syria between 2000 and 2002, and nearly the same amount in trade with Iran between 1996 and 2002.[8] Saddam therefore certainly had enough resources available to him to pursue his policy of patronage and enticement, while the UN continued to supply the basic needs of the Iraqi people with oil-for-food funds.

Hide-and-Seek with UNSCOM

Even though the economic situation was now being managed and the regime could continue to accrue additional wealth, Saddam still faced a serious problem when it came to dealing with the activities of UNSCOM. The Iraq–UNSCOM relationship had been characterized by mistrust on both sides since inspections commenced in 1991. Iraq was convinced (with good reason) that UNSCOM was a cover for the intelligence services of the US, UK and Israel to operate inside Iraq, and UNSCOM was convinced (again with reason) that Saddam was operating an extensive evasion and concealment scheme, preventing the inspectors from finding anything of real worth. Saddam's litany of deception against UNSCOM makes remarkable, and at times rather amusing, reading. For example, after Iraq disconnected UNSCOM equipment monitoring a former WMD production facility in October 1997, the Iraqis stated that the wires had been cut by a 'wandering psychopath' who might 'make a reappearance' (Baram 1998: 75).

While such excuses may have been met with nothing more than raised eyebrows, dealing with UNSCOM was a dangerous game of brinksmanship for the Iraqi leader. Delaying and obstructing the activities of the inspectors would run the risk of military reprisals (such as the January 1993 cruise missile attack by the US), but the regime became skilled at backing down at the last moment while still ensuring that the 'obstruction' work had achieved its aims of removing incriminating evidence beforehand. The final straw came when Rolf Ekeus's replacement, the more combative Australian diplomat Richard Butler, refused to certify that Iraq had destroyed its banned weapons (Niblock 2001: 123). Iraq then refused to cooperate with UNSCOM – something which it felt justified in doing due to its gaining evidence that the organization had been working closely with Israeli intelligence since 1994. By December 1998, and after several crises over inspections between Saddam and the UN (which, on one occasion, saw US bombers actually being airborne when Iraq backed down to UN demands on 14 November 1998), Butler withdrew UNSCOM from Iraq in the face of Iraqi non-compliance. As punishment, an ineffective air strike was launched by the US and British, known as Operation Desert Fox, between 16 and 19 December 1998 (Butler 2000: 231–2).

For Saddam, Desert Fox was of no particular concern and merely heightened the fact that the US policy aimed at removing him from power proved to be toothless. His actions had managed to rid Iraq of the pervasive and annoying presence of the inspectors, who were getting rather good at finding out his secrets, and his show of resolve against the international community had served to reconsolidate his standing amongst the security services and the Republican Guard (the latter had been purged after the failure of the INA-CIA coup attempt). Therefore, if Desert Fox was intended to force Saddam into accepting inspectors under the framework of UNSCOM, it failed badly. After the attacks, Iraqi resolve was strong and UNSCOM had been too discredited by its association with foreign intelligence services to enable the UN to further sanction its activities in Iraq. Combined with this was a resurgence of international criticism regarding sanctions and the perceived weakness of the provisions of the oil-for-food programme. With these problems in mind, SCR 1284, adopted on 17 December 1999, replaced UNSCOM with the United Nations Monitoring, Verification and Inspection Commission (the rather unwieldy-sounding 'UNMOVIC').

Essentially similar to that of UNSCOM, the task of UNMOVIC was to verify Iraqi compliance with SCR 687, rather than seek evidence of its non-compliance – a difficult task indeed. However, the main difference was the linking of compliance to the lifting of sanctions. If UNMOVIC and the IAEA confirmed that Iraq had cooperated fully with the remaining disarmament requirements of Resolution 687, and with monitoring and verification being operational for 120 days, then the Security Council would suspend the sanctions regime for periods of 120 days at a time, but with the proviso that sanctions could be reimposed if Iraqi double-dealings became apparent (Niblock 2001: 124–5).

For Iraq, however, the problem of SCR 1284 would be found in the details. Emboldened by the abstentions of three of the permanent members of the Security Council when 1284 was being voted on (China, France and Russia), the Iraqi regime rejected the resolution on the grounds that UNMOVIC was effectively UNSCOM with a different name. Iraq was also quite rightly sensitive to the fact that states deemed 'anti-Saddam' such as the US (with Clinton now publicly promoting a policy of regime removal) had the power to veto anything pertaining to the lifting of Iraqi sanctions. For Saddam, 1284 was good on paper but had no value in reality. For Iraq, the price of renewing a weapons-monitoring presence was the removal of the sanctions regime itself. Nothing less would do, but in the absence of such a change in policy, Saddam would make the US squirm as Clinton's administration doggedly attempted to force Iraqi compliance through UN channels. However, Saddam's US adversary was about to change. The cautious policies of Clinton were to be replaced with the Manichean simplicity of George W. Bush.

Towards Invasion

The 2003 US-led invasion of Iraq clearly had its roots in the Republicans' criticisms of the perceived lack of conviction showed by Clinton towards removing Saddam. Members of the first Bush administration who went on to hold key positions within the second Bush administration, such as Dick Cheney, had argued throughout the 1990s that regime change should be forcibly implemented (Dodge and Simon 2003 10). However, this was easier said than done, as George W. Bush had inherited the same problems which had hamstrung the Iraq policy of Clinton: the Iraqi opposition was in disarray, neighbouring countries were unsupportive and other crises were sapping US military resources, including most notably those in the Balkans. The new administration would therefore fall into the same policy malaise as its predecessor, until the terrorist attacks of September 11 in 2001 recalibrated US foreign policy aims.

Following the attacks on New York and Washington DC by al-Qaeda, figures that had previously been on the fringe of US policymaking circles, including the so-called neo-conservatives (neo-cons), seized the opportunity to invigorate the regime change policy. In what remains a prime example of the power of sound-bites, media manipulation and preying on an electorate's deepest fears, the fringe-right constructed a devastatingly seductive, if incongruous, nexus of September 11, al-Qaeda, international terrorism, Osama Bin Laden, political Islam, WMDs and Saddam's Iraq. Overnight, Saddam became synonymous with international terrorism, which in turn was magnified by WMD, which in turn led back to Saddam and the lack of weapons inspections in Iraq since 1998. The fact that Iraq had still not managed to account for immense stocks of biological weapons, including anthrax, allowed the publicity wagon to run riot, particularly after limited anthrax attacks occurred in the US itself. Saddam, by a careful and highly skilled process of psychological media association, was now the bogeyman, and it became clear that, after the US's attack against Afghanistan in the aftermath of September 11, the neo-cons would waste no time in advising their president to target Iraq.

After the US had tackled the Taliban regime in Afghanistan and destroyed al-Qaeda's bases, it was clear that Bush now had grand plans aimed at eradicating the threat posed to the US by undertaking an aggressive foreign policy. In addition, many observers viewed the US targeting of Iraq to be a purely opportunistic occurrence, driven by the desire to gain control of Iraq's oil wealth rather than any other concern (see, for example, Jhaveri 2004; Leaman 2004). The beginning of the countdown to what would be the Third Gulf War (the first being the Iran–Iraq War, the second the invasion of Kuwait) can be dated to 29 January 2002 when Bush delivered his State of the Union address to the US Congress (Dunne 2003: 270).[9] In this infamous speech, Bush branded Iraq along with Iran and North Korea as constituting an 'axis of evil' which threatened the national interests of the US and, indeed, the civilized world. On 10 October, the US House of Representatives (by a vote of 296 to 133) and Senate (by 77 to 23) authorized Bush to use military force against Iraq if necessary, based on an array of intelligence assessments that have since been shown to be flawed, if not actually false. Mirroring Bush's actions, British Prime Minister Tony Blair also moved towards using his country's military force to support the US if Bush chose to attack Iraq, for reasons which started with WMD, but were then augmented by arguments focusing upon the ineffectiveness of sanctions and the suffering of the Iraqi people (Bluth 2004: 872). With Prime Minister Blair at his side, Bush set about building a case for action to be taken against Iraq with unbridled vigour. However, the case as presented – which focused upon WMD – was never remotely convincing and was viewed as being a prime example of opportunistic foreign-policymaking, rather than being based upon any clear evidence of the status of Iraq's WMD stocks, nor was there any structured, coherent vision of a post-Saddam strategy for Iraq. Almost certainly due to the request of Blair, Bush renewed the debate with the UN regarding Iraqi WMD. Resolution 1441 was passed on 8 November 2002, signifying the commencement of the penultimate stage in the countdown to war. The resolution required Iraq to cooperate with UNMOVIC fully. Failure by Iraq to cooperate with UNMOVIC would lead to 'serious consequences' – a well-known diplomatic euphemism for military action.

Weapons inspectors of UNMOVIC and the IAEA returned to Iraq on 18 November 2002, under the leadership of Dr Hans Blix and Mohammed al-Baradei respectively. In some respects, weapons inspections were something of a waste of time. In circumstances of US and UK entrenchment regarding taking military action against Iraq, Saddam faced a difficult task in proving a negative – he had to show that he did not possess something. Blix's reports to the Security Council were expertly positioned 'on the fence' but tended to give more credence to the value of continuing with weapons inspections rather than declaring Iraq in violation of Resolution 1441. Such findings were never going to be enough to convince the

Security Council of the need to take military action against Iraq. France and Russia both stated that they would use their vetoes in the Security Council against a bill forwarded by the US, and China and Germany also made their opposition clear. Realizing that their attempts to gain UN support to take action against Iraq had failed, the US and Britain had no choice but to withdraw the bill. Instead, they embarked upon assembling a rather hotch-potch collection of forty-four nations into another 'Coalition of the Willing'.[10] With the UN fragmenting and the US unable to secure a resolution categorically sanctioning military action against Iraq, the US and UK went ahead irrespectively and began to undertake a military build-up in Kuwait. George W. Bush made one final ultimatum on 18 March 2003, demanding that Saddam Hussein and his immediate family leave Iraq. Saddam dismissed the ultimatum as ridiculous. Indeed, he had organized his regime and his military and seemed to be relishing the opportunity to have one final battle. On 20 March, the Third Gulf War commenced.

State and Society on the Eve of the Invasion of Iraq

With hindsight, Iraqi society had been subjected to transforming influences especially since the seizing of power by the Baʿth Party in 1968. The transformation of society occurred in several linked ways, and includes the re-tribalization of society, the tribalization of the state, the fracturing of society by the regime, and the crippling of society and the strengthening of the regime through the effects of the sanctions regime.

The first transformative element – the re-tribalization of society – is perhaps surprising if the pronouncements of the Baʿth government made in 1968 are considered. 'Communique No. 1', issued in July 1968, stated that '[w]e [i.e. the regime] are against religious sectarianism, racism, and tribalism', defining each of these as the 'remnants of colonialism' (Baram 1997: 1).[11] Yet by the 1980s, the regime itself would be promoting tribes, committing acts of genocide against Kurds and attacking the Shiʿi religious establishment. The reasons behind this seeming policy about-face relate to the fact that the Iraqi government was moving from being totalitarian back to authoritarian. As such, society could no longer be dominated as it had been in the 1970s – it now had to be managed.

The re-tribalization of the state could be seen particularly in the south of the country. The power of tribal sheikhs had been in decline throughout the twentieth century. The monarchy effectively weakened the power tribal leaders held over their kinsmen, and Qasim's agrarian reforms severely reduced the landholdings of the tribes. The Baʿth government of 1968 followed suit, enacting various reforms all designed to curtail the power of the tribes. However, inherently weakened by the effect of the Iran–Iraq War and then the ousting from Kuwait, Saddam's government turned to the tribes, seeing them as a means to maintain control through bringing them into partnership with the state. The reasons for this relate to the fact that Sunni tribes had assisted the regime in combating the Kurdish rebels in 1991, in the north, and Sunni (and some Shiʿi) tribes had similarly supported the regime in the south (Baram 1997: 8). Saddam also saw the tribes and their sheikhs (whether Sunni or Shiʿi) as being distinctively 'Arab', and therefore of use symbolically against the rise of the Shiʿi religious establishment with its associated links with Tehran. Tribes patronized by the regime would be granted large estates and given light weapons and resources from the state, to the extent that particular sheikhs could build their own private armies, ready to do the bidding of the regime when needed. All too often, such 'tribes' were not authentic – rather they were manufactured from heterogeneous elements, given an old tribal name and supported by the state. Such tribes were held in disdain by the Iraqi public, but were often empowered by the regime to hold positions of power in urban areas (Jabar 2003a: 94–5).

The flip side to this re-tribalization of society was that the Baʿth Party itself also become 'tribalized'. The tribal origin of party members, particularly in the leadership, became of fundamental importance. In an attempt to graft notions of Arabism and tribal honour on to the Baʿth Party, Saddam effectively worked to transform it from being an ideological political organization into being a tribe in all but name. The effect of this was to constrain the overall appeal of the Baʿth Party to Iraqi society, but to consolidate it internally. In order to maintain his hold over society at large, Saddam would depend increasingly upon the activities of the range of security organizations that watched Iraq's populations for any signs of actual or potential dissent (see Boyne 1997/8; Marashi 2003). The pervasiveness of the security apparatus meant that even day-to-day activities would often need the approval of one of the security offices. The result of this was the further weakening of the bonds of civil community in Iraq, with '[c]orruption, competition for influence and authority, and a rigid hierarchy [all rendering] this system highly effective in achieving one of its major objectives: promoting a sense of helplessness among the population' (al-Khafaji 1992: 16).

This fracturing of society, combined with the corrosive effects of the sanctions regime upon day-to-day life in Iraq, meant that localized political actors, including the tribes, the religious establishment and ethnic entrepreneurs, became of crucial importance in the lives of Iraqis, as these were the sources that could provide support, security and possibly even protection from the regime. On the eve of the invasion of Iraq in 2003, Saddam's regime was the force that was holding together what was a complex system managing and manipulating what had been turned into a fractious and unstable political structure. When the regime was removed, Iraqi society shattered into pieces.

7 Regime Change, 2003–2007

The 2003 invasion of Iraq pitted the most powerful military force ever seen against an Iraqi military that was a shadow of what it had been in 1991. The speed and efficiency with which US and British forces destroyed Iraq's military formations exceeded the expectations of military planners in Washington DC and London, and hopes were certainly high that the venture would prove to be relatively trouble-free – as many in the neo-con camp in Washington had been predicting. However 'regime change' logically has two parts to it. The first of these, regime removal, is arguably the easier and the awesome military might of the Coalition found the task of invading Iraq and defeating the Iraqi military straightforward enough. But the second part of regime change, which is regime replacement, proved to be more problematic and ultimately far more dangerous.

From the very first days following Saddam's removal, the Coalition struggled to put into place strategies for administering Iraq, to build an Iraqi government deemed 'legitimate' by its subjects, to create a security force that would act in the interests of Iraq rather than of particular communities, to counter a range of insurgencies and rebellions that would break out in both Sunni and Shi'i communities and to resist the influence of neighbouring powers in Iraq's affairs. The product of failings in all these has been to magnify the tendencies towards fragmentation already apparent in Iraq, but kept in abeyance by Saddam's authoritarian and totalitarian methods of government.

Understanding how Iraq moved from being unified under the heel of a dictator to being on the verge of possible collapse and fragmentation is the subject of this chapter. The military assault that would end Saddam's decades in power is described and analysed, as is the failure of Coalition forces to set up emergency institutions of government immediately following Saddam's demise. The political development of Iraq since 2003 is then addressed, with particular emphasis placed upon understanding why and how the administrative vacuum came to be filled by communally identified organizations and groups. The various reactive actions of the Coalition are also considered, as is the impact of their policies upon Iraqi political development. To begin with, the final analytical theme of this book is presented, which is the debate over transitions to democracy in post-conflict and divided societies, otherwise referred to as the *state-building and democratization debate.*

The State-Building and Democratization Debate

The final 'theme' relates to how authoritarian regimes, once removed by external powers, are then replaced with 'democratic' regimes of a design influenced, maybe even prescribed, by the occupiers. A key question to ask in this regard is whether the process of regime-change and (attempted) democratization in a globalized world enhances the consolidation of multi-ethnic states, or instead acts as a catalyst in their fragmentation and possible collapse.[1]

If theories of globalization are considered, one would expect that the role of ethnicity and religion in political life should be in decline (Hobsbawm 1990; Keating and McGarry 2001: 3–4). But the empirical evidence suggests that the weakening of state sovereignty by the forces of globalization can in fact encourage the political fragmentation of multi-ethnic states, particularly if the role of a central authority declines and groups become fearful for their physical survival in an environment characterized by heightened levels of instability.

Political power then often becomes devolved and localized, with groups competing for power (Lobell and Mauceri 2004: 3; A. Smith 2004: 24–5). The Soviet collapse, for example, led to the intensification of ethnic conflict in several successor states, including Georgia, Moldova and Azerbaijan, and changes in the ethnic balance of power in Yugoslavia quickly heralded that state's demise (Horowitz 2004; Williams 2004). Globalization therefore provides a context in which ties to the state can be loosened, and identities can be disturbed and reformulated (Agnew and Corbridge 1995: 98).

In addition to the spread of the influence of the global economy, a more aggressive component of globalization has emerged since September 2001, this being US unilateralism and the global effect that the foreign policy actions of the only superpower has in what is, at present, a unipolar world. Until 2003, Iraq had largely remained isolated from the transformative effects of the global economy due to the authoritarian nature of the state and the debilitating nature of the sanctions regime imposed on the country since 1991. But, from existing under one of the world's most oppressive regimes for nearly thirty years, the peoples of Iraq were liberated in little over a month, with the stated aims of the US being to democratize Iraq and to create a zone of 'democratic peace' at the heart of the Middle East (Anderson and Stansfield 2004: 186). But how likely was it that Iraq could democratize in line with the aims of US policy, particularly when the sudden removal of Saddam's regime granted the forces of localized communal identities the political space in which to flourish? Suddenly finding themselves without the strictures of the Baʿth-dominated political system, localized political forces emerged seemingly overnight, with neighbourhoods, city quarters, rural areas and even entire regions falling under the sway of authorities which identified themselves principally by reference not to an Iraqi civic nationalism, but to a religious, ethnic or tribal ideal.

Even when stability and security in Iraq deteriorated in the months and years following Saddam's removal, President Bush remained openly confident about the chances of democratizing previously non-democratic states, (almost) associating himself with every democratic development that had occurred since the era of ancient Greece. Speaking in November 2003, he declared that 'we have witnessed, in little over a generation, the swiftest advance of freedom in the 2,500 year story of democracy', noting that, in the early 1970s, there were 'about 40 democracies in the world', and, as the twentieth century ended, there were nearly 120 'and I can assure you more are on the way' (Carothers 2002: 5–6). Notwithstanding the president's optimism, the empirical evidence suggests that the introduction of democracy-by-force is a somewhat risky strategy to follow. Out of the eighteen forced regime changes in which US ground troops have been committed, only three deserve the 'democratic' title – Germany, Japan and Italy (Etzioni 2004: 6; Pei and Kasper 2003: 9). Furthermore, Etzioni contends that democracy is problematic to export, and that Germany and Japan are the 'exceptions that prove the rule' (Etzioni 2004: 13). Democracy was successfully exported to these two countries because (i) they were totally defeated, and (ii) there was no danger of the emergence of a civil war. Arguably, both of these conditions have been lacking in Iraq.

The often-cited mantra of the US being at war not with Iraq, but with the regime of Saddam Hussein, proved beneficial in terms of attempting to isolate the Iraqi government in international and domestic terms, but also meant that Iraqis did not suffer the same absolute defeat as that inflicted upon Japan and Germany. Indeed, the unwillingness of the Iraqi army to engage US forces only served to support the notion that Iraq had not been defeated, but rather liberated from Saddam's dictatorship. Thus, those organizations that had been given political space by the removal of Saddam set about resurrecting their authority and rebuilding their claims for a stake in controlling the direction of the state. The fact that sectarian (if not ethnic) identity as a politically mobilizing force had been in decline in Iraq, particularly since the mid-twentieth century, was quickly forgotten as the competition for the control of the state, and what Iraq would 'be', began in earnest. The US very quickly found out that the task of democratizing and reconstructing a multi-ethnic state was fraught with difficulties and dilemmas, particularly as their own, at times simplistic, methods of conceptualizing Iraqi society began to feed into, and affect, political developments on the ground. How the US and its allies attempted to build a state and to enforce a democratization process in Iraq is charted alongside the reaction of Iraqis to the policies pursued. The balance of the two – and the interaction between them – lies at the heart of the debate.

Operation Iraqi Freedom

The military campaign to end Saddam's regime commenced with an air attack against Baghdad on the morning of 20 March. A mere twenty-one days later, US forces would be in control of the capital, with Saddam reduced to hiding in the region known as the 'Sunni Triangle'. Before the invasion occurred, the possibility of a collapse of Iraq's military forces taking place was rarely acknowledged among commentators. Indeed, many had predicted that Iraqis, faced with an invading non-Muslim enemy, would rally as Iraqi nationalists in defence of their country and inflict horrendous losses upon Coalition forces. It was also expected that Saddam would deploy chemical and/or biological weapons as a last means of defence. His failure to do so proved that UNSCOM had largely achieved its objectives in the 1990s, making the reason to go to war in the first place invalid.

The opening salvo of the war was fired two days before it was timetabled to occur. In what would be the first of several opportunistic attacks aimed at 'decapitating' the Iraqi leadership, two F-117s (stealth attack aircraft) dropped bunker-busting bombs against seemingly non-descript buildings in central Baghdad in the early morning of 20 March, after US intelligence sources indicated that Saddam and his sons Uday and Qusay were all present (Murray and Scales 2003: 154–5). This attack was the start of a cat-and-mouse game between members of the Iraqi leadership and US forces that would ultimately see Uday and Qusay killed in Mosul on 22 June, and their father captured in a village near Tikrit some six months later on 13 December.[2] It would also see many innocent deaths as the US continued to respond to sightings of Saddam with the bombing of civilian areas.

The attack against Iraq surprised many observers, and probably Saddam, who were expecting the pattern to be similar to that seen in 1991, with an air assault against military targets taking place over several weeks followed by the committing of ground units. This was not to be the case. In 1991 the US mantra was one of employing 'overwhelming power' against Iraqi forces. This was changed in 2003 to 'overmatching power' – meaning that the enemy would be attacked across such a broad spectrum that its military would collapse. To achieve this, the Coalition would commence its land assault simultaneously with the air assault, rather than after. Furthermore, the land assault would not aim to seize territory. Instead, 'difficult' areas would be bypassed, with seizure coming only after Saddam was removed.[3]

The war therefore started in the south, and then progressed up the major highways towards Baghdad. Even so, Baghdad was hit heavily on the evening of 21 March. During the course of that night, 600 cruise missiles were launched and 1,500 missions flown, with 700 strike aircraft hitting 1,000 targets (Murray and Scales 2003: 169). This bombardment of immense proportions was named 'shock and awe' by the US administration, never one to miss a sound-bite. The rationale behind the tactic was simple: that faced with such force the regime would simply collapse. After this first night, Coalition planners had reason to be confident. Iraqi air defences proved ineffective when faced with the advanced equipment and overwhelming firepower available to the Coalition forces. No fixed-wing sorties were flown by Iraqi aircraft, and a pitiful number of surface-to-air missiles (SAMs) were launched.

Three weeks into the attack, US forces had captured Saddam International Airport to the west of Baghdad. In the south, much of Basra was in British hands. By 9 April Baghdad was largely under the control of the US military. Two days later, Mosul surrendered to US troops and Kurdish *peshmerga* units. Saddam's hometown of Tikrit was finally taken on 14 April. A triumphant George W. Bush declared an end to major combat operations from the deck of the aircraft carrier USS *Abraham Lincoln* on 1 May. Coalition casualties stood at a relatively low 125 Americans and 31 British killed. However, unofficial estimates put the number of Iraqi civilian casualties magnitudes higher at somewhere between 5,000 and 10,000, but Saddam and his two sons still remained at large.

The Chaotic Devolution of Political Authority

The alacrity with which the Coalition military defeated the Iraqi army was matched by their sluggishness in establishing emergency structures of governance and administration, whether at the local or the national level. Indeed, it appears that military planners overestimated the effort needed to defeat Iraq's military, and totally underestimated the effort needed to provide some form of civil executive authority in the aftermath period. The blame for this abject failing can be traced to policymaking circles in Washington DC, and particularly to the now dominant neo-cons. With their information being provided mainly from Iraqi opposition groups, including the INC, the INA and the Kurdish parties, the advisers to the US government seemingly bought into the opposition's depiction of Iraq as being essentially a democracy waiting to be rescued from the savagery of Saddam's regime. Ahmed Chalabi was particularly singled out as a prominent advocate of this position, and perhaps even as a future leader of the country. As one observer since noted, '[t]he Pentagon's plan for postwar Iraq seems to have hinged, until the war itself, on the idea that Chalabi could be dropped into Baghdad and, once there, effect a smooth transition to a new administration' (Rieff 2004: 23).

Once the dictator was removed, so the argument tended to go, then Iraqis would simply embrace the forces which liberated them and continue on their democratic path. The plan was stunning in its simplicity, but it had virtually no evidence to back it up as none of these groups, apart from the Kurds, had any substantive links with Iraqi society. Once this scenario was accepted as reality, then there would be no need to have a detailed plan, as a secure and stable Iraq would rapidly undertake the transition to democracy (see International Crisis Group 2004: 4).[4]

While the plan (or lack of it) could win awards for wishful thinking, its grounding in unreality was its undoing. Without the omnipotent organizations of the Baʿth regime in place, and lacking any immediate and credible emergency institutions, political authority chaotically devolved to those groups best placed to exercise power. Long subdued socio-political forces previously cowed by the combined effects of state patronage and coercion erupted across Iraq, with those parties benefiting from foreign sponsorship rapidly gaining localized power on the ground.

The Coalition had to respond quickly, and set in play the pattern of having to react to developments in Iraq rather than by implementing a plan thought through beforehand. The first attempt by the Coalition to bring some order back to Iraq and commence the rebuilding of the state was in the form of the Office of Reconstruction and Humanitarian Assistance (ORHA), led by retired General Jay Garner. ORHA entered Iraq in April 2003 and was tasked with implementing law and order as early as possible (Yordan 2004: 52). However, it soon fell victim to the civil war that was breaking out back in Washington DC between the State Department and the Pentagon, with some of the most knowledgeable foreign staffers being blocked from joining Garner's team, or being withdrawn once in place largely because of pressure from the Department of Defense (the Pentagon), and particularly from Rumsfeld, Wolfowitz and Feith (see Packer 2006: 124–5).

This feuding within the Washington DC beltway would continuously undermine US efforts to formulate a cohesive policy for Iraq's future, particularly as the most knowledgeable people in the State Department, with regard to Iraq and the Middle East, were unwelcome to the Pentagon because of their tendency to view the democratization of Iraq as a task of Sisyphean proportions. Rather than send the Arabist staffers of the State Department, with their professional understanding, the Pentagon would prove to favour those with far less experience but who sang from the same proverbial hymn sheet as Rumsfeld and his neo-con council (Galbraith 2006: 95).

Although picked because of his neo-con connections, Garner's strategy of using as much of the existing state apparatus as possible would soon see him at loggerheads with his DC-based backers. This strategy included working with civil servants and utilizing the remnants of the army. Even the Ba'th Party would probably have survived under Garner, with only the two highest echelons of membership being excluded from having positions of power. But, rather than be seen as working with the most appropriate materials available, this strategy would ultimately see ORHA fall foul of the Pentagon, particularly as Garner seemed less than willing to support the neo-cons' man of the moment, Ahmed Chalabi (Packer 2006: 128).

Still, Garner was popular among Iraqis, and especially the Kurds, as he had spent time in the north in 1991 during the setting up of the 'safe haven', but ORHA had arrived too late to stem the rapid descent into disorder (characterized at this time by widespread looting) that had already started before Garner had even reached Baghdad. The scale of the looting in Baghdad particularly was staggering. It was estimated that the economic cost alone was $12 billion – effectively taking up the projected entire revenues of Iraq for the first year after the war (Packer 2006: 139). With Garner proving unable to bring stability to Iraq, it was of no surprise that he was unceremoniously recalled to Washington DC in mid-May and ORHA disbanded.

The Coalition Provisional Authority and the Iraqi Governing Council

Ambassador L. Paul Bremer III and the Coalition Provisional Authority (CPA) replaced Garner and ORHA. Bremer, arriving in Baghdad on 12 May, was given far more authority than Garner enjoyed, and used it willingly. With the authority of the Pentagon behind him, he pursued a far more aggressive and transformative set of policies, often reversing the strategies followed by his predecessor. Upon his arrival, on 15 May, Bremer issued CPA Order Number 1 banning persons serving in the top four levels of the Baʿth Party from being in the government, thus purging nearly 100,000 from the newly formed administration. One week later, on 23 May, CPA Order Number 2 demobilized and dissolved the Iraqi army, forcing some 350,000 trained (and armed) soldiers into unemployment (Galbraith 2006: 119).

The two orders in effect removed the foundations of the Iraqi state. These decisions would very soon come back to haunt Bremer, as many of these soldiers would find their training and weapons of great value to the insurgency when it started some months later. In addition, the dissolution of the army and the illegalizing of the Baʿth effectively eliminated the only two structures that were truly 'Iraqi' (at least among the Arab component of society, if not the Kurdish), rather than communal. The US military, along with the CPA, also adopted a tougher stance against civilian unrest. While something needed to be done to bring order to Iraq's streets – Baghdad especially continued to be ravaged by insecurity – the result was that anti-occupation sentiment was heightened due to what was seen as heavy-handed tactics, and militant activity increased as a result. The first month of Bremer's tenure in office was marked by an increase of attacks on US forces, and with little apparent improvement in the provision of basic services as there were simply no working structures through which policies could be implemented. Bremer therefore needed Iraqi allies, and quickly.

In the political sphere, the CPA continued to work with parties and leaders from the previously exiled opposition. While this was understandable – neither the CPA nor the US military had managed to develop a more nuanced appreciation of which 'indigenous' actors to deal with in the post-Saddam milieu – it immediately structured the political system in a manner that mirrored that of the ex-Iraqi opposition movement. It also meant that the US was now committed to an overtly 'top-down' approach to state-building, rather than pursuing a 'bottom-up' strategy of working with local communities.

Furthermore, as the prominent forces of the ex-Iraqi opposition had mainly been in opposition because they failed to fit within the overtly Arab nationalist framework of the Ba'th narrative, they were, in the main, religiously or ethnically mobilized. Bremer's bringing together of Abd al-Aziz al-Hakim (SCIRI), Ibrahim al-Ja'afari (Da'wa), Massoud Barzani (KDP) and Jalal Talabani (PUK) underscores this fact. The leaders of the two 'centrist' parties, Iyad Allawi (INA) and Ahmed Chalabi (INC), were also included, along with a token Arab Sunni representative, Nasser al-Chaderchi, to form a Leadership Council.

But the manner in which the council was assembled saw Bremer for the first time being challenged by the highest Shi'i religious authority in Iraq, Grand Ayatollah Ali al-Sistani. Believing the Leadership Council to be illegitimate due to its unelected condition, and undoubtedly recognizing the fact that the Shi'i were in a numerical majority in Iraq, Sistani called for an elected national assembly and the writing by it of a constitution (Diamond 2005: 40–1). It would not be the last time that Bremer would be successfully challenged by the Grand Ayatollah.

With unrest continuing to grow across Iraq and with the insurgency in Sunni Arab areas now recognized as a serious threat, Bremer pushed ahead with expanding his Leadership Council into a broader body. By including other smaller parties alongside the 'Magnificent Seven' of the original council, a twenty-five-person Iraqi Governing Council (IGC) was formed on 13 July (Diamond 2005: 42). The composition of the council attempted to roughly mirror Iraq's societal composition, with thirteen being Shi'i, five Kurdish, five Sunni Arab, one Assyrian and one Turkmen.[5] It was, therefore, of little surprise that political life in Iraq moved from being ideologically based under Saddam to being interest and communally based following his removal. However, while the CPA was vociferously criticized for assembling the IGC in such a way, to be fair to Bremer, no other options were available. It was certainly the easiest action to take, but also the only realistic possibility on the table.

Even if the formation of the IGC was driven by necessity, it was seen from the outset as being a creation of the US, and every structure succeeding it, including the government formed after the January 2005 elections, suffered from this stigma. This lack of legitimacy was made even more serious by the role the IGC would play in decision-making. Not only was the IGC hand-picked by the CPA, but all of its decisions had to be sanctioned by the CPA, thereby reducing the IGC to little more than an advisory body in the eyes of most Iraqis. Interest-based agendas also dominated the proceedings of the IGC, with the most prominent members coming from the Shiʿi parties, or Kurds promoting their own people's autonomy in the north of the country. Meaningful Sunni Arab members (i.e., enjoying some measure of popular support) were glaringly noticeable by their absence.

The first task given to the IGC by the CPA was to draft a new constitutional law by 15 December. The proposed law would then outline a mechanism by which a constitutional convention would be elected. Following this, the convention would draft a constitution which would then be subjected to a referendum. Upon its acceptance in the referendum, multi-party elections would take place and sovereignty would be transferred to the new Iraqi government from the CPA. This sounded straightforward enough, but problems quickly emerged as each of the three most prominent groups (the Shiʿi, Kurds and Sunni Arabs) tabled their demands, with each group effectively presenting their own vision of what they considered a future Iraq should look like.

The Shiʿi, following the example set earlier by Grand Ayatollah al-Sistani, demanded that delegates to the constitutional convention be democratically elected, thereby reflecting their numerical dominance. The Kurds once again presented their vision of Iraq being bi-national, with them existing autonomously in their own region. Meanwhile, Sunni Arab members of the council remained divorced from their constituents. Instead, the opposition to what was seen as a process that was disempowering Sunni Arabs for the benefit of the Shiʿi and the Kurds was heard more through the increasingly aggressive actions of the insurgency. August witnessed a notable surge in violence in Baghdad. The Jordanian embassy was attacked on 8 August, with seventeen people killed, and the UN mission was destroyed on 19 August, with the UN Secretary-General's envoy to Iraq, Sergio Viera de Mello, being one of the victims. With increasing regularity, al-Qaeda and the name of Abu Musab al-Zarqawi began to be heard.[6] The assassination of the leader of SCIRI, Ayatollah Mohammed Bakr al-Hakim, by a car bomb left outside the Imam Ali mosque in Najaf on 29 August was taken by many as being the first indication of a sectarian conflict emerging in Iraq – whether he was killed by Sunni Arab insurgents or not.[7]

November 2003 was a critical month for Bremer. By then, it was clear to him and to his political masters in Washington DC that the deadline for forming a convention would not be met, due to IGC members adopting increasingly intransigent negotiating positions. If this was not problematic enough, the number of US casualties was rising quickly (with forty troops being killed in the first ten days of the month alone, and attacks rising threefold since July). Following a visit to Washington DC in November, Bremer was ignominiously forced to scrap the timetable and introduce in its place a new plan which was duly presented to the IGC on 15 November.

The new plan was even more complex than the one it replaced, requiring a Transitional Administrative Law (TAL) be drafted by 28 February 2004 which would act as an interim constitution. The plan then envisaged that a Transitional National Assembly (TNA) would be formed, again not by elections, but by a complicated three-stage selection process. Each of Iraq's eighteen provinces was to select an Organizing Committee of fifteen members appointed by the IGC (but approved by the CPA) that would then convene a Governorate Selection Caucus. This caucus would then elect representatives to the TNA by 31 May, which would then assume full sovereign rights on 30 June. The final stage of the plan involved the drafting of a permanent constitution, with final elections taking place sometime before 31 December 2005. If, in the words of Bremer himself, the first plan to convene a constitutional convention was 'straightforward and realistic', then this second plan was rather more complicated and unrealistic, particularly as the timeframe for action had been drastically reduced, and the actions of the insurgents were continuing to degrade the fledgling Iraqi security forces.

Once again, Bremer came up against the implacable figure of Grand Ayatollah al-Sistani. By ignoring him when the IGC was formed, Bremer had shown himself to be unaware of his status and the unchallengeable influence he held over his followers. Bremer had also succeeded in sensitizing the Shiʿi population to any new plan that had the fingerprints of the US upon it. Ayatollah al-Sistani immediately objected to the new plan for exactly the same reason as he had objected to the old plan – that a new constitution should be drafted by a democratically elected body. The Shiʿi therefore insisted that the proposed TNA not be selected by caucuses, but elected by the (predominantly Shiʿi) people. This time, however, the Kurdish parties also became increasingly noisy and pressed on the beleaguered Bremer their demands that federalism should be guaranteed and the status of Kirkuk resolved.

After fighting alongside US forces during the regime-change phase of military operations, the Kurds were becoming increasingly exasperated with what they perceived to be US inaction. They also had viewed with dismay the withdrawing of the pro-Kurdish Garner and his replacement by Bremer, who seemed at best to be lukewarm towards the Kurds. His stubborn refusal to be drawn on the potentially destabilizing issue of Kurdish autonomy, leaving it instead for the future Iraqi government to act upon, heightened the already acute sense of paranoia of Barzani and Talabani, who also had to satisfy the demands made upon them by the increasingly nationalistic 'Kurdish street'. Prominent Shiʿi leaders had also begun to speak against the Kurdish federal vision, including Muqtada al-Sadr and the leaders of Daʿwa. By the beginning of February, Kurdish sensitivities on this subject were at an all-time high. Ethnic tensions in Kirkuk had increased, and the Turkish government had begun to place a considerable amount of pressure on both Kurdish parties and the US in order to forestall Kurdish autonomy.

Within the north, however, Kurdish popular opinion had grown more nationalist with calls for federalism often being swamped by increasingly vociferous demands for secession. The bombing of KDP and PUK *Eid* celebrations in February 2004 claimed over 100 lives, including those of several prominent political leaders, but ultimately only served to harden the Kurds' resolve to get their own way.

Meanwhile, the Sunni Arabs remained distinctly unrepresented in the negotiations. The result was, again, predictable. Even though Saddam was captured alive in December 2003, the insurgency against Coalition forces and nascent Iraqi security forces continued unabated, with several considerable victories being achieved by the increasingly confident insurgents. The cleavages apparent within the political discussions were now becoming apparent in society at large.

The Transitional Administrative Law

Faced with deadlock in the IGC, and having the mantle of being the champions of democracy taken from them by Ayatollah al-Sistani, the CPA was once again forced to react to events rather than follow any preconceived plans. When rejecting Bremer's 'caucus' plan, Sistani had noted that he would only reconsider his decision if a UN mission came to Iraq (Diamond 2005 84). The fact that the US felt the need to turn to the UN for assistance indicates how desperate their situation had become. On 28 January 2004, UN Secretary-General Kofi Annan announced that he would send a mission to Iraq to establish whether elections could be held before the transfer of sovereignty on 30 June. The mission, led by Lakhdar Brahimi, arrived in Baghdad on 6 February. Remarkably, Brahimi managed to find a compromise solution that while not satisfying the different interest, mollified them for the time being. The Brahimi report gave credence to the US position on the impracticality of holding early elections, while supporting the Shi'i position of having elections at the earliest opportunity, which the UN mission believed would be December (Diamond 2005: 137). Brahimi further recognized the sensitivity shown by Sistani towards the caucus selection system, and recommended that it be scrapped. Instead, an interim, caretaker government would be chosen to govern following the handing over of sovereignty on 30 June.

With a compromise in place, the CPA and IGC still had to come up with an acceptable interim constitution – the TAL. The IGC negotiators agreed on certain fundamental issues, but in reality simply froze political negotiations until a later time. The Kurds succeeded in keeping control of their autonomous region (without Kirkuk), and the Shiʿi compromised in having Islam named as 'a source of legislation', rather than 'the' source. The Sunnis, again, were sidelined in the process.

Signed on 8 March, the TAL was more a postponement of fundamental issues rather than a result reached by compromise.[8] As such, it was riddled with ambiguities. Even issues of fundamental importance such as what the political structure of the state would be, and the role of Islam in the state, were basically fudged in order to pass the document and keep the political process on track for the transition of sovereignty to take place in June. A further peculiarity of the TAL was that it stipulated a provision whereby a majority two-thirds vote in any three governorates in a future referendum could block the adoption of a new constitution – a mechanism that would become known as the 'Kurdish Veto', even though, in effect, it was placed in the constitution to satisfy the Sunni Arab negotiators. Far from ideal, the TAL was adopted as the interim constitution of Iraq, to govern the affairs of state between 30 June and the formation of a new Iraqi government after elections in 2005.

With the TAL in place, attention could now be paid to the formation of an Interim Iraqi Government (IIG) which would succeed the CPA as the sovereign power. For the administration of George W. Bush, the timeframe to deliver success in Iraq was beginning to get perilously tight, particularly with his own election campaign beginning to gain momentum. The Brahimi report had stipulated that the IIG should be staffed by technocrats. However, keen to maintain their positions within the government, the parties of the IGC were in opposition to Brahimi's plan. Similarly, the CPA, faced with yet another upturn in violence, was becoming increasingly authoritarian in the way it acted, and Bremer was under pressure from his political masters to start delivering 'success' in Iraq immediately. The result was that Brahimi's recommendation of the nuclear scientist Hussein Shahristani was sidelined, and the CPA and IGC brokered the details and membership of the interim government between them.

The Iraqi Interim Government

Far from being technocratic, the IIG was staffed from top to bottom with politicians from the IGC. Indeed, its membership read as a 'who's who' of ex-opposition parties. In the best traditions of power-sharing, the main positions were divided out between the Shiʿis, Sunnis and Kurds. Ghazi Al-Yawer, a returning Sunni Arab exile from London, who was linked closely to the government of Saudi Arabia, and also hailed from the prominent Shammar tribe, became president of Iraq – a ceremonial position rather than one carrying any real authority. The most influential position of prime minister went to the leader of the INA, Iyad Allawi, and Ibrahim al-Jaʿafari of Daʿwa was made vice-president. Although Kurds were appointed to prominent positions within the cabinet, they were left disappointed as both Barzani and Talabani had expected a Kurd to be made either president or prime minister (see Bremer 2006: 355–6). Their failure to gain either of these positions heightened secessionist sentiments in Kurdistan, forcing both leaders to be increasingly strident in their demands for Kurdish autonomy in the future.

On 8 June, the UN Security Council passed Resolution 1546, and unanimously gave its blessing to the IIG. While Iraq lurched from one round of negotiations to another – and all to produce an IIG and TAL that enjoyed only limited popular support – the threat posed by Sunni Arab insurgents and rebellious Shiʿi groups (and principally the Jaish al-Mahdi of Muqtada al-Sadr) had now reached new levels of seriousness. Reflecting just how difficult the security situation had become, sovereignty was formally transferred to the IIG not on 30 June as planned, but two days earlier in a low-key ceremony in the Green Zone of Baghdad. Ambassador Bremer left the same day and CPA staff became advisers to the IIG operating through the auspices of the new US embassy (see Bremer 2006: 392). The CPA legacy to the IIG was one in which power had chaotically devolved to localities; where militias were the pre-eminent forces dictating social actions; and a range of insurgencies had flourished under conditions almost comparable to those of a failed state.

Shiʿi Rebellion and Sunni Insurgencies

Opposition to the Coalition presence started in the months following the invasion of Iraq, and particularly from May 2003, and can be roughly divided into two categories.

The first, geographically located in the 'Sunni Triangle' between Baghdad and Mosul, was, and remains, composed mainly of Sunni Arabs but also had Kurds and Turkmens within its ranks. Often referred to as 'an' insurgency, it is more correct to refer to it in the plural. Indeed, there are several insurgencies ongoing within Iraq that are associated with the Sunni Arab community, ranging from ex-Baʿthists, neo-Baʿthists, Arab nationalists, home-grown Islamists or al-Qaeda associated factions.

The second opposition category has its strongholds in Baghdad and the Shiʿi south, and is composed of radicalized Shiʿis that have occasionally rebelled against the Iraqi government and Coalition authorities. I choose to identify their actions not as an insurgency, but as a rebellion, partly to distinguish it from the Sunni Arab insurgencies, and partly as its aims are more to do with influencing the Shiʿi-dominated government already established, rather than removing it from power as is arguably the case with the insurgencies.

As we have seen, SCIRI and Daʿwa assumed a prominent position early on following the arrival of the Coalition in Baghdad. From being involved with the exiled Iraqi opposition movement, both parties were recognized as important actors by the US, and SCIRI also benefited from its close links with the Iranian government. In addition to these political organizations, the Hawza al-Marja'iyya had emerged as a force capable of influencing popular sentiment, and Ayatollah al-Sistani showed he could act politically when he needed to.

There was, however, another force among the religiously minded Shiʿi that did not fall under the control of SCIRI or Daʿwa, and viewed Ayatollah al-Sistani with a certain degree of suspicion, if not disdain. To understand this force, we need to go back to the late 1990s. Saddam had been having particular trouble with the most prominent Shiʿi cleric, Grand Ayatollah Mohammed Sadiq al-Sadr and so ordered his assassination. Along with his two eldest sons, the *marja'* was killed in a hail of bullets in Najaf in February 1999 (Cole 2003). Sadiq al-Sadr had been an immensely popular figure, and particularly among those youths who had been marginalized and dispossessed by the inequities of Saddam's regime. One concentration of the poorest of Shiʿis in Iraq was in the rather inappropriately named Saddam City on the west bank of the Tigris next to Baghdad, where as many as 2 million people lived in appalling conditions (Napoleoni 2005: 136). The killing of the Grand Ayatollah sparked off violent clashes between the followers of al-Sadr and Saddam's security forces. Hundreds died, but the fire of rebellion had been lit among these followers of Sadr, and would grow following Saddam's removal. In March 2003, Sadiq al-Sadr's surviving son Muqtada, a young cleric with a fiery turn of phrase, emerged as the leader of the Sadr Movement.

As the inheritor of a large and wealthy movement, Muqtada was well positioned to fill the administrative vacuum left behind by Saddam's defeat and Coalition mismanagement. Saddam City was quickly renamed Sadr City, and Muqtada and his movement organized local services, food distribution and security while the effect of Garner's actions remained unseen – indeed, it seems that Muqtada's forces had expelled Iraqi forces from Sadr City before Saddam had even been defeated. As a figure who had stayed in Iraq and suffered under the dictatorship, Muqtada had little time for the returning exiled politicians and resolutely opposed the presence of foreign occupiers in his country. As a proud Iraqi nationalist, he also had viewed with contempt SCIRI and Daʿwa, with their ties to Tehran. Finally, as a son who had lost his father, he also was critical of his father's successor, Sistani, due to the latter's unwillingness to air his views and criticize the atrocities committed by Saddam. With so many grievances, and with such a large and devoted following, it would only be a matter of time before Muqtada came into conflict with those around him.

Muqtada's rise was totally unpredicted by the US and the Iraqi government. But his heightened influence in, and even control over, large parts of northern Baghdad, combined with his attempts to spread his message of radical Shiʿism and anti-occupation rhetoric to other areas of the country on the run-up to the 28 June handover of sovereignty meant that neither the CPA nor the IGC could ignore him.[9] Believing him to be little more than a young cleric with an obvious ability to rabble-rouse, the CPA attempted to intimidate Muqtada into compliance. His newspaper, *Al-Hawza*, was closed down on 28 March and one of his deputies, Sheikh Mustafa al-Yacoubi, was arrested in Najaf (Etherington 2005: 168).

Within days, the Sadr Movement was revolting across the south of Iraq and in Baghdad. Rather than following the Sunni Arab insurgents' tactics of guerrilla attacks, the Mahdi army was more brazen in its approach and attempted to fight US forces in the open. The plan was always destined to fail militarily, as there was no way that the ramshackle Mahdi army could hope to defeat such a superior military force. But the plan succeeded for Muqtada in a political sense. His taking refuge in the holy city of Najaf meant that the US could not attack him in case it provoked a wider-scale Shiʿi revolt, and Muqtada not only survived the fighting but also escaped arrest – in effect, he had stood up to the Americans. The Sadr Movement was weakened in the short term by picking a fight with the US military, but in the longer term its popularity was on the rise as new supporters saw Muqtada as the one leader who would not bow down to the authority of the occupiers.

While Muqtada was organizing his followers in the slums of Sadr City, Sunni Arab insurgent movements were beginning to coalesce in the days following the demise of Saddam's regime. Several different trends emerged but each was unified in their opposition to the occupiers and, to a greater or lesser degree, the Shi'i-dominated government.

The first of these groups were essentially the remnants of the deposed regime. As it became clear that the state had, for practical purposes, evaporated, and the Coalition had failed to replace it, the remnants of the deposed regime's security services, elite military outfits and paramilitary organizations regrouped (Dodge 2005: 10). Initially, many of these insurgents did not take up arms against the Coalition forces. Rather, 'they wanted to see whether the Americans were going to be liberators or occupiers' (Hashim 2006: 19). With the harder security line taken by the incoming CPA, many would soon see the occupying forces in the worst possible light. Undoubtedly buoyed by Bremer's demobilizing of the army, these groups benefited from the existence of stockpiles of weaponry across the country, and had access to the vast financial resources of the Ba'th Party. Former regime supporters and ex-military figures recommenced fighting the Americans in particular, unified in their aim to defend Iraq against an external aggressor.

The second set of Sunni Arab insurgencies had its origin within radical Islamist groups in Iraq itself. But, rather than there being one root, there were in effect two trends that came together: a 'regular' religious network of charities, mosques and organizations, and a 'radical' influx of militants. With regard to the former category, Iraq, along with all other Middle East countries, had experienced an upsurge in the growth of Islamist sentiment. One of the established Islamist political organizations was the Iraqi Islamic Party (IIP) led by Muhsin Abd al-Hamid. The party's history can be traced back to 1960 but, due to the potential threat it posed to the military regimes of the period, it was effectively banned and only appeared publicly following Saddam's downfall (Hashim 2006: 21). A further group that would achieve considerable notoriety was the Association of Muslim Scholars (AMS) led by Dr Harith al-Dhari. Both the AMS and IIP focused initially upon social and charitable works – essentially providing vital services for their communities. But the invasion of Iraq by non-Muslim forces and its subsequent occupation provided the spark which ignited this sentiment into a volatile opposition movement.

The 'radical' element of the 'home-grown' Islamist insurgency can be traced to the Kurdish mountains towards the end of the 1990s. Following splits in the most prominent Kurdish Islamist movement, the Islamic Movement of Kurdistan, a new and extreme group emerged from them known as Ansar al-Islam, dedicated to the overthrowing of the secular KDP- and PUK-dominated Kurdistan Regional Governments. The destruction of their bases in the Khormal region of Kurdistan by US bombers in 2003 served to change the focus of Ansar from their provincial concerns towards fighting the occupiers. The survivors ventured south to join forces with like-minded insurgents who were coalescing around the AMS and, to a lesser extent, the IIP. Together, these disparate groups formed the Jaish al-Ansar al-Sunnah (Partisans of the Sunnah Army).[10] Other groups that managed to blend radical Islamism with nationalist sentiment also appeared, including the Jaish al-Islami fil-Iraq (Islamic Army in Iraq), which merged *salafi* discourse with patriotic ideals, perhaps indicating the involvement of former regime elements (International Crisis Group 2006: 2). Each of these groups, along with many others, claimed the allegiance of multiple 'brigades' and, over time, developed from being badly organized and uncoordinated terrorists to proficient insurgents capable of striking the new Iraqi security services and their Coalition allies seemingly at will.

In addition to a home-grown set of Islamist insurgencies, the presence of US forces in Iraq and the lack of a state apparatus acted as a magnet for foreign fighters, commonly assumed to be members of al-Qaeda, travelling in from neighbouring countries. The main 'foreign' insurgency group was dominated by the late Abu Musab al-Zarqawi and was called Tandhim al-Qaeda fi Bilad al-Rafidain (al-Qaeda's Organization in the Land of the Two Rivers), formerly know as al-Tawhid wal-Jihad (Monotheism and Jihad) (International Crisis Group 2006: 1–2). This group gained infamy for undertaking the kidnapping and execution of Western contract workers, and was also blamed for suicide and bombing attacks against Shi'i targets, particularly from 2004 onwards.

The reputation of this group would suggest that it remains the main opposition force in Iraq and is primarily responsible for the majority of attacks that have taken place – and continue to take place – against Coalition forces and Iraqi government offices and individuals. This, however, would seem to be inaccurate and is perhaps a product of the focus placed upon this group by the US administration. Keen, indeed desperate, to show that Iraqis welcomed the Coalition as liberators, the US in fact benefited from the existence of a foreign al-Qaeda-associated group, as it allowed blame for attacks to be attributed to 'non-Iraqis'. It would seem, however, that while al-Zarqawi's group, even following his killing in June 2006, is powerful and effective, it is but one of many. Rather than being the core of the insurgency, the foreign element remains a small but deadly sideshow, with the most important component of the insurgency being indigenous Iraqi in origin.

The focus of the activities of the Sunni Arab insurgencies remained resolutely in the Sunni Triangle, until 2005. For the Coalition, there existed several troublesome towns and regions in the Triangle, including Ramadi, Balad and Tikrit. However, it would be the town of Fallujah that would become the focal point of the world's media in 2004. After initially being a relatively quiet town following Saddam's removal, confrontations between insurgents in Fallujah and US forces reached a climax with the killing and dismemberment of four contract workers in March 2004. Their particularly gruesome killing, and the broadcasting of pictures by the world's media, would see Fallujah made an example of by the US military. But, after a month-long military assault, US forces could still not enter the city. It was only after a siege that US Marines entered Fallujah in November, claiming to kill as many as 1,000 insurgents, but, in reality, much of this number was more likely to have consisted of innocent civilians.

Fallujah was a turning point in Iraq and 'renders a cautionary lesson on using military force to signal resolve in an unconventional conflict' (Malkasian 2006: 423). With

Muqtada Sadr's followers already rising against US forces, the US military and CPA were faced with a perilous situation. Rather than seek the support of the IGC, which was already seen as ineffectual by the CPA due to the inability of representatives to find common agreement on issues of importance, it seems that the decision to invade Fallujah, and to attack Muqtada's forces in southern Iraq, was taken unilaterally by the US (see Bremer 2006: 317–22). By doing so, the US pushed those Iraqis still uncommitted to the insurgency into joining their countrymen in their struggle to expel what was now seen as a dangerous and brutal occupier. The insurgency spread rapidly across Al-Anbar governorate, and Fallujah became a symbol of the resistance to the continued foreign presence and, in the wider Arab and Islamic world, evidence of the level of brutality to which the US military would go in order to force its vision on the new Iraq down the barrel of a gun.

January 2005 Elections

The elections for the Iraqi National Assembly occurred on 30 January 2005 amid fears of insurgent attacks. Zarqawi's al-Qaeda outfit had issued warnings not to participate in the elections, viewing those who did as legitimate targets.[11] The warning achieved its desired effect, but only in Sunni Arab-dominated areas. Certain indisputable trends could be seen in the voting pattern. Most notably, the turnout in the Kurdish and Shiʿi areas was very high – perhaps as high as 80 per cent in Shiʿi areas, and an astonishing 90 per cent in Kurdistan. Meanwhile, the turnout in the Sunni Arab areas was as impressively low. Indeed, the turnout in Mosul was as low as 10 per cent, and most of those would have been Kurds. The pattern was repeated in Tikrit, Baquba, Ramadi (where only 300 votes were cast), Fallujah and even parts of Baghdad. The communalization of Iraqi political life was now codified by the results of the elections. Those who voted did so as Shiʿis or as Kurds. Those who did not vote did so as Sunnis (Anderson and Stansfield 2005: 7).

This skewed pattern of voting would have implications for the distribution of seats within the national assembly. Of the 275 seats, 140 went to the United Iraqi Alliance (UIA, a coalition of Shi'i parties enjoying the support of Ayatollah Sistani). The next largest bloc in the assembly was the Kurdish Alliance (a union of the KDP and PUK, along with several other smaller Kurdish parties). Trailing in behind these was the 'Iraqi List' of Iyad Allawi, with forty seats. The most seats any Sunni Arab list secured were the five of Ghazi al-Yawer's 'The Iraqis'.

Table 7.1 Results of elections to the Iraqi National Assembly, 30 January 2005

Alliances and parties	*Total votes*	*Vote percentage*	*Seats*
United Iraqi Alliance	4,075,292	48.19	140
Kurdish Alliance	2,175,551	25.73	75
Iraqi (National) List	1,168,943	13.82	40
The Iraqis	150,680	1.78	5
Turkmen Front	93,480	1.11	3
National Independent Cadres and Elites	69,938	0.83	3
People's Union (Communist)	60,920	0.83	2
Islamic Group of Kurdistan	60,592	0.72	2
Islamic Action Organization (Shi'i)	43,205	0.51	2
National Democratic Alliance	36,795	0.44	1
National Rafidain List (Assyrian)	36,255	0.43	1
Reconciliation and Liberation Bloc	30,796	0.36	1
Others	444,819	5.65	0
Total	8,456,266		275

Source: Independent Electoral Commission for Iraq

This polarization of voting patterns manifested itself as an imbalanced Council of Representatives, with legislative and executive power being held mainly by parties sponsored by the Shiʿi religious establishment, and the political parties of Kurdistan. In practice, and keeping in mind the history of political representation in Iraq, those who had been marginalized under successive Sunni-dominated governments were now dominating the process in Baghdad, while the previous dominant grouping was firmly marginalized and dependent upon the charity of the Shiʿi and the Kurds for any representation and executive power in the new arrangement.

The new cabinet gave further credence to the view that power in 'the new Iraq' was being divided between the leading Shiʿi and Kurdish parties, at the expense of the Sunnis. The long-time Kurdish leader Jalal Talabani was elected president of Iraq by the TNA on 6 April, followed the day after by one of the leaders of Daʿwa, Ibrahim al-Jaʿafari, assuming the position of prime minister due to the predominance of UIA members in the TNA. Jaʿafari's subsequent granting of seventeen cabinet posts to Shiʿis, including the crucial interior and oil portfolio positions, with seven positions allocated to the Kurds (including foreign affairs) and eight to Sunni Arabs, was a clear attempt to try and form a government representing the three major political groups.[12] However, Sunni Arabs remained distinctly unimpressed both by how Jaʿafari had negotiated the formation of the new cabinet, and the final result. Discontent quickly percolated through to society at large as prominent Sunni clerics aimed their sermons at the new government, with the influential leader of the AMS, Sheikh Harith al-Dhari, accusing Jaʿafari of marginalizing the Sunnis. Worse was to come, however, as the anger caused by the forming of a new cabinet would pale into insignificance when it came to writing the new constitution.

Constitutional Negotiations

For the Sunnis, the drafting of the new constitution in the summer months of 2005 illustrated to them the dangers of existing under a state dominated by the Shiʿi, with a prominent Kurdish voice. Early promises that the Sunnis would be included in the process and that a draft would be achieved by consensus soon fell by the wayside, first because most potential Sunni negotiators were fearful of the insurgent threats against any 'collaborators', and second because the Shiʿis and the Kurds soon forgot about their agreement to find a consensus as they entered negotiations with a range of non-negotiable positions. While the Kurds and the Shiʿis could, between them, find a working agreement, if not a consensus, the same could not be said for the Sunnis.

Two issues were of particular concern. What had originally been the most contentious issue – the role of Islam in the constitution – remained so but it rapidly became a secondary concern to the issue of federalism. Believing that a federal system of government would protect at least the autonomous region they currently administered, the Kurds continued to place federalism before all else in their negotiations with other Iraqi groups. Even though the Sunni Arab negotiators never liked the idea of the Kurds being autonomous from the rest of Iraq, believing perhaps with good cause that such an arrangement would be but the first step leading to the accretion of Kirkuk to the federal region, followed by the secession of Kurdistan from the state, they grudgingly accepted that no authority inside Iraq could forcibly reintegrate the Kurds back into a unitary state. Sunni Arab negotiators however reacted with horror when SCIRI announced that it too supported the federal plan, but for all of Iraq, envisaging the creation of a southern Shiʿi-dominated province. The Sunni Arabs could all too easily envisage the break-up of Iraq, with the oil-rich north and south falling out of the orbit of Baghdad and the Sunnis left with a resource-poor central region.[13]

As 15 August came and went, there was still no progress towards finding a consensus between groups. The deadline for the drafting of the constitution was extended several times, until the Kurdish and Shiʿi negotiators simply passed the draft to the national assembly, effectively bypassing their Sunni counterparts. The draft constitution was subjected to a referendum on 15 October. The rules of the TAL stipulated that an overall majority vote was required to accept the draft constitution. However, the passage of the constitution could be blocked if more than two governorates had 'no' votes of two-thirds. The so-called 'Kurdish Veto' was now viewed as being a potential 'Sunni Veto', particularly as the Sunni Arabs were increasingly supported in their opposition to the draft constitution by the irrepressible Muqtada al-Sadr.

The Referendum

Electoral specialists were soon modelling how the votes would be cast in key marginal governorates, but the result was a more controversial and close-run affair than many imagined. As expected, the two provinces dominated by Sunni Arabs, and with a reputation for being home to the most vehement anti-occupation sentiment, rejected the referendum by more than the required two-thirds margin. Salahadin's 'No' vote stood at 82 per cent and Anbar's was even higher at 97 per cent.

But the vote in the more mixed provinces was perhaps even more damaging for the future unity of the Iraqi state as it was heavily polarized and therefore threatened to further the sectarian conflict which had already broken out in Iraq's mixed and contested regions. In Baghdad, the 'No' vote was just over 22 per cent, with most of these votes being cast in Sunni suburbs. In Tame'em province (Kirkuk), 37 per cent were against, with most of those voting in favour of the constitution being Kurdish. In Diyala, the vote was almost 50:50 and roughly divided between Sunnis and Shiʿis. The pattern that emerged was telling. In the twelve provinces where there existed a majority Kurdish or Shiʿi population, the 'Yes' vote ranged between 95 and 99 per cent. In those where Sunni Arabs were more numerous, the 'No' vote increased proportionally. With two governorates voting against the referendum with more than a two-thirds majority (Anbar and Salahadin), the situation in the northern governorate of Ninevah, with its capital of Mosul, became crucial. After a ten-day delay, the 'No' vote was declared at 55 per cent – a majority, though not greater than the required two-thirds – but this has never been accepted by the Sunni Arabs as legitimate. Indeed, accusations of electoral rigging were perhaps not merely knee-jerk reactions to losing.[14]

The result of the referendum can be read in one of two ways. The first way is that the constitution was accepted by a legal referendum. The second is that it was rejected by a significant proportion of Iraqis, who were predominantly the Sunni Arabs and Turkmens, while being overwhelmingly accepted by Kurds and Shiʿis. Both, of course, are correct, but the reality described in the second version has seemed to be a more appropriate guide to how political life in Iraq has since developed. Indeed, the referendum seemed to further the forces of sectarian and ethnic-based conflict. From a Sunni Arab perspective, the result emphasized to them the futility of attempting to affect change in Iraq through the ballot box as, even when they did vote (and they did so in considerable numbers), they still failed to defeat what was perceived to be a constitution drafted by Kurds, Shiʿis and Americans. Even worse, by participating in the vote, they gave the referendum a legitimacy which the results of the elections of January 2005 never enjoyed. Therefore, by participating, they supported the process, but still lost.

Arguably, the process of drafting and ratifying the constitution served to exacerbate the already centrifugal dynamics that were gripping the country. With hindsight, this should not have been unexpected. After all, the constitution was drafted by groups that considered their communal identity first, with an 'Iraqi' interest independent of their provincial positions not being high on their respective lists. As such, the draft constitution was something of a mess – promising all things to all groups, yet satisfying no group in particular, disappointing everyone and presenting a series of ambiguities which promised to haunt those who have to interpret its meaning in the future.

December 2005 Elections

With the constitution accepted, 'final' elections were held on 15 December 2005. Iraqis would now vote for a particular list, with 230 seats proportionately distributed across Iraq's eighteen governorates. A further forty-five 'compensatory' seats were allocated for distribution based upon the performance of parties in the election. The system was designed in order to give more weight to the Sunni vote, in the hope that it would result in more Sunni Arab representation in the national assembly, even if their vote remained low.

The final result, while seeing a clear increase in the number of seats going to Sunni Arab representatives, unsurprisingly still saw the same basic pattern emerge as that of the elections of January. The UIA dominated the assembly with 128 seats. The Kurdish List secured the second largest bloc with fifty-three seats. However, the Iraqi Accord Front, a union of various Sunni Arab parties formed in October 2005, managed to secure the third largest bloc in the assembly with forty-four seats. The gaining of a further eleven seats by Saleh al-Mutlaq's Iraqi Front for National Dialogue effectively gave Sunni Arabs representation that simply could not be ignored by the Kurds and the Shiʿis. However, the existence of a more balanced assembly seemed to complicate the political process rather than ease its running. Two months after the election had taken place agreement still had to be reached upon the composition of the new Iraqi government, and the identification of key figures including the president and prime minister. While it seemed likely that the Kurdish leader Jalal Talabani would remain as president of Iraq, it was far from clear who would be prime minister or who would be appointed to the sensitive ministries of interior, defence, and oil.

Ibrahim al-Jaʿafari had successfully managed to lose the support of the Kurds, who accused him of making decisions without undertaking the appropriate consultation, and who were furious with him for making a trip at the end of February 2006 to Ankara, without the (Kurdish) foreign minister, Hoshyar Zebari. Sunni Arabs were also opposed to Jaʿafari continuing as prime minister as attacks by Shiʿi gangs, commonly associated with the Interior Ministry, had risen during his time in office. A stand-off developed between the UIA on the one hand, and the Kurds and the Arab Sunnis on the other, over who should be appointed prime minister.[15]

Table 7.2 Results of elections to the Iraqi National Assembly, 15 December 2005

Alliances and parties	*Total votes*	*Vote percentage*	*Seats*	*Gain/loss*
United Iraqi Alliance	5,021,137	41.2	128	–12
Kurdish Alliance	2,642,172	21.7	53	–22
Iraqi Accord Front	1,840,216	15.1	44	+44
Iraqi (National) List	977,325	8.0	25	–15
Iraqi National Dialogue Front	499,963	4.1	11	+11
Kurdistan Islamic Union	157,688	1.3	5	+5
The Upholders of the Message	145,028	1.2	2	+2
Reconciliation and Liberation Bloc	129,847	1.1	3	+2
Turkmen Front	87,993	0.7	1	–2
National Rafidain List (Assyrian)	47,263	0.4	1	0
Mithal al-Alusi List	32,245	0.3	1	+1
Yazidi Movement for Reform and Progress	21,908	0.2	1	+1
National Independent Cadres and Elites			0	–3
Islamic Action Organization			0	–2
National Democratic Alliance			0	–1
Total	*12,396,63*		*275*	

Source: Independent Electoral Commission for Iraq

A product of this political uncertainty was the deterioration of security. Undoubtedly the most worrying development in the post-election period was the rapid intensification of what could already be described as a civil war between Sunnis and Shiʿis. Throughout 2005, suicide bombers had been targeting Shiʿi population centres and committing acts of violence against prominent members of the Shiʿi community. Iraq's security forces seemed to be totally incapable of preventing these attacks, more often than not blamed upon brigades associated with al-Zarqawi, but likely to be dominated by indigenous Iraqi resistance groups. In response, Shiʿi militias, most commonly associated with SCIRI's Badr Army and the Jaish al-Mahdi of Muqtada al-Sadr, were accused of undertaking retaliation killings against Sunni Arabs.

Staring into the Abyss

In February 2006, the situation took on a dangerous new dimension. In what was by all accounts a well-organized and expertly executed plan, unknown forces (but almost certainly from some component of the Sunni Arab insurgencies) destroyed one of the holiest shrines of Shiʿism – the Askariyya shrine in Samarra which housed the tombs of the tenth and eleventh Imams.

The symbolism of the attack could not be overstated. By the spring of 2006, with a government still not formed and with Sunni–Shiʿi killings being increasingly commonplace, Iraq was staring into the abyss of civil war. In the weeks following the destruction of the shrine, it was estimated that 500 people were killed in sectarian-related violence, with the Shiʿi-dominated Ministry of the Interior being implicated in the planning and undertaking of revenge attacks against Sunni Arabs. Meanwhile, the Coalition forces seemed powerless to prevent the ongoing violence. In the hope that Iraqi security forces would be capable of defeating the Sunni Arab insurgencies, and at least managing the various Shiʿi militias, the responsibility for policing Iraq's cities had been transferred to a great extent from the Coalition forces to their Iraqi counterparts. However, these counterparts, far from being able or willing to act as Iraqis in the interests of Iraq, instead often used their position to promote the interests of one group (normally the Shiʿis) over the other (usually the Sunnis). Kurdish *peshmerga* too were implicated. With Kurds serving in the Iraqi military ostensibly as 'Iraqis' but in reality as

Kurds, their actions were perceived by those in the communities policed by them as being dictated by their own particular ethnic agenda.

The political stand-off over the position of prime minister was resolved after a lengthy period of negotiations between the Shiʿi parties, involving the religious establishment and Ayatollah Sistani. On 22 April, the deputy leader of Daʿwa, Nouri al-Maliki, was appointed prime minister of Iraq. His cabinet, finally agreed on 8 June, is perhaps the most important in Iraq's modern history. By the spring of 2006, the future of Iraq was looking very precarious indeed. From being an almost impossibility under Saddam, the spectre of not one, but several, civil wars loomed large. Sectarian violence between Sunnis and Shiʿis had spread across Baghdad; Kirkuk experienced an upsurge in tension between Kurds and everybody else; and Basra and the south had become the scene of an intra-Shiʿi conflict over power, and Shiʿi militias were forcing out of the region the many thousands of Sunni families resident there. Worryingly, ethnic cleansing throughout Iraq's traditionally mixed cities was beginning to break out and gain momentum.

Whether a civil war was always inevitable in Iraq is a pertinent question to ask. The existence of Iraq as a state throughout the twentieth century would tend to suggest that it was not, but there is one important proviso to recognize: the prominence of authoritarian governments in Iraq's modern history indicates that non-democratic mechanisms of governance have been the norm and there remains scant evidence that Iraq can successfully chart the difficult waters of democratization. Maliki's government had perhaps the last opportunity to show that the trends of the authoritarian past could be consigned to history and Iraq could begin to take its first steps towards embracing and, most importantly, institutionalizing a democratic culture and system of government. But Maliki would ultimately fail to seize this opportunity. Instead, following a further US-led intervention to quell the civil war, the political and social fabric of Iraq would be rent apart in ways that were even more catastrophic than the events unfolding in 2007.

8 From the Brink to the Brink, 2007–2014

Many analyses of Iraq have been written since 2003 which comment upon a particular period – such as 2003 and the invasion, or 2005 and the passing of the Constitution – as being seminal, transformative times that would then facilitate the ongoing rehabilitation of the state and strengthening of the national project. Often, unfortunately, these seminal events have also been of a negative sort, such as the destruction of the Askariyya shrine, which instead heralded the rapid unravelling of Iraq rather than its consolidation. Viewed back from 2015, following the rise of the Islamic State, it would be tempting and reasonable to expect that the period leading to the fall of Mosul and the disintegration of Iraq would be punctuated with a litany of destabilizing and destructive events.

To be sure, there have been many. But what is fascinating, and tragic, about this period was that the road that led to the appalling situation apparent from 2014 was not one of successive unmitigated disasters. Indeed, there were many successes, in terms of events that brought Iraqis of different hues together, and especially peaceful elections, which suggested that Iraqi elites had managed to take advantage of the opportunities given to them by US-led actions against insurgents and at work in a consensual fashion. However, there were also many signals that all was not well in Iraq, and that one critical element – trust – was nowhere to be found.

The US was also complicit in allowing the politics of sectarianism and ethnicism to take hold even further, by supporting prime minister Maliki's continued premiership despite his loss of elections in 2010, which then saw him pursue policies of increased reactivity against Sunni Arab politicians and activists. Still, with the US maintaining a military presence in Iraq, the ability of Washington to influence events proved vital in keeping the political system operating. The US ensured that compromises would be reached between Maliki and his political opponents, that Arab Sunni movements would maintain their non-aggressive posture towards the government, and that the Kurdish leaders would ultimately compromise with the government of Iraq on sensitive issues, such as military operations in the disputed territories and the management of the Kurdistan Region's hydrocarbons sector.

But this managed consensus would be rapidly undermined following the end of the US military presence in December 2011 and the withdrawal of forces thereafter. Refusing to countenance a new Status of Forces Agreement (SOFA), Prime Minister Maliki had changed from being seen as a relative unknown, caretaker-style figure who replaced Ibrahim al-Jaʿafari in 2006, to rapidly becoming the new 'strong man' of Iraq – and he was in no mood to honour the many promises made by the Americans to Sunni Arabs about sharing power and reconfiguring the security services. Similarly, Maliki viewed the Kurds as being increasingly problematic, perhaps because he could do little about them in their northern stronghold apart from target their economy – a tactic that he employed with increasing effect. With the withdrawal of US forces in December 2011, it became clear that any notion of consociational politics – the politics of elite accommodation – continuing to survive in any meaningful way was wishful thinking. These political developments happened in a context of the Iraqi state continuing to be one of the most corrupt in the world, with public service provision across the country being poor and deteriorating – irrespective of the billions of dollars and trillions of dinars spent since 2003 – and with the Sunni Arabs in particular having to find their own ways of surviving in a system whereby the government of Iraq was dominated by the Shiʿi, while the Kurds existed in their own autonomous region in the north.

This first half of this chapter addresses a period that sits between the end of one civil war and the early stages of another. It is a period in which the possibility of a new, democratic Iraq was on the verge of being embraced, only for it to be squandered by Iraqi politicians and ignored by Western countries. There was a strong possibility that the 'Iraq project' – to build a unified, democratic, pluralist state – was still achievable, arguably until 2010, following the parliamentary elections, and possibly even later into 2011, as Iraqi elites struggled to find a working compromise between them. But this chapter, ultimately, presents a defeat snatched from the jaws of victory. Iraqi politicians and their Western supporters made successive mistakes that would lead not to a unified, democratizing country, but to a bitterly fragmenting entity that provided the theatre in which regional powers would pursue their own national interests. Before this unhappy situation emerged, however, the US succeeded in quashing the threat posed to Iraq by the Sunni insurgency, as President Bush gambled on saving his legacy in Iraq by sending thousands of US personnel back into the rapidly destabilizing situation. But his short-term solution would have disastrous longer-term consequences due to raising the aspirations and hopes of the Sunni Arabs, only to see them not only disappointed but exposed to the recriminations of an increasingly reactive and fearful Iraqi state dominated by the Shiʿi.

The Sunni 'Awakening', the US 'Surge' and the Targeting of Insurgents

The rapidity with which the sectarian conflict spread in Iraq following the destruction of the Askariyya shrine in Samarra was alarming for several reasons. Clearly, the daily death toll was devastating, evidenced by the appearance of bodies in Iraq's multi-communal towns, which had been transformed into sectarian-cleansing zones, or in the Tigris, which had become such a common dumping place that the inhabitants of Baghdad began to fear drinking its waters. By August 2006, civilian fatalities averaged more than 1,500 a month and the US military monthly losses stood at 100 dead and 700 wounded.[1] If the numbers of actual deaths were not grim enough, then the manner in which the murderous acts had been committed, on both sides, were designed to impart maximum psychological damage upon their foe. Beheadings were common, particularly by Sunni insurgents, while Shiʿi militias developed a penchant for executing their opponents with power drills. Any remnant of cross-sectarian societal cohesion that might have survived was further undermined due to the practice, by both sides, of leaving the remains of their victims for their families to find. But the descent into violence caused concern among the Coalition for a more prosaic reason. The government of Iraq was proving singularly unable either to counter the insurgent groups that were by now successfully challenging the hegemony of the state, or to broker any form of political compact between the different elites as represented in parliament, in government or in the informal yet far more powerful circle of political leaders that existed and operated above the level of the state. If Iraq was to survive the sectarian conflict, then the Coalition would need to break the insurgency and remove the very real and immediate threat to these formal and informal political and governmental systems. To do this, the US adopted a multi-pronged approach. They supported Sunni Arab tribes and militias that had already begun to mobilize to defend their locales against what was seen as the foreign threat of al-Qaeda Iraq, in a strategy that became known as the Sunni 'Awakening'. At the same time, Shiʿi militias, particularly the Jaish al-Mahdi of Muqtada al-Sadr, were targeted and put on notice that their actions, too, would be met with overwhelming force if they continued (see Krohley 2015: 4). The third prong of the approach was to ferociously target those insurgents who had refused to accept US support against AQI, or refused to heed warnings to stand down, with an extremely focused, comprehensive and unrelenting programme of targeted assassinations by Coalition special forces.

The decision taken by the Bush administration to increase troop numbers in Iraq was made in a nationwide television broadcast by the president on 10 January 2010. It had, however, been the subject of extensive discussion in US policy circles for some months before, with the Iraq Study Group report of December 2006 arguing strongly for a significant increase in US military personnel and a report published by the American Enterprise Institute (AEI) in January calling for US military forces to 'surge' and to secure and protect critical areas of Baghdad.[2] The plan would see a significant reorganization of the US military under the command of General David Petraeus, with five additional army brigades deployed to Iraq, adding a further 28,000 troops to the 150,000-strong army already present. With his mission being to defeat the insurgency and restore an environment over which the government of Iraq could once again take control, Petraeus would not only have to defeat the insurgency but also to tackle the main drivers of the conflict – in effect focus on the causes of Sunni aggression towards the new state, and of Shiʿi antipathy towards the Americans. As Toby Dodge notes, Bush's hope was that a new counter-insurgency doctrine would 'remove the perpetrators of violence from Iraq's streets, rebuild state capacity, rework the elite settlement shaping Iraq's politics, and find a way to reduce sectarian tensions'.[3] Clearly, these were astonishingly difficult tasks to achieve in isolation, let alone together. Yet Petraeus very nearly succeeded, only to see the fruits of his labours wasted in future years.

The strategy pursued by Petraeus developed following an assessment of US failings between 2003 and 2007, with an acknowledgement that new ways of securing towns and territory in Sunni areas in the north – especially in Tal Afar – were producing interesting results. In Tal Afar – a town in Nineveh, close to Mosul – Colonel H. R. McMaster and the 3rd Army Cavalry Regiment had pursued a strategy of sealing the town, followed by heavy patrolling, combat and the establishment of twenty-nine outposts across the town, operated jointly by US and Iraqi personnel, with the sole aim of keeping the insurgents out and neighbourhoods safe.[4] Inadvertently, Petraeus had stumbled upon a strategy of hybrid statemaking/compromised peacebuilding, combining a top-down approach with a bottom-up strategy of engaging local elites.[5] Bringing the theory of counter-insurgency together with the practice as evidenced by isolated successes in Iraq, Petraeus restructured US counter-insurgency doctrine to focus upon the rebuilding of the legitimacy of the state, with such legitimacy being garnered not by a show of military force but by the 'provision of basic economic needs', 'essential services' and the 'sustainment of key social and cultural institutions', with local elites and structures being used to deliver them.[6]

The first stage of the surge strategy, to secure neighbourhoods in Baghdad and establish Joint Security Stations, continued throughout the first half of 2007 and the death rate in Baghdad declined swiftly, although critics of the strategy noted how the segregation of communities, often behind blast-walls, only served to further the sectarian division of Baghdad.[7] The second stage of the strategy began in June, when the US military began more regular operations targeting insurgent bases on the outskirts of Baghdad, a process which again seemed to be successful, with many insurgents being killed and many more captured and imprisoned, including in Camp Bucca, where one Ibrahim Awwad al-Badri – who would emerge as the leader of ISIS – had already been in residence since his capture in Fallujah in February 2004.[8]

While Petraeus was successful in bringing stability back to Baghdad and its environs, there remained serious warning signs that the durability of what had been put into place was questionable. Having built a series of neighbourhood security areas, the rehabilitation of these areas – in terms of their economy and service provision – should have been financed and increasingly managed by the Iraqi government. But it was not. Rather, the US military found itself to be the provider of resources as well as being the underwriters of security. Without this core element of what Petraeus himself had identified as being an essential part of the plan – of having the government take over the responsibility of managing and supporting the new outfits while also taking forward the improvements in the provision of social service provision in largely Sunni Arab-populated neighbourhoods – then the successes of the US in 2007 and 2008 could only ever last for as long as the US military remained engaged.

This unwillingness of the Maliki government to engage with the structures and dynamics established by the US military was even more stark when it came to the second component of the plan to undermine ISI.[9] Even before US policymakers were discussing the possibility of increasing troop numbers, events had been unfolding in Anbar province without any intervention from either the Iraqi government or the US military. Previously the focal point of the nationalist insurgency against the US and the Iraqi government, the tribes of Anbar had found themselves caught in an uncomfortable relationship with the austere Salafists of ISI, and were beginning to rebel against the attempts by ISI to dominate their affairs. Furthermore, the tribal leaders began to view the insurgency against the Iraqi government and their US backers as being doomed to fail. When ISI announced an independent emirate in Iraq in October 2006, the largely nationalist-minded Anbar tribal leaders began to rebel against them. With US support, the Anbar Awakening Council was formed under Abdul Sittar al-Rishawi (Abu Risha), who became the figurehead of a rapidly expanding Iraqi tribal rebellion against what was seen as a foreign-dominated Islamist takeover. In effect, the US had stumbled upon a tactic of embracing locally designed solutions to resolve local problems. The US military would fund those best placed to stand against ISI and to provide security in their localities, and the new forces would agree to not attack the US military or institutions of the Iraqi state. Anbar and other Sunni-dominant governorates would be divided up into different *sahwat* areas, all with their own direct tie to the US military and not to the Iraqi state, and with them all being on the US payroll.

Far from embracing the successes of the Awakening Councils, or even the stability brought about by the 'surge' of US forces in Baghdad, the Maliki government viewed these developments with considerable fear and antipathy. Their concern had several overlapping facets. There was a deep-rooted fear of the Ba'th and the return of elements of Saddam's regime. There was also, of course, an even deeper angst concerning the expansion of Sunni *jihadists* and their visceral hatred of the adherents of Shi'ism. But, in effect, these fears merged into one. It would be difficult to exaggerate the level of concern that was felt among circles of Shi'i politicians in government of the possibility of the Ba'th, which was now becoming conflated with 'Sunnis', returning to power. Even among Kurds, the leaderships in Erbil and Suleimani saw the hands of the Ba'th at every political juncture and insurgent assault. And so while the US military had implemented a very successful counter-insurgency plan in Baghdad (which still had its flaws in terms of dividing up the city and solidifying sectarian divisions), and had seized upon the events in Anbar and built a new, loyal set of Sunni Arab tribal forces, the power holders in the post-2003 state were determined to suffocate these developments simply by ignoring the structures that had been created. From Maliki's perspective, the US military was asking the impossible. By December 2007, the US had placed some 75,000, mainly Sunni, fighters on their payroll, at the princely sum of $350 per fighter per month. Rather than succumb to US pressure, Maliki instead brought the entire scheme under his control and took possession from the US military of the biometric data of every recruited *sahwat* member – data that would be used to later round up and target leading Sunni Arab tribal figures and commanders. Awakening forces were not integrated into the police, military or security services, and were not empowered further by the Iraqi government to provide security for their tribal domains. Rather, leaders were arrested and imprisoned, and Maliki brutally and effectively disassembled the structures that had been used to defeat the burgeoning AQI/ISI presence in Iraq. For those who had thrown their lot in with the US and formed Awakening groups, the failure of the US to protect them from the government would be a salutary lesson: for the Sunni community as a whole, re-entering Iraqi political life as equals with the Shi'i was shown to be almost impossible.

Maliki's Survival and the Targeting of Shiʿi Opponents

Bringing the US military's most obvious success story – the Awakening forces – under his control, and subsequently unravelling what had been built, illustrated Maliki's emergence as a force to be reckoned with. It also exposed a significant weakness in the way the US now saw Iraq going forward – that the stability of the government was recognized not by what was happening across Iraq at large, but by which elites were occupying the senior offices of state. Inadvertently, maybe, the US administration had fallen into the established pattern of post-2003 Iraqi political life: of government by elite accommodation and extra-constitutional negotiation.

But how did Maliki achieve such a position of prominence? Principally, he enjoyed the legitimacy inherited by being the grandson of a notable tribal leader who had fought the British in the 1920s.[10] He also had been a long-standing member of the Daʿwa Party, with his family losing relatives at the hands of Saddam's security forces – something that had already coloured his view of Baʿthists and, by association, Sunnis.[11] Yet he was still a relatively unknown member of the Iraqi parliament when the US moved to replace incumbent Prime Minister Ibrahim al-Jaʿafari, in 2006, due to fears of his policies effectively sanctioning sectarian war with Sunnis and weakening the relationship with the Kurds. But it was exactly because he was comparatively low-key and perceived as relatively weak that he was deemed acceptable to the Shiʿi parties and politicians, the Kurds and those Sunnis still engaged with the state apparatus.[12]

During his first two years in office, Maliki was prime minister largely in name only, as real power rested with the US ambassador, Ryan Crocker, and the US military commander, David Petraeus. But this was to change in March 2008. Conditioned from his years of working covertly against Saddam's regime, Maliki seemed to possess a deeply suspicious view of his counterparts on the Iraqi political stage, and was always concerned about the possibility of a Sunni/Baʿthist revival. But his first outing as the new 'hard man' of Iraqi politics was not against Sunnis. It was instead against his Shiʿi counterpart, Muqtada al-Sadr.

As the head of the powerful and wealthy Sadr family network, following the assassination of his father, Ayatollah Mohammed Sadiq al-Sadr, by Saddam's security services in 1999, Muqtada had emerged as a powerful and at times dangerous force in Iraqi politics. With his own Iranian-backed militia, the Jaish al-Mahdi, Muqtada had led a Shiʿi rebellion against US forces to great effect, proving to be at least the equal of the threat posed by the AQI/Sunni nationalist rebellion attacking the US forces at the same time. For a time, Muqtada was perhaps a willing pawn in the hands of Maliki, who exploited the Jaish al-Mahdi's fighting prowess to counter the advance of Sunni insurgents in Baghdad – thus enveloping the capital and its environs in a sectarian struggle that was a critical element in forcing the US military to 'surge' its forces.[13] But the relationship between Sadr and Maliki was undermined by the prime minister's concern that the scion of one of the most important Shiʿi religious families, with a powerful militia and the support of Iran, would ultimately mount a challenge against him. With elements of his militia now targeting the ISF, Sadr found himself facing both the US military and their Iraqi allies.[14] Heeding the strong US threats to desist from attacking US forces during the surge in Baghdad – with Muqtada announcing a ceasefire in August 2007 – he subsequently went into a self-imposed exile in the Iranian seminary city of Qom, while his militia moved to the south of the country, to Basra, which had already become the stronghold of the Jaish al-Mahdi following the withdrawal of British forces from the city to the airport, leaving Basra in the nominal control of the ISF, but in reality in the grip of the militias of Muqtada.[15]

Maliki, now more secure following the surge of US forces and the quelling of the Sunni insurgency in Baghdad, turned his attention to Muqtada, in a move that took the US and Coalition forces by surprise but made perfect sense in terms of internal Shiʿi politics. The rise of Muqtada and the Sadrist movement, and their move to Basra, threatened the power base of other Shiʿi parties, especially the Islamic Supreme

Council of Iraq (ISCI) and its militia, the Badr Army. Throughout 2007, skirmishes between the two militias resulted in rising numbers of deaths, and the ongoing spread of the movement was of great concern to Maliki himself, not least because provincial elections were to be held in October 2008 – which would be the first opportunity for Maliki to begin building his popular power base. Throughout the second half of 2007, Maliki began to reinforce army units in the south, moving several brigades into Basra, including a special forces battalion, and establishing a Basra Operational Command under Lieutenant General Mohan al-Furayji. However, impressive though these moves looked, the Iraqi army under General Mohan still proved unable to challenge the rule of the Jaish al-Mahdi in Basra city itself, and the British forces were still very much isolated in their airport base.[16] Throughout the first quarter of 2008 the situation in Basra deteriorated, with Maliki taking an increasingly forceful view as to what should be done to remove the sources of instability. In a move which surprised everyone – including General Mohan, his British advisers and the US military leadership – Maliki assumed direct control of the situation, flying to Basra on 24 March to lead Operation Charge of the Knights. The operation was a messy affair with the ISF struggling to make headway against Sadr's militia, and with the US military being used to launch airstrikes against Sadrist targets. But it was the involvement of Iran that brought the conflict to a conclusion, and particularly the role played by General Qassem Suleimani of the IRGC – a figure who would become very significant in combating the threat posed by the Islamic State in subsequent years. Negotiating between Sadr on the one hand and the Iraqi government, ISCI, and the Badr Army on the other, Suleimani secured – or maybe more accurately ordered – a ceasefire in Basra. Jaish al-Mahdi militiamen melted away, while Maliki's forces re-established their control over the city and its environs. Maliki claimed victory over the Jaish al-Mahdi and used the operation as proof of his military acumen and his uncompromising approach to bringing security to Iraq's cities by quashing the rule of the militias – whether Sunni or Shiʿi. Yet, in reality, the situation was quite different. The events of 2007 and 2008 had bought time for the Iraqi government by suppressing the Sunni insurgency, breaking ISI and stymying the efforts of Sadr. But these were mere symptoms of far deeper pathological dynamics that ran through Iraq's political culture – dynamics of sectarianism, ethnicism and deep mistrust – with only the presence of the US military and, increasingly, the deft manipulation of the Iranian IRGC, keeping the facade of a unified country in place.

Losing the Election, Keeping Power: The Failure of Democracy in Iraq

The period following 2008 was, compared to the years between 2003 and 2007, relatively peaceful. The US military had successfully reduced the threat posed by Sunni militants and were now setting about in earnest to rebuild the ISF so that US forces could leave at the end of 2011, as agreed by President Bush with the Iraqi government in 2008. The Sadrists, too, seemed to be much less vocal following their removal from Basra, with Muqtada himself probably seeing considerable benefit in having his increasingly disobedient militia commanders removed from the scene. And the Kurds were beginning to enjoy something of a warmer relationship with the government of Iraq, including with Maliki himself, continuing to view him as a relatively weak figure who they could control and influence as needed. To be sure, there were still major issues of contention between Baghdad and Erbil – especially over the status of the disputed territories, including Kirkuk – but, by any measure, Baghdad–Erbil relations in 2008–9 were probably better than they had ever been since 2003.

But this enhanced stability was built upon a status quo of identity-based politics holding sway, and of Sunni Arabs being significantly under-represented in the government. Both of these factors would be challenged in the elections of 2010. First, the provincial elections of 2009, organized in such a way as to allow for the choosing of both parties and individuals in what was known as a 'modified list' system, had generated new debates among voters, focusing on government effectiveness, public service provision and economic development, rather than questions concerning religious or ethnic identities. The collapse in the vote for ISCI in these elections, as it campaigned on distinctly Shi'i sectarian lines, served as a warning to all parties about what to expect in the forthcoming parliamentary elections.[17] Second, the re-entry of the Sunni community into mainstream political life, largely facilitated by the engagement with and promises made by the US military during the establishment of the *sahwat* organizations, would also alter the balance of voting in the national elections. Recognizing the possibility of bringing together a significant Sunni-dominated vote alongside a possible constituency of Shi'is and Kurds who had grown tired of voting for 'traditional' Shi'i and Kurdish parties, was Iyad Allawi. A Shi'i by birth and a dissident Ba'thist in opposition, Allawi presented a secular face to Iraqi voters. By building an alliance with prominent Sunni politicians – including Tariq al-Hashimi, Saleh al-Mutlaq and Rafi al-Issawi – under the banner of the Iraqi National Movement, or Iraqiyya, Allawi was well placed to take advantage of the changing outlook of Iraq's voters.

Maliki, too, was busily positioning himself for the 2010 election. Keen to portray himself as an 'Iraqi' rather than 'Shi'i' leader, Maliki brought together the State of Law coalition (*Dawlat al-Qanun*) and presented himself as a leader who was able to provide security for Iraqis and to control militias and armed groups. He also presented himself as working in the interests of a unified Iraq, with a centralized government, while his opponents, including ISCI and their Kurdish allies, were criticized for wanting Iraq to be federalized into regions. Illustrating how far he had come from being an institutionally weak prime minister, who the US believed they could control, to being the most important politician in Iraq, Maliki adopted a tough stance in negotiations with the US over the Status of Forces Agreement (SOFA) that would allow a smaller US troop presence to remain after 2011. Having performed strongly in the provincial elections of

2009, and having continued to bring under his direct control key government offices and the security apparatus, Maliki had good reason to feel confident in his ability to hold on to power in the elections of 2010.

However, it was his inherent suspicion of other Shiʿi parties that led to his undoing. Refusing to join the Shiʿi coalition of the Iraqi National Alliance, headed by his prime ministerial predecessor Ibrahim al-Jaʿafari, who headed parts of the Daʿwa Party, and which also included ISCI, led by Abdul Aziz al-Hakim, Maliki had in effect split the Shiʿi vote. In so doing, he facilitated a narrow victory for Allawi's Iraqiyya. With ninety-one seats to Maliki's eighty-nine, and with Jaʿafari's coalition holding a further seventy seats and the Kurds holding a significant forty-three, and with 163 seats needed to form a government, the scene was neatly set for Allawi to return as prime minister in what was turning into an unforeseen victory for a party that was seen as the representative of the Sunnis.[18] Yet Maliki was unmoving. He made allegations of electoral fraud and ordered a recount – the result of which upheld the results. With parliament reconvened on 14 June 2010, it would not be until 11 November that a new government would form, following the reaching of an agreement in Erbil, mediated by the Kurdistan Region's President Massoud Barzani. The Erbil Agreement contained nine parts and forty-eight paragraphs, and promised far-reaching changes across significant government portfolios, including the divesting of control of the military, security and intelligence apparatus away from Maliki – who would remain as prime minister – to Allawi, who would become the head of a new security council.[19] But the agreement was too extensive in scope, too vague in detail and therefore easy to ignore. Once in post, Maliki did not implement a single part of the Erbil Agreement, and no one could force him to do so. Instead, he appointed close advisers to the sensitive security positions that had been promised to Allawi, while keeping the Ministry of Interior and control of the military very much under him. The centrepiece of the Erbil Agreement, the National Council for Security Policy, which was to be headed by Allawi, was never formed.[20]

Iraq had held a democratic election in which all communities voted, which in itself was an admirable achievement coming so soon after the major upheavals of 2007–8. Furthermore, the result was deemed valid by all participants except the incumbent prime minister, and validated by Iraq's Independent High Electoral Commission (IHEC), which operated with the support of the UN. Yet the results were sidelined by the defeated Maliki, who had managed to accrue significant powers in the period running up to the election and who used them to maintain his premiership. Why, then, did outside powers, and especially the US, not intervene in the interests of preserving the democracy that they had invested so heavily in? And why did other Iraqi leaders not challenge Maliki more forcibly? With regard to the US, the answer was simply one of lack of interest, as the focus of the new Obama administration had moved away from Iraq. Having promised on the campaign trail to 'end the war' in Iraq and to withdraw all combat forces by the end of 2011, the US government had little interest in pressing for Maliki to stand down if the result might be civil war, as Maliki's threats seemed to suggest. In a similar vein, the US viewed as unwelcome attempts by the Kurds to tie Iraqi government formation to the resolution of their own long-standing, and deeply destabilizing, grievances concerning the ownership of the disputed territories. And so the US government remained impassive as Iraq's engagement with democracy unravelled.

The Iranian government, too, had little interest in encouraging Iraqi politicians to respect the results of the elections. Not only was Iraqiyya seen as a haven for Sunni voters; it was also seen as a new manifestation of the Baʿth. Furthermore, Allawi was not their creation and was not a man who Iran, even through the IRGC, could influence. Throughout his period heading a leading opposition movement to Saddam, the Iraqi National Accord (*Al-Wifaq al-Watani al-Iraq*), Allawi had been closer to Western governments and intelligence agencies. This, combined with his secularism and non-sectarian appeal, meant that the Iranian kingmakers would follow their US counterparts and simply let Maliki bully his way back to the premiership. As for the lack of opposition from other Iraqi leaders, they had probably calculated that it was in their interests to allow business as usual, in the form of constructing governments according to communal interests and through a process of elite negotiation. Other Shiʿi leaders, such as the newly appointed Ammar al-Hakim who succeeded his father Abdul Aziz after his death in August 2009, needed time to re-establish their position, while Sunni leaders, such as Atheel and Osama al-Nujaifi of the Hadhba Party dominant in Nineveh, saw an opportunity to return to carving out their own power base in the Sunni Arab provinces by using Maliki's continued tenure to mobilize a Sunni vote around them – a strategy that succeeded but would ultimately benefit ISIS. The Kurds, as ever, viewed events from a Kurdistan-centric position, seeing the demise of democracy in Iraq and the rise of Maliki as ultimately serving their ambitions to hive further powers from Baghdad to Erbil while continuing to present themselves as the only democratic success story to any Western power that would listen.

The US Departure and Maliki's Consolidation

The Status of Forces Agreement (SOFA) between the Iraqi and US governments, which had been in place since December 2008 and which allowed for the basing of US combat troops in Iraq, expired on 31 December 2011. With no follow-on agreement in place that would allow for a US combat presence to remain, US forces had begun to withdraw from Iraq by 16 December. While often seen as evidence of the US losing influence in Iraq, in effect neither the US administration nor the Iraqi government was particularly keen to see the arrangement continue. President Obama did not seem fully engaged with the process, with Iraqi officials sensing considerable apathy coming from the White House.[21] Maliki, too, was distinctly lukewarm to the idea of signing a further SOFA due to the very significant opposition that existed to the idea in all parts of Iraq, excluding the Kurdistan Region where the Kurds would have accepted as large a US military presence as they could possibly accommodate, such was the positive view of the US in the Kurdistan Region. But as a populist prime minister, Maliki was merely responding to Iraqi popular sentiment, which was very much opposed to seeing the US occupation continue. For Maliki, supporting a new SOFA that would extend the stay of US forces would be to commit political suicide. And so Iraq entered a new phase, a post-American period, in which the overwhelming coercive force of the US military evaporated and in which the ISF could no longer call upon US assistance when fighting determined opponents. Those Iraqis that had been increasingly forgotten about – defeated *jihadists*, subordinated tribes and the remnants of Saddam's military and security apparatus – began to see opportunities on the horizon.

The withdrawal of US forces also satisfied the popular opinion of a US public that had been emotionally drained by the trauma of the Iraq experience. But it did little to further the rehabilitation of the Iraqi state following the perverting of the 2010 election result. The absenting of the one power that could act as an arbiter among Iraqi stakeholders, even if not necessarily unbiased, and even if pursuing policies that some stakeholders found unacceptable, made cooperation not only less likely, but also made the situation more polarized and dangerous. The political scientist Barbara F. Walter notes, '[o]nly when an outside enforcer steps in to guarantee the terms do commitments to disarm and share political power become believable. Only then does cooperation become possible.'[22] In the case of Iraq, following the withdrawal of the US military, Walter's thesis would be proven in reverse: when the outside enforcer steps out, then commitments to disarm and to share political power become unbelievable, and cooperation becomes impossible. Still, even seasoned Iraqi observers armed with such theoretical insights were shocked by the speed with which the political fabric of Iraq unravelled – an unravelling that was triggered by elites in Sunni-dominant provinces attempting to apply the constitutionally mandated principles of federal region formation that would, if successful, see power shift from the government of Iraq to provincial regional governments. It was not a shift that Maliki was prepared to see happen.

Whenever federalism is mentioned in Iraq, it is generally the case that the Kurds are involved. Following the 2010 election, if not before, the Kurdish leadership around Barzani was beginning to sense an opportunity to further their own cause – of enhancing their own stability and security – by encouraging neighbouring Sunni Arab provinces to embrace the federal components of the Constitution. This was a clever move as the Constitution gave the legal right to provinces, or groups of provinces, to form a Region, which would then enjoy the same levels of autonomy as the Kurds had, and thus would weaken the authority of the central government of Iraq.[23] Building upon their already strong links with Iraqiyya leader Allawi, the Kurdish leadership around Barzani reached out to Sunni Arab leaders who had, only months before, been their implacable enemies. The leader of the powerful Hadbha Party, the governor of Nineveh, Atheel al-Nujaifi, along with his brother, the Speaker of Parliament Osama, put their enmity towards Barzani aside and instead started working in close alliance with the Kurds. Reaching out to elites across Sunni-dominated Iraq, the idea was received positively in Salahadin, Anbar and Diyala provinces, and even the Shiʿi-populated oil-rich provinces of Basra and Wasit saw the benefits of being a Region and managing their own affairs.

The situation came to a head on 27 October 2011. Witnessing a rise in government arrests of Sunni opponents in the provinces north of Baghdad, the provincial council of Salahadin acted in accordance with the Constitution and voted to hold a referendum on the question of forming a Region.[24] Diyala did the same in December, with Anbar looking as though it would follow suit. Facing what was not only a challenge to his power, but a legal, constitutionally mandated threat, Maliki reacted forcefully, though still mindful of the US presence that remained in place. He increased the activities of his loyal security services in these provinces, using the *sahwat* data obtained from the US to target the most prominent figures for arrest, and stymied any possibility of referenda being held. Not content with stopping the Sunni federal initiative, he then raised the spectre of it being a

Baʿthist plot to justify the unleashing of even greater and less discriminating repression against Sunni elites and their supporters – leaving them with no option but to acquiesce or to rebel.

Worse was to come. Still scarred by the show of Sunni popular opinion in the 2010 election, and fearful of any reorganization of a Sunni/Baʿthist movement, Maliki pulled as hard as he could at the most sensitive threads that had kept the Sunni Arab community in the shaky compact that had held while the US had been an in-country power. In what can only be described as an utterly brazen move, Maliki in effect rewrote the rules of how 'post-American' Iraqi politics would be conducted, and directly targeted political elites. On the evening of the leaving ceremony marking the departure of US forces from Iraq, on 15 December, troops commanded by Maliki's son, Ahmed, surrounded the homes of the vice-president of Iraq, Tariq al-Hashimi, the minister of finance, Rafi al-Issawi, and the deputy prime minister, Saleh al-Mutlaq. Accused of organizing terrorist acts, Hashemi was placed under house arrest, although was subsequently allowed to leave for the sanctuary of Erbil.[25] It was fortuitous for him that he did. Following public confessions by Hashemi's bodyguards that were almost certainly gained through torture and who died while in prison, of his involvement in organizing a death squad in Fallujah, Maliki ordered the arrest of Hashemi on terrorism charges – charges that carried the death penalty. Fleeing to Turkey, Hashemi was subsequently tried and sentenced to death *in absentia*.

With Hashemi removed from the scene and the politicians of Iraqiyya cowed by Maliki's show of force, two new realities began to emerge that would set the scene for the further undermining of Iraq's coherence. The first was the heightened marginalization of the Sunni community from the state. In a misguided move, Iraqiyya's reaction to the targeting of its leaders was to boycott parliament and withdraw its ministers from cabinet meetings until February 2012. But this strategy played into Maliki's hands. He simply used their disengagement as an opportunity to further consolidate power around him while also managing to persuade parts of Iraqiyya into joining his own coalition. With little chance of parliament being able to mobilize a vote of no confidence against him, Maliki continued to consolidate power and to make key state institutions of interior affairs, defence and intelligence his own personal preserve, using their resources to further project his power against his opponents. These developments, however, did not end opposition in the Sunni-dominant provinces; they rather facilitated a rebellious environment that would provide fertile ground for more radical, violent actors to emerge.

The second new reality – which had in fact been in existence for some time – was that of Kurdish strength, and the ability of the Kurdistan Region's leadership to challenge the authority of Maliki not only militarily in the north, but politically in Baghdad. The two Kurdish leaders – Talabani of the PUK and Barzani of the KDP – operated in a 'good cop, bad cop' fashion towards Maliki and the government of Iraq. Talabani, as the president of Iraq and arguably the elder statesman of Iraq's political elite from across all parties, found it relatively easier to deal with Maliki, not least because he and his team felt more at ease dealing with their Arab counterparts than did Barzani and his associates. Barzani, on the other hand, had always felt uncomfortable even visiting Baghdad and much preferred to remain as the president of the Kurdistan Region – indeed, from his perspective, there was far more honour to be had in being president of Kurdistan than the president of Iraq. And, as such, he would often take a far harder line against the government of Iraq and Maliki. With Kurdistan safe from military attack (a belief that was largely shared by Kurds and Iraqis alike, and also by the international community – and which was exposed as being deeply flawed following the near defeat of Kurdish forces by IS fighters in August 2014), and with their ability to manipulate the politics of Baghdad, the Kurds became the effective leaders of the opposition to Maliki with the demise of Iraqiyya. Their opposition to Maliki, and his reaction to the Kurds, would see the Kurdish trajectory in Iraq move from one embracing federalism, to one that would be focused upon the heightened possibility of secession and independence.

Kurdistan Rising

Two matters exercised Kurdish leaders in their dealings with post-2003 governments in Iraq, and both could be traced to the interpretation and application of parts of the Constitution of relevance to the Kurdistan Region. The first was the status of the disputed territories, particularly with reference to the future of Kirkuk. The second concerned agreeing upon the competences of the KRG, including the right to maintain the *peshmerga* as the military force of the Kurds and the right to develop a hydrocarbons sector capable of exporting oil and gas independently of Iraq, which would give the Kurds an independent revenue stream and therefore economic sovereignty. On both matters, the Kurds would find themselves confronted by Maliki and his allies. In the case of implementing Article 140, Maliki could afford to be passive in his opposition – in effect, not engaging with the Kurds through the Article 140 mechanism would simply mean that nothing would get done. But in the case of containing Kurdish attempts to accrue sovereign powers to their KRG from Baghdad, Maliki could apply economic pressure on the Kurdish leadership by limiting their revenue provided from Baghdad. The problem was, however, that the Kurdish leadership interpreted such a tactic as reinforcing the necessity of securing an independent revenue stream, and thus a vicious circle was established, with Baghdad's attempts to control the Kurds increasing the determination of the Kurds to enhance their autonomy and independence.

Famously, the Kurds had insisted on the incorporation of a specific Article in the constitutional negotiations that would prescribe a method for the resolution of the question of the disputed territories. Article 140 rearticulated the process outlined in Article 58 of the earlier Transitional Administrative Law (TAL) of 2004, which put forward a three-part method of 'normalization' (returning deported populations back to their places of origin), then the holding of a census, followed by a referendum, that would take place following the ratification of a permanent constitution, but with one key difference.[26] At the insistence of the Kurds a time limit of no later than the end of 2007 was imposed on the implementation of the Article, as they did not wish to see negotiations strung out over many years. But those opposed to the Kurds' plans knew they only had to delay matters until the end of 2007 – which was very easy for them to do – in order to obscure the process by pushing it beyond its implementation period.[27] Needing a partner with whom to negotiate, the KRG found no one to engage with in Baghdad. As December 2007 passed, the tension between Erbil and Baghdad grew, leading to the involvement of the UN envoy Staffan de Mistura who negotiated a six-month extension. But this, too, came to nothing. From the perspective of Erbil, Article 140 remained active. From the perspective of Baghdad, it had become void as its implementation had run out of time. For the Kurdish leadership, the situation was not only intolerable; it was deeply embarrassing and destabilizing for them inside the Kurdistan Region. Having accepted the passing of the Constitution of Iraq in 2005, and having encouraged Kurdish voters to vote overwhelmingly in favour of staying in a federal Iraq on the basis of the inclusion of Article 140, the failure to achieve anything in the following years called into question the judgement of the leadership. It also raised serious questions about whether the Kurds should continue to work towards being a component of federal Iraq, or to find a way to secede from Iraq altogether. This position would be further strengthened as Maliki brought more economic pressure to bear on the Kurdistan Region in a bid to scupper the plans of the Barzani leadership.

A key plan of the Kurdish leadership since 2005 had been the building of an independent oil and gas sector, and they contended that the federal components of the Constitution gave them the right to do this by developing 'new' fields in their territory. Following the appointment of Ashti Hawrami – a figure with many years of experience in the oil sector – as minister of natural resources, the KRG made available fifty-four exploration blocks in the Kurdistan Region to international oil companies (IOCs). The intention of Hawrami and his prime minister, Nechirvan Barzani, was clear – that in the first stage of the building of the KRG's oil sector, he would attract to the region smaller companies that were more risk averse than larger international oil companies (IOCs). As oil was discovered and the attraction of the Kurdistan Region moved from being speculated to proven, then other, larger IOCs would be tempted to sign contracts with the KRG. Ultimately, the plan would see the KRG present a fait accompli to the government of Iraq which would, by then, be incapable of limiting the Kurds' aspirations, whether they chose to remain in federal Iraq on their own terms or to declare their independence.

By the end of 2008, Hawrami's strategy seemed to be bearing fruit, with twenty IOCs operating in the Kurdistan Region, increasing to thirty-eight by the beginning of 2010. Kurdistan was seen by IOCs and their funders as a favourable place to invest, but there remained one very significant problem: the government of Iraq viewed the KRG's actions as being unconstitutional, and refused to acknowledge the legality of the contracts signed with IOCs. At the end of 2007, Iraqi oil minister Hussein Al-Shahristani had decreed that IOCs signing agreements with the KRG would be 'blacklisted' by the government of Iraq, making it impossible for those IOCs to work in the rest of Iraq and also exposing them to possible legal action. Undeterred, the KRG continued with its policy, exporting crude oil to Ceyhan in Turkey and providing oil products for domestic consumption in the Kurdistan Region. The tension between Erbil and Baghdad, already apparent due to the ongoing dispute over Kirkuk and other territories, was heightened. Barzani and Maliki began to sabre-rattle, with their media making pointed attacks on each other and their military forces undertaking aggressive manoeuvres in the relatively confined space of the disputed territories.

The result was predictable, with a serious military confrontation occurring in the town of Khanaqin in Diyala governorate. Outside the Kurdistan Region, but with a large Kurdish population largely loyal to the PUK, Khanaqin was a prime target for Maliki to focus upon because of the significant numbers of Shiʿis and Turkmens that also resided in the area.

The Kurds responded by deploying more *peshmerga*, and it would take the involvement of the US military to broker a peaceful outcome.[28] By now, at the end of 2008, with the gaze of Iraq's politicians turning towards the elections of 2010, the antagonism between Maliki and Barzani was escalating. To make matters worse, the dispute was only partially about oil. It also concerned federal and regional powers, and involved the resolution of the status of the disputed territories.[29] And it was deeply personal. By 2010, the enmity between Barzani and Maliki was palpable, with each lambasting the other in their pliant media outlets, and each using increasingly bellicose rhetoric.[30] This was mirrored by their ministers in charge of oil and gas – Hawrami for the KRG and Sharistani for the government of Iraq. Neither was minded to back down, and their mutual animosity would make it impossible for Erbil and Baghdad to find common agreement on a much-needed Hydrocarbons Law that would then lead to the normalization of the Kurdistan Region's oil and gas production and export.

Even so, the terms offered by the KRG made investing in their oil and gas sector an attractive proposition, not only for small companies hoping to find significant reserves that they could then sell on, but increasingly for larger companies that had the resources to invest in a project that might take years, or decades, to overcome the political problems and come to fruition. The world's biggest oil company, ExxonMobil, announced its entry into the KRI in November 2011, taking several prime blocks in the north-west of the region, with Chevron following in July 2012.[31] The response of Maliki and Shahristani to these and other developments was to put in place an economic embargo against the KRI, with transfers of funds stopping in May 2011. Military pressure was brought to bear as well, with the *peshmerga* and ISF taking up positions against each other in the north of Nineveh province at Zummar, and with Maliki creating a new ISF Dijla (Tigris) Operational Command, based to the west of Kirkuk and in clear striking distance of the major cities of the KRI.[32] Since then, although Erbil and Baghdad found temporary agreements that involved Erbil exporting certain amounts of oil and payments being made by Baghdad, the situation has been one of Baghdad's regular uses of fiscal pressure against Erbil. The response of Erbil has been to further expand its oil and gas sector and to push for independent exports to cover the costs of their region. By the spring of 2014, neither side looked likely to back down and the engagement between Erbil and Baghdad had become more tense than at any time since 2003.[33]

The Targeting of the Sunnis

By the beginning of 2014, the political fabric of Iraq was in a terrible condition. Prime Minister Maliki had continued to consolidate his hold over the key institutions of the state, and attempts by his opponents – including the Kurds in alliance with Sunnis and Shiʿis opposed to him – had proved ineffective. Most notable among the failures to limit the powers of the prime minister was an attempt led by Kurdish leaders Barzani and Talabani. On 28 April 2012, Barzani hosted a political summit in Erbil, bringing together Jalal Talabani, Iyad Allawi, Muqtada al-Sadr and Osama al-Nujaifi. Together, they issued an ultimatum to Maliki, demanding reforms to be implemented within fifteen days or face a vote of no confidence in parliament. Ultimately, however, and almost certainly due to Iranian intervention, Sadr withdrew his support, thus ending the possibility of gaining a parliamentary majority and exposing Maliki's opponents as being weak and divided.

With his standing in parliament secured, Maliki continued to centralize power around him and his cohorts – known collectively as the *Malikiyoun* – bringing the military under his direct control by directly appointing loyalists to key positions, whether they had military experience or not. This would prove useful for the quelling of demonstrations that would come about at the end of the year, but would prove disastrous when the ISF had to fight a far more determined and well-organized foe in the form of ISIS fighters in 2014.

But few foresaw the scale of the problem that was beginning to emerge, nor that the continued oppression of Sunnis would promulgate a serious backlash. This oppression would increase to a new level at the end of 2012, when Maliki took advantage of the confusion caused by the sudden leaving of the political scene by President Talabani in mid-December. By 2012, Talabani was seventy-nine years old and holder of one of the most stressful of jobs. But his energy had remained undiminished and he had continued to act as one of the few figures in Iraqi political life who could genuinely reach out across the ethnic and sectarian divides and find compromises – even with figures such as Maliki – when situations seemed dire. But his life's work had taken a heavy toll on him and, on 18 December, after what was reported as an extremely confrontational meeting with Maliki earlier in the day, he succumbed to a major stroke.[34] Although he survived, he would no longer be able to play such a critical role in the politics of either Iraq or Kurdistan, and Baghdad lost perhaps the only figure who had sufficient leverage over the principal actors to push them into compromise rather than conflict.

For Maliki, the time spent on worrying about his presidential partner was limited. Within hours of Talabani's medical evacuation to Germany, Maliki once again found an opportunity to reignite the sectarian flames with his Sunni opponents. This time, the respected and admired Rafi al-Issawi was targeted, with his bodyguards arrested on charges of terrorism. The targeting of Issawi was seen as even more unacceptable among the Sunni Arab community than had been the targeting of Hashemi the year before, with the arrests prompting large demonstrations across Anbar and a concomitant rise in insurgency attacks against the Iraq government's civilian and military personnel. Sensing a change in the posture of the Sunni Arab community to the status quo of Iraq, ISI units once again became operational, with ISI announcing a new offensive in July that saw coordinated bombing attacks take place against Shiʿis throughout the rest of the year. The protests spread quickly to Salahadin, Diyala and Nineveh provinces in the north, and they also took place in Baghdad itself. Indicative of the mood of the demonstrators was the treatment of Sunni Arab political grandee Saleh al-Mutlaq. Sitting as deputy prime minister from the Iraqiyya block, and recognized as a vociferous opponent of Maliki, Mutlaq would have usually expected a warm welcome from a largely Sunni Arab gathering. Yet their mood had changed and his attempts to address protestors in Ramadi, on 30 December, were met by a barrage of bottles and stones. Clearly, parts of the Sunni Arab community present at the demonstration viewed Mutlaq, and what he stood for, as failing to uphold their demands – or even to be cooperating with Maliki himself.[35] With Sunni Arab political elites in Baghdad being disconnected from their constituents who were now expressing their frustrations via increasingly militant protest, a political space was opening for the return of an increasingly violent, sectarian-focused group to take a more physical fight to Maliki and what was now very much seen as a Shiʿi, *safavi* government.[36]

The situation deteriorated further into 2013, with demonstrations taking place across the country and with the ISF response becoming more violent. The response of the state security forces matched this violence, with prominent figures from the *sahwat* organizations and those associated with organizing demonstrations being assassinated by assailants who were unknown but commonly presumed to be agents of Maliki. In the town of Hawijah – a famously militant Sunni Arab town to the west of Kirkuk – the pressure that had been building between the demonstrators and the government exploded with devastating consequences. Following the killing of an ISF officer on 19 April, the ISF launched an assault against insurgents of the Jaish al-Rijal al-Tarika al-Naqshabandiyya – otherwise known as the Naqshabandiyya Army (JRTN) – led by Saddam's deputy, Izzet Ibrahim al-Douri. But the assault also targeted the Sunni demonstrators' camp in Hawijah. By the end of 23 April, some sixty protestors had been killed, with footage leaked from the scene revealing the harsh treated meted out to the demonstrators by ISF personnel.[37] Revenge attacks took place throughout the north, with the ISF responding in an ever more brutal fashion.

By the end of the year, the situation between Sunnis and Shiʿis had become dangerously polarized, and the relationship between Shiʿi and Sunni politicians had been poisoned by distrust, with accusations of Sunni militants being either Baʿthists or al-Qaeda *jihadists* being regular aspects of the narrative of an increasingly paranoid and reactive Prime Minister Maliki. Sunni leaders inside the provinces rebuked these claims and openly referred to the sectarian nature of the Iraqi government and its security forces. Neither Maliki nor his opponents realized that the reality was far worse. What Maliki had failed to appreciate was that there were Baʿthists, al-Qaeda *jihadist* remnants and secular Iraqi nationalists re-emerging among the Sunni community, but they were not isolated from each other. In reality, the boundaries between these groups had already become blurred, and had been doing so even towards the end of the 1990s, leading to the emergence of a new initiative that brought together these strands of Sunni militancy. This new network – by now operating under the banner of the Islamic State of Iraq and al-Sham (ISIS), under the leadership of Abu Bakr al-Baghdadi – would now find fertile ground in Iraq's Sunni-dominant provinces in which to nurture their already significant societal roots and to challenge the government and their military forces not only in Iraq, but ultimately across Syria, the Levant and North Africa. But the Sunni leaders, including Abu Bakr, had also perhaps failed to appreciate the sheer scale of the Shiʿi dominance of Iraq, and its underwriting by Iran. With no options apart from capitulation left for the Sunnis, or for a Maliki government that remained fearful of any meaningful return of Sunni influence, the scene was set for Iraq to enter a new and even more violent period in its post-2003 journey. It was this period that would see the fallacy of a unified Iraqi nationalist project exposed and the very territorial integrity of the state effectively broken.

By 2014, several key questions had been brought to the surface of the boiling political mess of Iraq. Key among these was the Kurds' demand to be able to export oil independently of Baghdad, and thus become economically self-sufficient in their autonomous region. They also demanded the resolution of the status of the disputed territories, and especially of Kirkuk. By the beginning of 2014, the failure of Erbil and Baghdad to find an agreement on the oil question, and the failure of Baghdad to engage with Erbil on the territorial question, had seen the rhetoric of the Kurdistan Region's President Barzani and Iraqi Prime Minister Maliki becoming dangerously threatening and war-like. Yet it was the situation south of the Kurdistan Region, in Sunni Arab-dominated provinces, where the beginnings of Iraq's disintegration could be most clearly witnessed. As Maliki sought to break the ability of the Sunnis to threaten his regime by taking increasingly oppressive actions against elites and those Sunnis who publicly stood against him, of whom there were many, the scene was set for the rise of a new, anti-government, anti-Shiʿi movement that would seek to redress these abuses. Few could foresee, however, the brutally exclusionist and transformational nature of the new rising force of ISIS.

9 The Islamic State, the Kurdistan Region and Shiʿi Iraq

The rise of ISIS and the pronouncement of the Islamic State in 2014 has become the focal point of interest in Iraq, such has been the scale of the activities, atrocities and instability generated by Abu Bakr and his followers. But the unravelling of Iraq was also apparent in two other regions: in Kurdistan and the Shiʿi-dominated area. With ISIS undeniably serving as a catalyst in this process, both Kurdistan and the Shiʿi area further internalized their already overwhelmingly strong communal identities, resulting in Iraq being divided into three de facto states – the Kurdistan Region, the Islamic State and, for want of a better name, the Baghdad-Basra region controlled by the government of Iraq. Map 3 illustrates the immense extent of ISIS in 2015, and the division of Iraq into three entities. This chapter focuses upon a relatively short period in Iraq's recent history, addressing primarily the period from the end of 2013 with ISIS's taking of Mosul and subsequent domination of most of Sunni Arab-populated Iraq. To do so, however, the story of ISIS is contextualized by placing it within a broader story of Sunni disenchantment, suppression and oppression at the hands of the new Shiʿi masters of the state, and fear that had been growing since the fall of Saddam. Only then does the full scale of the ISIS phenomena – of it being a movement with social roots rather than merely a radical organization imposing itself on a subjugated and vulnerable people – become apparent.

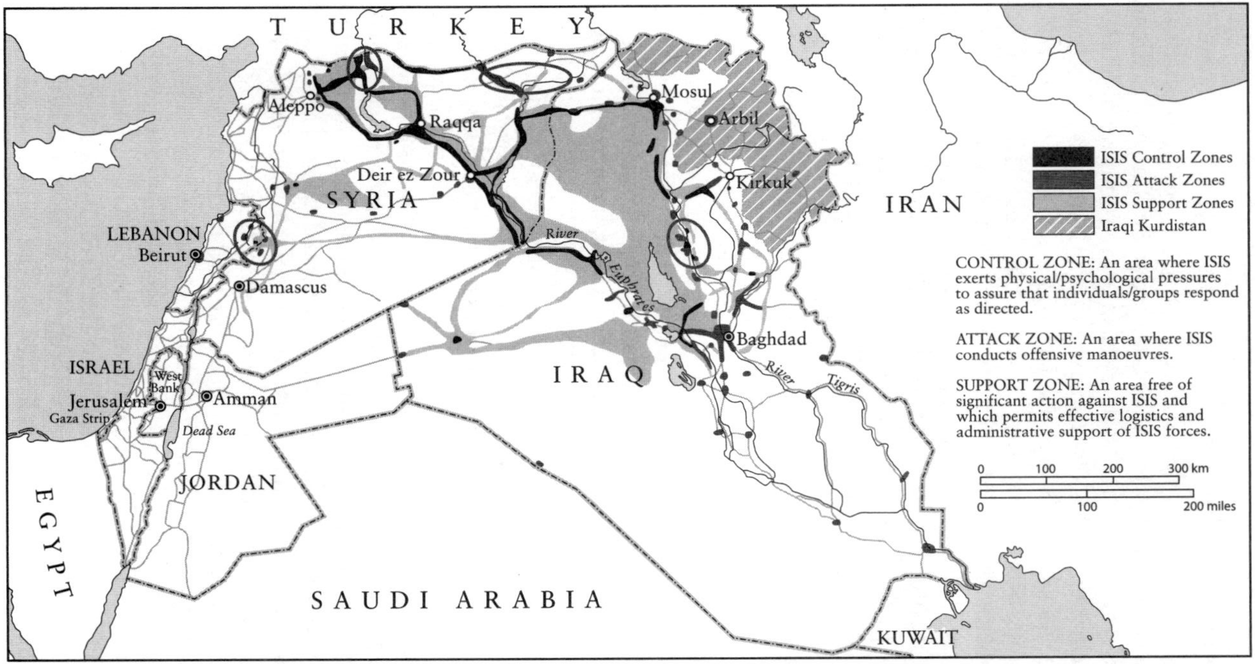

Map 3 The extent of ISIS, 2015; adapted from The Institute for the Study of War, ISIS Sanctuary: March 2015

The Origins of ISIS

The precursor to the Islamic State (IS – or, in Arabic, al-Dawla al-Islamiyya) was the Islamic State of Iraq and al-Sham (ISIS – in Arabic, al-Dawla al-Islamiyya al-Iraq wa al-Sham), which itself was a development of the Islamic State of Iraq (ISI). As such, ISIS was the latest in a line of Sunni *jihadist* organizations to operate in Iraq, but was also a complex amalgam of a range of different Sunni insurgent groups brought together over a period of years.[1] Broadly, ISIS was a coming together of a range of different political and insurgent trends from within the Sunni community of Iraq. These entities spanned a wide gamut of ideologies and motivations, from the *jihadist* to the nationalist, and from the disaffected tribal fighters through to the city-based neighbourhood guards nurtured by the US during the 'surge' campaign. They were similar in one respect, though, and that was in their opposition to the government of Iraq and to the increasing dominance of the Shi'i community. They had also become disenchanted with politicians purporting to represent them in Baghdad – from Iraqiyya, namely – seeing them as being loyal to their political class rather than seeking a redressing of the Sunnis' position. Fertile ground existed among the Sunni Arab community, particularly from 2010, from which organized opposition to the government of Iraq could grow. What was needed, however, was a leader who could find a way to bring these disparate trends together and build an insurgency against seemingly overwhelming forces, succeeding where previous attempts had failed. The odds of this happening were remote, but this is exactly what did come to pass and from a situation that, from the perspective of a Sunni Arab insurgent, would seem to be astonishingly weak.

IS should be viewed as the latest, and by far most successful, of a line of Sunni Arab-dominated *jihadist* insurgent movements that began to form in the Middle East under the guidance of the al-Qaeda organization of Osama bin Laden from the late 1990s. In terms of the direct lineage that led to ISIS, it is to the activities of Jordanian militant Fadl al-Nazal al-Khalayleh – otherwise known as Abu Musab al-Zarqawi

– that we must turn. Unlike the future leader of ISIS, Abu Bakr al-Baghdadi, Zarqawi was a figure who had no real standing, either as a leader of Islamists or as a military thinker, coming from a life of obscure petty criminality to heading what was at the time the most dangerous insurgent group in Iraq. Having secured a small amount of funding from al-Qaeda, Zarqawi created Jama'at al-Tawhid wa al-Jihad (Organization of Monotheism and Jihad, commonly referred to as 'Tawhid').[2] Tawhid relocated to Afghanistan to fight alongside al-Qaeda and Taliban forces, following the September 11 attacks of 2001 on the US. From there, Zarqawi moved Tawhid again, through Iran, to the mountainous border area of the Kurdistan Region of Iraq controlled by a Kurdish *jihadist* group with ties to al-Qaeda – Ansar al-Islam.[3] With the invasion of Iraq in 2003, Tawhid emerged as a dangerous insurgent group, destroying the UN mission's headquarters in Baghdad on 19 May, and killing the UN Secretary General's representative Sergio de Mello. They then turned their attention to the Shiʿi, assassinating the spiritual leader of the Supreme Council of the Islamic Revolution in Iraq (SCIRI), Ayatollah Mohammed Baqr al-Hakim, in the Shiʿi religious stronghold of Najaf on 29 August.[4] Tahwid continued to expand its operations in Iraq, targeting Coalition forces and government targets, and earning international notoriety by kidnapping and beheading foreign hostages. By 2004, Tawhid was the most powerful of the *jihadist* groups operating in Iraq and, in September 2004, Zarqawi pledged allegiance to al-Qaeda. Tawhid was renamed Tanzim Qa'idat al-Jihad fi Bilad al-Rafidain – the Organization of the Base of Jihad in the Land of Two Rivers, otherwise known as 'al-Qaeda Iraq' (AQI).[5]

AQI became the scourge of Coalition forces and the Iraqi government alike, with Zarqawi expanding the size of the organization by merging smaller groups into it and creating a broader council – the Majlis Shura al-Mujahidin (Mujahidin Advisory Council, or MSM) – to coordinate the rapidly growing insurgency against the Iraqi government and its US supporters.[6] However, Zarqawi's luck ran out. Upon identifying Zarqawi's spiritual adviser, Abd al-Rahman, US forces quickly identified Zarqawi's safe house in Hibhib, north-east of Baghdad, and, on 7 June 2006, a US F-16 aircraft dropped two laser-guided bombs on it, mortally wounding the AQI leader.[7] Without Zarqawi, AQI recovered under the new MSM leader, Abu Ayyub al-Masri, who renamed AQI as the Islamic State of Iraq (ISI), then pledged the allegiance of the MSM itself to the new ISI leader, Abu Omar al-Baghdadi. Within Iraq, these pledges of allegiance, *bay'a*, were important as they consolidated the Sunni insurgency in the aftermath of Zarqawi's killing. But there was one *bay'a* missing, and that was from ISI to al-Qaeda itself. Without a formal pledge from Baghdadi to bin Laden being made, ISI would begin to move away from doing al-Qaeda's bidding, thus setting the scene for ISI's successor, ISIS, to overshadow al-Qaeda itself.

Within the setting of US-occupied Iraq, however, ISI was too successful for its own good. By late 2006, the organization had the means to project its power across Sunni areas and into Baghdad, was largely self-sufficient in terms of income and even controlled territory in the Sunni triangle north-east of Baghdad. Their success was rapidly undermining the integrity of the Iraqi government, and this spurred the US into action – in the form of the surge of US forces into Baghdad and Anbar province. ISI's control of territory, too, saw a reaction from tribal sheikhs who, while no friends of the government of Iraq or the US, were still unwilling to allow their territory to be taken by Sunni *jihadists* that were increasingly seen as being foreigners brought in by al-Qaeda. This backlash saw the tribes of Anbar and other provinces take action that would lead to the Awakening movements that were subsequently utilized by the US military.

The end result saw Iraq become too hostile for ISI. Its leaders were ferociously targeted by the US military, whose increasing organization of the Sunni tribes enabled the Sunnis to reassert their local control against what were seen as foreign fighters. By the end of 2008, ISI had become a shadow of what it had been, but Abu Omar still made decisions that would prove formative for ISI's successor. In a bid to recentralize their leadership, ISI moved its headquarters to Mosul and implemented a new, tighter administrative structure. Moving to Mosul also brought the ISI leadership into a closer relationship with former Saddam regime figures – as Mosul had been home to the most important military colleges in Iraq, and many former military figures had continued to reside there. Lastly, the ISI leadership sought to further legitimize themselves – perhaps against al-Qaeda as much as other Iraqi competitors – in terms of religious authority. Emphasizing Abu Omar's membership of the Quraysh tribe of the Prophet Mohammed, and thus suggesting that Abu Omar had the necessary prerequisites to be the caliph, unlike the Egyptian leader of al-Qaeda, Ayman al-Zawahiri, with hindsight ISI was already beginning to lay the building blocks for the Islamic State itself to be declared. But it would not be Abu Omar who would make this pronouncement. Following his killing in Tikrit by US and Iraqi forces, on 18 April 2010, another descendant of the Quraysh tribe assumed control of ISI. The relatively unknown Ibrahim Awwad Ibrahim Ali al-Badri al-Samarra'i, otherwise known as Abu Du'a, Dr Ibrahim, or now Abu Bakr al-Baghdadi, would take ISI from what was by now a greatly marginalized position in Iraq to build an organization that would unleash new levels of violence across a country that had already experienced the worst that dictatorship, occupation and civil war could bring.

Abu Bakr al-Baghdadi

There is still relatively little known about the self-proclaimed caliph of the Islamic State, Abu Bakr al-Baghdadi. Most accounts would have him born in 1971 in Samarra, a largely Sunni town north of Baghdad, but with a significant Shi'i population centred around the Askariyya shrine housing the remains of the tenth and eleventh Imams venerated by Shi'is. The sources available, however, are few and far between – indeed, Abu Bakr has seemingly done his utmost to remain an enigma, especially when compared to his media-hungry predecessor, Abu Musab al-Zarqawi. How, then, can his rise from obscurity be explained, from being a thoughtful student of Islamic studies in the 1990s, to being a leader that Patrick Cockburn, writing in the *Independent* newspaper at the end of December 2013, lists as the 'Middle East leader of the year' in recognition of his rebuilding of ISIS following the crushing of ISI by the US-led 'surge'?[8]

Few aspects of Abu Bakr's background, profile and character stand out as being particularly noteworthy – which is of course of some interest in itself. His family is described as 'lower middle class', although it claimed to descend from the Prophet Mohammed, which then bestows upon Abu Bakr one of the key attributes necessary for becoming caliph – an attribute not possessed by Osama bin Laden, or his successor as leader of al-Qaeda, Ayman al-Zawahiri (Atwan 2015: 105). He appears to have been a thoughtful boy and adolescent, seemingly scholarly and focused upon his studies of Islam. Witnesses suggest that he carried himself with quiet authority, although they are likely to be influenced by explaining what he became rather than what he actually was. There is a suggestion that his family – even Abu Bakr himself – may have been members of the Ba'th Party, which would not have been at all unusual for a Sunni Arab from Samarra. Indeed, apart from the comments regarding Abu Bakr's quiet, commanding authority and presence, there is little to suggest that he was in any way unusual or different from those other pious youths who would have been in their early twenties in 1990s Iraq.[9]

Brookings scholar William McCants, in one of the more detailed biographies available, places Abu Bakr in Baghdad in 1996, where he graduated from the University of Baghdad in Islamic studies. He continued with his studies, enrolling at the newly founded Saddam University for Islamic Studies – an institution that was very much a product of the regime's attempts to cloak itself in the mantle of Islam – where he received a Master's degree and then a PhD in Islamic studies. During this time, he became exposed to the Muslim Brotherhood, but viewed them as being 'people of words, not action', and he began to advocate a more muscular approach to *jihad*. His willingness to act was realized following the defeat of Saddam and the occupation of Iraq by the US in 2003. Under the pseudonym Abu Du'a, Baghdadi joined one of many insurgent groups forming to target US forces, and would find himself arrested in 2004 and imprisoned in the Camp Bucca detention facility in southern Iraq (Atwan 2015: 109). His identity – as a member of an insurgent group – seems not to have been realized by his US captors, however, who allowed him the relative freedom in the camp enjoyed by 'civilian detainees' (McCants 2015a). During his ten-month stay in Camp Bucca, it is difficult to say whether Abu Bakr became more radicalized than before his incarceration. It would seem that he was already quite convinced of the necessity of promoting violent *jihad*. But Camp Bucca did give him two important elements necessary to assume a leadership position upon his release: a network of other *jihadists* and insurgents, including al-Qaeda fighters and former regime elements, and his exposure to them as a figure of quiet confidence, reflection and authority.

Upon his release, probably in 2006, he formed a new group called Jaish Ahl al-Sunnah wa al-Juma'ah (Army of the People of the Sunnah and Solidarity), which operated around his place of origin in Samarra. Upon Zarqawi's death in 2006, Abu Bakr brought the group into the new ISI entity led by Abu Omar al-Baghdadi and, as a classically and highly trained Islamic scholar, Abu Bakr was appointed to the Sharia Committee (Atwan 2015: 110). Upon Abu Omar's death at the hands of the US in 2010, again through an air strike, Abu Bakr was chosen as the new Emir above many who were older and more experienced than him. From this point on, any notion of the quiet, reflective and bespectacled scholar of Islam would fade as the new leader restructured the activities of ISI from being an organization that had suffered successive defeats at the hands of its opponents to being the most feared, dangerous and potentially transformative entity to have emerged in the twenty-first century.

The Reformation of Sunni *Jihadism* in Iraq

It is tempting to view the progression of Sunni *jihadist* organizations in Iraq on a timeline starting with Tawhid and ending with the Islamic State. But such an approach would miss two critical factors that explain the Islamic State's emergence. The first is that the nature, character and competence of ISIS, and then IS, owes nearly as much to the involvement of non-*jihadist* trends and legacies – and particularly those that emanated from Saddam's regime – as it does to ISI and its predecessors. The second is that ISIS did not merely emerge as the next iteration of Sunni *jihadist* insurgency, taking over from where ISI had left off. Indeed, if ISIS had simply carried on working to the same doctrine as ISI had before the assassination of Abu Omar, then it is likely they would have been further marginalized. What made ISIS different was its willingness to learn not only from the successes and mistakes of ISI and AQI, but also from the way in which the US military from 2007 onwards had undermined and ultimately tamed the threat of ISI. It was this ability to learn and to then refine their actions that made Abu Bakr and his lieutenants far more dangerous than any previous Sunni militant leadership and, unbeknown to observers, a new and far more deadly organization was being created from 2010 onwards.

With hindsight, from the outset ISI under Abu Bakr behaved differently to the ISI of Abu Omar. Abu Bakr was aware of the need for ISI to have deep roots into Iraqi Sunni communities, and to ensure that local conditions and grievances were understood. He also seems to have recognized the necessity of not being overly reliant on foreign fighters, and acknowledged the sensitivity of tribes to losses of territory, resources and prestige. His response was to devolve the actions of his fighters, improve the social grounding of the organization by recruiting local notables and to ensure that ISI was 'Iraqified' as much as possible. If there were still opponents within the community, they would be dealt with swiftly and brutally – with their treatment serving as a warning to others. These techniques were evident in earlier years – particularly in the ISI of Abu Omar – but they had also been honed by recognizing how the US military had broken ISI in 2008, and how the US had understood the power of facilitating local actors to resolve local problems, and killed those who refused to surrender. ISI also began to fight differently. Their actions became more targeted, and more devastating, throughout 2009 and 2010, and they also began to operate more publicly and openly, particularly when the US military withdrew at the end of 2012. In effect, ISI began operating as though it were a regular military, conducting raids against *sahwat* and government opponents that bore the hallmarks of regular and special military training, and having the foresight of knowledge that indicated the existence of an expertly designed intelligence organization. The hallmarks of former Saddam regime elements were beginning to be felt. Lastly, Abu Bakr himself behaved differently from his predecessors. Not for him were the public pronouncements of Zarqawi and the undisciplined use of telephones and computers. Abu Bakr disguised his identity and his whereabouts, to the extent of being known as the 'Ghost' among his men.[10]

ISI's behaviour under Abu Bakr became more expansive, and more successful, in Iraq. New techniques of multiple, clustered attacks, employing suicide bombers in conjunction with vehicle-borne improvised explosive devices (VBIEDs, or truck bombs), suggested a new offensive doctrine was in play – one that advocated the use of overwhelming destructive force against opponents to not only kill and maim, but to terrify and demoralize those who were left. With hindsight again, ISI was also following a carefully thought-through plan: one that would aim to build the organization, to demoralize their opponents and to regroup under its banner as many supporters as possible. As part of their campaign to undermine their opponents, they also declared what their plans were. Starting in July 2012, ISI began the 'Breaking the Walls' campaign, with the stated intention of freeing its captured members from Iraq's prisons. This they did, launching eight attacks on Iraq's major prisons, culminating with an assault on the infamous Abu Ghraib prison in July 2013, in which 500 prisoners escaped.[11] The second twelve-month plan, from July 2013 to July 2014, was called Operation Soldier's Harvest, and was aimed at draining the ISF and security forces through targeted assaults, assassination of key figures and widespread intimidation. By the time Abu Bakr's fighters were ready to confront the ISF in Mosul in June 2014, they had already managed to weaken the resolve, and the capabilities, of their opponents.

The final aspect allowing ISI to transform itself into the brutally capable organization of ISIS was that of the opportunities provided by the eruption of civil war in Syria in 2011. The interaction of Syrian and Iraqi *jihadis* in earlier years had been extensive, with President Bashar al-Asad of Syria facilitating the travel of many *jihadis* to Iraq to fight the US military.[12] And so it was a straightforward decision for Abu Bakr to take advantage of Syria's war, not least because controlling territory in the east of Syria, in close proximity to Anbar and Nineveh provinces, would provide him with strategic depth for when the situation in Iraq was not as amenable to his operations. Syria would be a strong recruiting base and would also turn into a safe haven for ISIS in the years ahead, when Abu Bakr established Raqqa as one of their two 'capitals' in the future Caliphate. Dispatching his Nineveh commander Abu Muhammad al-Jowlani, ISI brought together local *jihadi* groups into a new entity called Jabhat al-Nusra, at the end of 2011. In the chaos of the Syrian civil war, the well-organized and resourced Jabhat al-Nusra became one of the most established fighting forces, conducting operations around the country, and with an ever-expanding cadre of fighters. Watching his creation from Iraq, where his own successes were slower to achieve, Abu Bakr sought to realign Jowlani's creation within an ISI-dominant framework. On 9 April 2013, Abu Bakr announced that Jabhat al-Nusra would be subsumed within an expanded ISI organization called al-Dawla al-Islamiyya fi al-Iraq wa ash-Sham – the Islamic State of Iraq and al-Sham, or ISIS. Jowlani, however, rejected the edict, thus setting Jabhat al-Nusra and ISIS on a collision course. Abu Bakr re-entered Syria with a new ISIS force and engaged in ferocious fighting with Jabhat al-Nusra and other Islamist groups. Refusing to accept the mediation of al-Qaeda emissaries, Ayman al-Zawahiri effectively excommunicated Abu Bakr and ISIS from the al-Qaeda network. Yet this did not weaken them. Rather, it invigorated the organization and further consolidated their power base in Iraq, where the spectre of al-Qaeda and foreign influences had only served to weaken homegrown *jihadist* forces. The act also freed up Abu Bakr to challenge the uncharismatic Zawahiri for the accolade of being the pre-eminent leader of the global Sunni *jihadist* movement.

The Conquest of Mosul

Far from being unpredictable, the conquest of Mosul in June 2014 by ISIS fighters had been some time in the making. Already, Abu Bakr had begun to re-establish ISIS as an insurgent state, taking control of Fallujah and Ramadi along with much of Anbar province in January, and magnifying the targeting of the ISF as part of Operations Soldier's Harvest. In Syria, ISIS had consolidated their hold on Raqqa and the border area with Iraq, thus giving them access to immense stockpiles of Syrian Army weaponry, strong supply lines and a strategically placed safe haven. It also meant that ISIS fighters had high morale, compared to their ISF opponents.

The predictability of the assault was also causing concern in the Kurdistan Region. With their strong links to the governor of Nineveh, Atheel al-Nujaifi, who was openly complaining about his inability to counter the growing presence of ISIS cells in the city, and with their own intelligence networks watching developments there closely, Kurdish intelligence officials had been warning Baghdad and Western governments of the threat rising in Mosul for several months beforehand.[13] ISIS cells had already begun leveraging taxes for protection, operating a significant black economy across the city.[14] But neither Prime Minister Maliki nor Western capitals acted upon these warnings.

The beginnings of the ISIS assault commenced on 4 June, when hit-and-run convoys successfully overcame the city's checkpoints, which had been largely depleted of heavy weapons due to the repositioning of ISF forces in Anbar. Attacks continued over the next few days, with villages on the outskirts being targeted. Even so, with ISIS forces estimated at being no more than 1,500 strong and the ISF contingent in the city being some fifteen times more than this, the ISIS manoeuvres were seen as irritating rather than threatening. This was to change on 8 June when dozens of vehicles stormed into the city, and sleeper cells became active from within, with several neighbourhoods falling to the ISIS insurgents even before the main invasion actually began. Worse was to come the next day. By 9 June, the situation had moved from being concerning to alarming as the officers from the ISF evacuated the city, leaving their military units leaderless. In the ensuing chaos, some five divisions of ISF soldiers fled the city, allowing ISIS and its allies (including Jamaʿat Ansar al-Islam, and the Baʿathist front, the Jaish al-Rijal al-Tarika al-Naqshabandiyya – JRTN) to move quickly through the city of 3 million people, taking over government buildings and controlling key areas and sites. The insurgent forces quickly moved towards the east, pushing into Arab-dominated areas of Kirkuk, namely Hawijah, Abbasi, Zab and Riyadh.[15]

The speed with which ISIS advanced shocked even the Kurds, who had been forewarning of an attack. In an instant, the territories to the south of the KRI had been emptied of ISF divisions, with nothing stopping ISIS forces from not only occupying the areas vacated by the ISF, but claiming their huge stockpiles of weapons and taking control of territory deemed of vital interest to the Kurds – and especially Kirkuk. The Kurdish leadership therefore moved quickly and ordered the deployment of *peshmerga* brigades to the Kurdish-dominant parts of Kirkuk. By 10 June, the Kurds had largely gained all of the lands they had demanded as part of the constitutional negotiations of 2005, which had never been granted. With their forces garrisoned in Kirkuk and controlling the oilfields that run to the north-west, the KRG was then content to impose a dividing line with ISIS that was simply defined by what the KRG considered to be Kurdish and Arab territory. The western, Arab districts of Hawijah and Riyadh were ceded to ISIS, while the *peshmerga* moved to secure Makhmour and as much of eastern Nineveh province as they could. Lastly, the *peshmerga* reinforced their positions in Diyala governorate, at Jalawla, in order to protect the approach to Khanaqin, and keep open the eastern highway between Kurdistan and Baghdad.

But ISIS did not stop in the north. With alarming speed, their forces moved south, capturing Tikrit on 11 June and surrounding the refining centre of Baiji, thus depriving northern Iraq of petroleum products and limiting the supply of electricity to Baghdad. By 15 June, the JRTN had captured Tal Afar near Mosul, with ferocious fighting breaking out in Baquba between ISIS and the ISF, due to the strategic importance of the town on the approach to Baghdad. By the end of the month, Anbar governorate had fallen to ISIS, giving them full control of the border crossings into Syria, apart from the Rabia crossing still controlled by the *peshmerga* and their Syrian Kurdish counterparts in the People's Protection Units (YPG) of the Democratic Union Party (PYD).[16]

From ISIS to the Islamic State

Abu Bakr was now in control of a territory as large as England, Scotland and Wales or, in US measures, a territory that spans from Illinois to Virginia.[17] Arguably, the most logical action would then have been to consolidate his position, and so few envisaged the ISIS pronouncement on 29 June of the establishment of the Caliphate, or the Islamic State, with Abu Bakr taking the title of Caliph Ibrahim.[18] His announcement was viewed by many observers as being an act of unbelievable hubris, and evidence of the political and religious ignorance of Abu Bakr. Looking at this from the outside, it is understandable why this was the mainstream analysis. By announcing the Caliphate, Abu Bakr had attempted to realize an ideal, something that was either deemed unattainable, or unnecessary, by the vast majority of moderate Sunni Muslims. And so it seemed logical that his spectacular overreach would be his undoing, as Sunnis from across the world would oppose it as an absurdity and an abomination.

Yet this did not happen inside the new Islamic State. Abu Bakr, perhaps remembering the success of Abu Omar in forcing the allegiance of other *jihadi* groups to ISI, and certainly having recent memories of how the US military exploited cleavages among the Sunnis in 2007–8, had in effect forced all other insurgent groups to give *bay'a* – allegiance – to him as the caliph. From the perspective of internal, domestic Iraqi Sunni politics, the move forced Abu Bakr's partners and allies – whether *jihadist*, Ba'thist or tribal – to recognize his supremacy before they became too strong to challenge it, with the announcement being a combination of theatre, threat and perfect timing. The alternative would be to fight what now appeared to be an invincible and terrifyingly brutal force that was laying waste to everything that stood against it. By announcing the Caliphate, Abu Bakr had changed the nature of the Sunni insurgency in Iraq, from being fractured and disparate to being cohesive and focused; it emboldened Islamic State fighters in Syria, and it served as a rallying call for more foreign *jihadis* to enter the fray. His actions also constituted a direct threat to the Iraqi government and their Iranian backers and, with the mass executions of captured Shi'i soldiers in the ISF now being spread instantly by the internet, fanned the flames of sectarianism among Shi'is to heights arguably not seen even during the civil war.

Government Formation Following the May 2014 Election

The timing of ISIS's assault on Mosul could not have been worse for the Iraqi government. Having held parliamentary elections at the end of April 2014, Iraq's political elites were still embroiled in heated argument over the formation of the next government. The results of Iraq's national elections were announced on 25 May. There were, at first sight, few surprises with incumbent Prime Minister Maliki doing as well as had been expected, securing just over 24 per cent of the vote and ninety-two out of 328 seats. His Shi'i opponents, however, fared worse than expected, with the Al-Ahrar bloc associated with cleric Muqtada al-Sadr and the Muwatin coalition dominated by the Islamic Supreme Council of Iraq (ISCI) of Ammar al-Hakim securing only 7 per cent each of the vote, Ahrar gaining thirty-four seats and Hakim thirty-one. Predictably so, the Sunni-associated vote was heavily fragmented between the three main groupings: the Mutahidun of Usama al-Nujaifi gained 5 per cent and twenty-eight seats, the al-Wataniyya of Iyad Allai gained twenty-one seats, and the Al-Arabiyya group of Deputy Prime Minister Saleh al-Mutlaq gained just 2 per cent and ten seats.

Among the Kurdish parties, overall the picture was as predicted, with them gaining sixty-two seats, but the internal division of the spoils provided some surprises. Leading the field, as expected, was Barzani's KDP, securing some twenty-five seats (though down four seats from the previous election). Of some note was the second placed party, with Talabani's PUK performing particularly well and securing twenty-one seats – up seven. Coming third was Gorran, with nine seats and nearly half the votes of the PUK. Showing particularly strongly in Kirkuk, and with Gorran being punished in Erbil for its willingness to negotiate with the KDP to form the next KRG, Gorran's seemingly inexorable rise was tempered by the Kurdish electorate, while claims of the PUK's demise seemed to be premature.

In Iraq, meanwhile, the electoral numbers provided some interesting scenarios to consider. As the most acceptable figure heading the most popular bloc by quite some margin, Maliki's claim to be prime minister for a third time running was quickly reasserted. However, his opponents proved unwilling to support him to do this. Needing a bloc in parliament of 165 to ensure a majority, the sums made difficult reading for the incumbent prime minister. In short, to become prime minister by adhering to the established rules of the government-forming game, Maliki would need to find agreement with at least two sets of elites out of three, yet all three of them had expressed their deep unease at the prospect of him remaining prime minister, and all three groupings had met before the elections to agree upon strategies to follow to prevent Maliki from securing the keys to the prime minister's office.

However, the electoral numbers, if worrying for Maliki, looked even more concerning for the anti-Maliki blocs. Together, Ahrar, Muwatin, the Sunnis and the Kurds could bring together some 186 seats at the very most, more than another sixteen being needed, and with little room to manoeuvre (with most leaders wanting some 200 seats to be sure of parliamentary approval). Furthermore, the chances of being able to assemble this theoretical number would be slim. With so many parties each competing for influence and position, the opportunity for Maliki to entice some of them to at least not work against him, even if they could not support him, was significant. Also, building a government without the most popular figure at its head, from the most popular bloc of the most populous community, would be a deeply destabilizing move for any of the others to decide on, however enticing it proved to be.

The first meeting of parliament in Baghdad illustrated the inherent chaos that seemed to have taken hold in the capital. Acting as though it was business as usual, the parliament failed to appoint either a prime minister or a speaker, instead holding back on the decision for subsequent days. At the same time, Maliki, who was by now a caretaker prime minister, continued to act as the 'actual' prime minister and the commander in chief of the army, making it blatantly clear to everyone that he had no intention of relinquishing power without a struggle.

In this setting, the president of the Kurdistan Region, Massoud Barzani, moved quickly to stake Kurdistan's right to self-determination, tasking the Kurdistan National Assembly (KNA) on 3 July to prepare for a referendum on independence.[19] With Turkey seemingly on side, as long as Ankara would be kept informed of progress, and with Israel and some Arab states expressing varying degrees of support, President Barzani began to present himself not just as the president of the Kurdistan Region of Iraq, but as the focal point of the Kurdish nation as it moved towards independence. The two problems he faced – of overt opposition from Iran, and the US clinging to the notion of still being able to build a government of national unity in Baghdad – seemed of lessening importance to him. However, Barzani's leadership would very soon be sorely tested as Abu Bakr unleashed his fighters not on Baghdad, but on the Kurdistan Region's capital of Erbil.

The Near Death Experience of the Kurds

The leadership of the KRG tended to view the fall of Mosul as being a distant event – something that was 'over there', in a different country, rather than constituting a threat to the KRI itself. Indeed, in the weeks following the fall of Mosul, it was clear that the focus of the leadership of the KRG and the KDP was not primarily upon the threat posed by the Islamic State. It was, instead, focused upon the exposure of Maliki's military weakness in the north and what was clearly a powerful restatement of the sectarian divide that ran through the Arab community of Iraq. From the perspective of President Massoud Barzani, Prime Minister Maliki had been shown to be bluffing – while his talk and posture had been threatening up until June 2014, a ramshackle group of badly organized and poorly equipped *jihadis* had simply frightened away a military force many times larger and equipped with the finest materials the US could offer. But Barzani and his security team misjudged the threat against the KRI. Still confident in the martial abilities of the *peshmerga* – a force that in reality had a chain of command fragmented according to party allegiances, was poorly trained and even more poorly equipped, and had not been battle-tested against an attacking enemy for nearly two decades, with the last time being during the last round of KDP–PUK fighting in 1997 – the Kurdistan Region was woefully exposed to a sudden, overwhelming and uncompromising attack along what was now a border of over 1,000 km with the Islamic State.

July was a peculiar month in the Kurdistan Region (KR). Very quickly, it seems, the threat posed by IS seemed to have travelled down the list of issues of most importance to the leadership of the KR, with them focusing again far more intently on the political gaming around the nomination of an individual to be president of Iraq, or watching carefully the Shiʿi discussion over whether Maliki should be prime minister. Only in Jalawla, in the far south-east, was there a concerted focus on fighting IS, and this was largely due to the local necessity of protecting Khanaqin and ensuring the

Iranian border was safe. Meanwhile, in Erbil and Dohuk, the Kurdish leadership and the *peshmerga* seemed to be increasingly confident in their abilities to counter any threat posed by IS. They had good reason to be so. In limited engagements between IS and *peshmerga*, the Kurdish units had done very well indeed, leading many in the leadership to consider the IS threat as being dangerous and ever-present, but one that would not erupt, at least not in the immediate term.

But just as IS had surprised observers not only with their taking of Mosul, but with their moving on Anbar and taking Tikrit in Salahadin, their attacking of Kobane and their taking of Deir Az-Zur in Syria, they then suddenly deployed impressively large forces in Nineveh, bringing them into a conflict with the Kurds that virtually every analyst had predicted they would avoid. Moving with alarming speed, IS fighters moved into the Kurdish-controlled Zummar region north-west of Mosul city. They attacked the Kurdish-held Kesik military base that had formerly been held by the ISF, and also targeted a range of Christian and Yezidi towns and villages across Nineveh, including the area of Jabal Sinjar – a region with a large Yezidi population.

With only some 200 *peshmerga* defending a very large military base, and with the example of the Syrian Army Base 17 (to the west of Raqqa) where IS had beheaded every Syrian soldier they captured just days before, the *peshmerga* withdrew from Kesik and Zummar, expecting an Iraqi Air Force attack that ultimately did not take place. This, however, set up a pattern for the next few days, of the *peshmerga* evacuating civilians from villages and towns being targeted by IS, before then evacuating themselves, leaving IS to take ownership. When the *peshmerga* did make a stand, they were outgunned by IS forces, with their recently acquired military equipment from the ISF. One senior Kurdish figure noted with disdain that the *peshmerga* could not get close enough to even fire their guns at IS, with IS having the ability to fire on them from some 2 kilometres.[20] Even when they did manage to engage IS vehicles, they found it extremely difficult to stop their Humvees with AK-47s. And, even when they did stop them, they realized that IS fighters were not affected by the destruction of their vehicles around them. Indeed, it seemed to make them even more determined to press ahead, such was their high morale and commitment to the cause.

The situation took an even more worrying turn on 5 August. With attention being paid to fighting in Nineveh governorate, IS moved against villages around the town of Gwer – a town located not in Nineveh but in Erbil governorate and very much in 'traditional' KRG-controlled territory. Further to the south, still in Erbil, IS also moved against the large district town of Makhmour. Again, the *peshmerga* evacuated residents and then themselves, leaving Gwer and Makhmour under IS control. It was at this moment that the international community seemed to have become far more aware of the danger posed by IS, not only to areas to the south of the Kurdistan Region but to the Kurdistan Region itself. With the opening of a second front in Erbil, the Kurdish *peshmerga* were dangerously stretched, and the presence of IS in the governorate suddenly brought home to the population of the Kurdish capital that what had happened in Mosul could easily happen there. Very quickly, residents of Erbil made moves to leave the city, causing traffic jams on the roads to Shaqlawa and Koy (to the north and east), and even to Kirkuk. Far from seeming invincible, the *peshmerga* were now seen as failing, and the morale of them and Kurds at large was beginning to unravel.

Needing to regroup, Barzani ordered the withdrawal of *peshmerga* into focused parts of Nineveh, including at Tel Kayf, and established the Great Zab river – which is the natural boundary between Nineveh and Erbil – as the front line. The river-crossing town of Eski Kelek (Kelek) was fortified with earth berms and military fortifications. It was at this very dark moment for the Kurds that the Obama administration announced, on 7 August, that it would sanction military action against IS, but in a very tightly focused manner: if US diplomats were deemed to be under threat in Erbil, then US forces would be used to protect them; if IS columns approached Erbil, then they would be attacked. Nothing was said about the providing of the *peshmerga* with weapons or other equipment. Indeed, even though Obama was seemingly giving a lifeline to the Kurds, it was one that would allow them to do little more than, at best, maintain the status quo of an expanded IS.

Fortress Baghdad

Meanwhile, in Baghdad, Nouri al-Maliki finally succumbed to the intense pressure that had been brought to bear on him by his opponents and stood down as prime minister on 14 August 2014. His replacement, Haidar al-Abadi, who was also from Maliki's Da'wa Party, inherited a broken country. The Kurds were more independently minded than ever before, and now had the de facto support of Western powers, following their supporting of Erbil when ISIS had attacked in August. And, of course, a huge block of territory covering Anbar, Salahadin, Nineveh and Diyala provinces had now become the preserve of Abu Bakr's Islamic State and, in August 2014, the possibility of an attack on Baghdad was not only feared, but expected.

These problems were serious for Abadi. But they were secondary to a far more pressing concern for him, and that was his own weak position within his Shi'i community. With the rise of IS and the threat to Baghdad, Shi'i political life had seen a massive resurgence in sectarianism. Following the fall of Mosul, the supreme spiritual leader of the Iraqi Shi'i, Ayatollah Ali al-Sistani, pronounced a *fatwa* on 13 June that was carefully worded so as not to be seen as sectarian. In it, he called upon Iraqis to take up arms to defend 'their country and their people and their holy places'. He also urged Iraqis to join the security forces.[21] What became known as the 'righteous *jihad fatwa*' succeeded in rallying Iraqis to fight against IS, but it was interpreted by the majority of Shi'is as being a call by their *marja'* to take up arms as Shi'is against Sunni fighters of IS. A range of different Shi'i militias were already in existence, including the Peace Brigades of Muqtada al-Sadr, the Badr Organization led by Hadi al-Amiri, the Asa'ib Ahl al-Haq led by Qais Khazali and the Kata'ib al-Imam Ali led by Shibi al-Zaydi. They all had long histories of fighting the US occupation after 2003, of fighting AQI and ISI, and at times of fighting each other. And the majority of them were tied to Iran.

These groups were brought together under an umbrella called the Hashed al-Sha'abi – the Popular Mobilization Forces, or Hashed – in an attempt to provide coordination among them and to find some way of legitimizing them within the framework of the Iraqi state. Yet the ties of the Hashed leadership with Iran illustrated where real control lay. In the case of Iran, the most important figure by far was the general commanding the Al-Quds force of the Revolutionary Guards Corp of Iran (IRGC), Qassem Suleimani. A veteran of many campaigns and deployments to areas of national interest to Iran, including Iraq, Afghanistan and the Syrian civil war, the influence of Suleimani in the post-2003 politics of Iraq cannot be overstated. Previously, however, he had tended to work in the shadows, influencing both Shiʿi and Kurdish politicians with carefully timed interventions, and being a force that even US General Petreous found to be invidious. In 2015, however, with no US presence in Iraq, Suleimani's role became much more obvious. He worked directly with ISF and militia forces to push back IS from Amerli, close to Tuz Khurmatu in the north-east, and thus important for Iran to remove as a threat to its border, and he was present on the battlefield in several locations. He also was responsible for putting into place plans to defend Baghdad from IS, which in itself presents a remarkable turn of events when compared to the last defence of Baghdad in 2007. Then, it had been the US military organizing the defence. Less than a decade later, it would be the Iranian military doing so. With militia units based at each of Baghdad's entry points, with ISF forces in reserve, the remit of the Abadi government was between Baghdad and Basra, and, even then, the power of the state was not absolute. To the north of Baghdad, the Iraqi state had basically evaporated. Iraq had become divided by conflict into a country of three states, with each one of them now defined by an exclusivist sectarian or ethnic agenda, and with the prospects of Iraq being reconstituted as a unitary state looking less likely than its continued collapse.

Conclusion: The Passing of Thresholds and the Emergence of Three 'States'

The original conclusion to this book focused upon reviewing the various debates that had been presented and pointed to an uncomfortable and pessimistic endgame for Iraq. I suggested that various societal thresholds were on the verge of being passed, or perhaps had been passed already – thresholds of violence inflicted by Iraqis of differing sect and ethnicity upon each other – that had caused communal cleavages to harden, leaving the notion of any sense of a unifying Iraqi national identity unlikely to survive. This was very much an argument that was taking place in the 2007–8 period, as academics and analysts tried to make sense of what was, at that time, a country gripped by internal conflict the like of which had rarely been witnessed, and which saw those writers who had watched a strong, secular, Iraqi identity form in the decades before 2003 struggle to explain not only what was emerging five years after regime change, but where it would lead.

Writing in 2015, it is sadly no longer the case that the question of the 'passing of thresholds' is any more a question. It seems that it is a reality, but that the thresholds were not passed in 2007–8. Indeed, these thresholds were perhaps not breeched permanently during this time, and were repaired to a degree by subsequent Iraqi-led and US-supported efforts, in the form of the Awakening Movement and the Surge of US forces. But these thresholds were passed thereafter, following the wasting of the opportunities provided by these initiatives by the government of Iraq and by their international supporters, and then through the catalytic and transformative impact caused by the rise of the Islamic State and the subsequent heightened, and often violent, sectarian and ethnic responses of the Shiʿi and Kurdish communities to this new, existential threat.

In the conclusion to this new edition, it is still useful to return to reviewing the salience of the debates that structured the original book. They provide four informative investigations into some of the key aspects of the nation- and state-building project of twentieth-century Iraq, and they come together to form an understanding of the political and social landscape of the country on the eve of the US-led invasion in 2003. I will then attempt to look forward, presenting a view of what Iraq has become since 2014 and the passing of the societal thresholds beyond which Iraqi society would struggle to reconstitute itself into a political whole. In effect, Iraq has become a country with three 'states' – the Baghdad-Basra region controlled by the named government of Iraq from Baghdad, the Kurdistan Region controlled from Erbil, and the Islamic State centred upon Mosul and the Syrian city of Raqqa. The future of Iraq is now very much dependent upon the trajectories taken by each of these three entities, the interaction between them and the role played by external powers.

Making Sense of the *Debates*

Starting with the *artificiality debate*, it is undisputable that 'something new' was created in Iraq following the demise of the Ottoman Empire, this being the state. As such, it is logically correct to call the state 'artificial' but, as pointed out in Chapter 2, all states are artificial to some degree. The problem for countries such as Iraq is that 'those [states] fashioned in the Middle East display their scaffolding more than most' (Cole 2004) and, for Iraq, this scaffolding was imperial in design and support, exclusionary in the manner in which power was distributed and the narrative of the state controlled, and coercive towards those who struggled to find a place within it. This did not necessarily predetermine that the state would collapse. Indeed, the growth of Iraqi nationalism in the twentieth century and the positive impacts of socio-economic development upon Iraqi society until the mid-1980s all suggest that the weaknesses of the early state were being successfully rendered less important as the years progressed.

But the issues surrounding Iraq's artificiality are now intrinsically interwoven with the volatile and emotive subject of identity. In other Middle Eastern countries which also emerged from the ruins of the Ottoman Empire, but are largely homogeneous in terms of population structure, the legitimacy of the existence of the state has rarely been called into question – consider Jordan, for example. In Iraq, however, with its complex societal patterns that have changed over time, the memories concerning the artificial nature of the state at its founding have become combined with how Iraqis themselves view their pasts, and increasingly their futures.

A further angle to consider regarding the question of Iraq's artificialness is the role played by the 'new' architects of the post-Saddam state – the US-led coalition. Indoctrinated for a variety of reasons with an understanding that Iraq was artificial and its problems were therefore products of its inorganic/imposed founding, US policymakers proved adept at analysing Iraq by viewing its parts, rather than the sum of them. Perhaps they were right to do so; maybe they were wrong. With regard to the Kurds, it is difficult to see how a different approach could have been used. But it is questionable whether this approach was the best for appraising which strategies to implement across Iraq south of Kurdistan's borders.

If today's Iraq is considered, the opposing positions of the original *artificiality debate* are now somewhat academic. These poles, with Elie Kedourie, for example, arguing that 'Iraq was a sham', on the one hand, and Hala Fattah claiming that the state 'developed indigenous roots in fertile soil', on the other hand, are certainly relevant in ordering an assessment of Iraqi political development in the twentieth century.

But do they have any application today, with particular reference to forwarding solutions to Iraq's woes? Arguably they do not, as sentiments such as 'Iraq was artificial, therefore let it fall apart', or 'Iraq managed to become a strong, successful state, therefore it must be maintained', are increasingly irrelevant, even misleading, starting points in building an understanding of what is happening in Iraq, and where Iraq is going. The trauma inflicted upon Iraqi society since the consolidation of Saddam Hussein's position in 1979, and particularly during the 1990s, through the actions of a reactive and defensive dictatorship and the devastating impact of UN-imposed sanctions, combined with the deconstruction of the Iraqi state in 2003, has meant that the situation is now quite different from those which characterized Iraq throughout the mid-twentieth century. Quite simply, Iraq as it was cannot be reconstructed, as the parts which were used to assemble it in the first place are no more. An attempt can only be made to allow Iraqis themselves to form something new and quite different, whether by purposeful design or civil war, or for the international community to assist in the building of a new state from scratch that would look quite different from its predecessor. The problem is, of course, that the British state-builders and their Iraqi allies of the early twentieth century had the luxury of a metaphorical canvas that was reasonably 'clean'. Over eighty years of history as a state means that the new state-builders of the post-Saddam period have a canvas that is cluttered with the legacies of this history.

These legacies can be discussed in terms of how Iraqis perceive themselves and others, and, most importantly for assessing Iraq's future, how they mobilize politically. In outlining the *identity debate*, a basic pattern could be seen in Iraq's history. The first part of the pattern was one whereby political mobilization was initially a function of communal association. This is not to say that the mobilization caused such inter-communal problems as we see today – indeed, the cities of Ottoman Iraq were vibrant, cosmopolitan places displaying an eclectic mix of communities living more or less in harmony – but rather that such identities were the primary social markers in the early years of Iraq's history as a state.

What then occurred was the transformation of swathes of Iraqi society, particularly in the years following the commercial exploitation of oil resources. Urbanization increased with influxes of people coming from the rural areas, and Iraq rapidly modernized. With the state promoting various manifestations of Iraqi and Arab nationalism under military-dominated governments, and with Iraq existing in the wider political setting of the post-Second World War Middle East, with the new state of Israel, as well as the global environment dictated by the Cold War, other political forces including communism and socialism also made significant headway. These 'new' political developments never eradicated the old forces of communal mobilization. Indeed, at times the latter were reinvigorated as could be seen with the Shiʿi religious establishment's promotion of Hizb al-Daʿwa to combat the appeal of the ICP. But such developments did overshadow and undermine them for several decades.

As Iraqi society developed, so too did the urban middle class and it is this group in particular that analysts in the West often refer to, explicitly or tacitly, as proof that Iraqi nationalism was a potent and real force, non-sectarian and non-communal in nature, and essentially secular and progressive. The analysts are right to refer to the middle class in this way, and it remains an educational experience to hear from urbane educated Iraqis about what life was like in Baghdad, for example, and how the inter-communal violence of today is a world away from the peaceful coexistence enjoyed in the mid-twentieth century. But the sad fact today is that Iraq's middle class has been weakened to the point of extinction by emigration caused by the pressures of living under authoritarian and totalitarian regimes, by war, by sanctions and economic hardship, and now by the actions of the US and her allies and the rise of Islamist movements and their expected future consolidation. The middle class was the bastion of the 'one Iraq' idea. With the middle class now a shadow of what it used to be, the notion of 'one Iraq' is being subsumed by many contending visions of what Iraq is, and what it should be in the future.

Now, the pattern has again changed. From being almost wholly communal, political life was then transformed and was dictated by the state-led ideologies of Iraqi and Arab nationalism. From the ideological, Iraqi society is reverting back to the communal and mobilizing according to local identities of ethnicity, sect and tribe. The question is, will the pattern ever oscillate back to seeing the ideological superseding the communal once again?

These changes do not happen suddenly. Indeed, throughout Iraq's history we have seen that patterns overlap, with new political and social structures being heavily coloured by those that they replace. The rise of the new communalism fits with this observation. Political Shiʿism, Kurdish nationalism, Sunni Arab exclusivism and Christian isolationism did not simply appear in March 2003. Rather, the reasons behind the strengthening of these forces can be traced back to how the state interacted with Iraqi society, and how society then related to the state. Of importance here is the impact upon society of the Iraqi state becoming more authoritarian in nature, particularly from 1968 following the ascendance of the Baʿth regime.

The *dictator debate* argued that Iraq, as an artificial state composed of different peoples living in different geographical spaces, was *predisposed* to succumbing to authoritarian rule. It was, however, not *predetermined* that this should occur. The catalyst in the development of authoritarianism was imperial meddling in Iraq's affairs and the reaction to this of the most 'advanced' organization in Iraq – the military. Because of historical legacies, the military emerged as the bastion of Arab, secular nationalism in a state numerically dominated by Shiʿis, and with a large minority of non-Arabs present within its boundaries. The arrival of the Baʿth regime, and particularly Saddam's assuming of supreme power in 1979, coincided with an influx of vast revenues accrued from oil. Saddam's political nature, combined with the manipulative power a rentier economy gives the state over society, resulted in Iraq moving from being governed by an authoritarian regime to one that was totalitarian in nature.

It was during this transition in the 1970s that the seeds of the re-communalization of political life were sown. The Kurds, continuously rebellious in the mountain fastnesses, would secure their own autonomous region in the early years of the decade, and the Shiʿi religious establishment would see the continued rise of parties such as Daʿwa, winning supporters away from both the Baʿth and the ICP. War with Iran only served to enforce the re-communalization of Iraqi society, with the Shiʿi *hawza* suffering at the hands of Saddam's security services, while the Kurds were subjected to actions of genocidal proportions during the *Anfal* Campaign. Meanwhile, Saddam's trusted circle remained firmly rooted among various tribes and communities almost always Arab in ethnicity, and nearly always Sunni in sectarian allegiance.

The penultimate proverbial nail in the coffin of ideological political mobilization in Iraq, and the end of 'one' Iraqi nationalism, came during the 1990s. Following Saddam's ill-advised venture into Kuwait and his subsequent defeat at the hands of the US-led coalition, the first obvious manifestations of the communalization of political mobilization in Iraq occurred in front of the world's media. These were the Shiʿi *intifadah* and the Kurdish *rapareen*. Although he survived these rebellions, Saddam's weakened position meant that by necessity he would have to follow a strategy of dividing Iraqi society even further, empowering 'new' tribes over old ones, tactically dealing with Kurdish parties to foment and magnify dissension within their own ranks, and accommodating pliant clerics while liquidating more troublesome ones.

In addition to this political strategy of fragmenting Iraqi political and social structures, an even more powerful socio-economic dynamic was having a devastating effect. This was, of course, the impact of the sanctions regime. Never before had a country been subjected to such a comprehensive sanctions package, and the impact of it was appalling in terms of the deterioration of health and socio-economic indicators. If the war damage inflicted by Iran and the US-led coalition since the 1980s had not pushed Iraq back decades, then sanctions surely did. Politically, the effect of sanctions was to strengthen the regime vis-à-vis Iraqi society, but they also served to resurrect the social bonds of local identities, as localized mechanisms of social provision, relief and political activism began to form. The emergence of a Kurdish de facto state is perhaps the clearest example of the death knell of an all-encompassing Iraqi nationalism in the 1990s. Indeed, it is possible that future historians of Iraq may be tracing Iraq's possible partition or collapse to October 1991, when Saddam withdrew the offices of the Iraqi state from Kurdistan, allowing the de facto Kurdish state to form. But similar trends were also emerging among the Shi'i community, with parties and organizations associated with the religious establishment gaining prominence and building increasingly prevalent support bases.

It remains clear, however, that no combination of localized political forces could have removed Saddam from power at the beginning of the twenty-first century. Even though his regime was grossly weakened, it still remained the pre-eminent force in Iraq. It was the removal of Saddam's regime by external powers in 2003 that would unleash the communal forces that had been growing in Iraq throughout earlier decades. The *state-building and democratization debate* attempted to assess the chances of post-Saddam Iraq transiting from a state of authoritarianism through to democracy. The comparative evidence suggested that, even in the best of circumstances, it would always be a very difficult task to achieve. But faced with the simple fact that the normal building blocks for a democratic state – political parties, a political culture with some semblance of democratic ideals, and a reasonably unifying political will – were weak if not actually lacking, Iraq seems to be a harder prospect than most other places one could imagine.

The subsequent analysis of the post-2003 environment went some way to illustrate these difficulties and outlined how a combination of Iraqi political realities (including communalization) and US-led Coalition mismanagement contributed to bringing Iraq to the edge of a fully fledged civil war by mid-2006. The response of Iraqis and then by the US ended what was a very significant threat to the integrity of the state, but in so doing set up even greater problems for the future. The short-term consequences of the US making promises to Sunni Arab tribes, fighters and communities as a whole that were then not honoured, or forced to be honoured, by the Iraqi government of Prime Minister Maliki cannot be described as anything other than an immense formative influence in the subsequent rise of a new, far more militant, well-organized and determined Sunni *jihadist* insurgency, in the form of ISIS. And the rise of ISIS has seen the heightened sectarianism of the Shiʿi, alongside the Kurds pushing for even greater sovereignty over their own affairs. Since the ties that bound Iraqis of different ethnicities and sect together have now been very much eroded, the future of the country is likely to be one of the interaction of three distinct regions, with each one representing a dominant 'nation'.

Making Sense of the Islamic State

The conquering of Mosul by ISIS fighters in June 2014 awoke a complacent international community to the stark reality that the attempt to instil democratic norms had failed. ISIS was not a cause of this failure, but was merely a very understandable, and predictable, manifestation of decisions made in and for Iraq principally since the government-formation process following the 2010 election, but also reaching back further to the days following the invasion of Iraq in 2003. From the deconstruction of the Iraqi army by the CPA in 2003 and the targeting of thousands by the de-Baʿthification process, to the manner in which the Constitution was drafted and then ratified, through to the broken promises made to Sunni tribes and militias by the US as they sought to break the power of AQI/ISI, the Sunni community had few positive experiences to point to following the demise of Saddam, and many examples of disappointment.

It was into this setting that actors among the Sunnis, thought to have been eradicated by US actions in 2007–8, began to regroup. Baʿthist remnants, including survivors of Saddam's Republican and Special Republican Guards, along with members of his once-feared security services (the *mukhbarat*, the *estikhbarat*, and the notorious *jihaz al-amn al-khas*) and young men who had previously been in the *fedeyeen* or the *ashbal Saddam*, now found common cause with those tribes of Anbar, Salahadin, Diyala and Nineveh that had confronted the threat of al-Qaeda, only to be left by the US to the mercy of Maliki's security services. Acting as the catalyst and the glue that brought these groups together, however, were the survivors of AQI and ISI – figures who had witnessed at first hand the tactics and strategies of the US counter-insurgency programme unleashed against them, and who had also seen how civilian populations and military forces alike responded to the use of overwhelming force. They also learned from their mistakes, and absorbed the lessons of Coalition counter-insurgency tactics, arguably at a time when the Coalition partners were fast forgetting them. They understood the Coalition force's tactic of 'clear, hold and build' in captured territory, they appreciated the power of a policy of winning 'hearts and minds', or at least controlling these through sheer brutality, and they recognized that the next struggle would be fought in the media as much as on the ground. This new iteration of extremist Sunni leadership, and their ideas and tactics, became forged in the crucible of unrelenting violence. They would take what they had learned to another, even more terrible, level. With hindsight, the failure to honour the results of the election of 2010 proved to be a formative moment for what would happen in Iraq in 2014, with the rise of ISIS and the return with a vengeance of the Shi'i militias. From the perspective of Sunni Arabs – and particularly those who had fought the US military and Iraqi government, who had later fought against ISI as the *sahwat*, and who had then believed the promises made to them by the US and chosen to re-engage with the political process – the lessons of 2010 were harsh and telling in the extreme: you can participate in elections but, even if your party of choice wins, the institutions of the government of Iraq will still be controlled by the Shi'i.

The blowback did not only come from the Sunnis, either. Maliki, too, had been burned by the experience of the election. Always prone to believing that conspiracies were being implemented against him personally, Maliki viewed with alarm the ability of Allawi and his Sunni counterparts to mobilize Sunni support to such an extent. He also viewed with fear the political aspirations of the Sunni to return to positions of power, and even to hold the premiership,. No longer would Maliki wait for the Sunnis to come to him – either through the ballot box or on the street, and no longer would he suffer the indignity of his authority being challenged in the disputed territories by Massoud Barzani, with the threat of the vaunted *peshmerga*. As soon as circumstances allowed, Maliki would pursue new policies aimed at removing existential threats to continued Shiʿi dominance in Iraq, and those circumstances came about with the withdrawal of US forces from Iraq in 2011.

The rot caused by the disenchantment from 2010 onwards was not contained solely within the Sunni community. Rarely, if ever, had Iraqi political elites worked together to overcome the most serious and contentious issues that confronted them. These problems were admittedly very great and included the need to create a new, all-encompassing nationalist project, the targeting of the inordinate levels of corruption that afflicted every layer of the state and the resolving of the deeply rooted grievances of the Kurds with regard to the status of disputed territories and their own federal existence within Iraq. The lack of action on these, and other, key points was as much to do with vested interests among the elites in maintaining a status quo that allowed for the continuation of inter-communal disharmony, given that these elites had been empowered by this very dynamic, and keeping in place the opportunity to siphon state resources to their own private accounts. But Western powers were also complicit in this, choosing to turn a blind eye to the worse excesses of abuses of position in the Iraqi state and not using their still considerable leverage to work towards resolving these worsening problems. Rather, a pattern emerged of Iraqi elites and their international friends overcoming moments of dispute by delaying making decisions and pushing the issue into the future, for future governments to address. While this might have made sense at the time, the end result was that Iraqi leaders had failed to resolve any major issue of concern that had emerged since 2003.

The Passing of Thresholds and the Emergence of Three States

Does history, or more accurately the modern history of the state, now actually *matter* in Iraq? By this, I mean to ask whether the legacies created by the transformation of society, which include the existence and prevalence of a vibrant, largely secular, non-communal middle class alongside the urbanization of society, now have any relevance in assessing how Iraq might develop in the forthcoming months and years. Consider, for example, two dynamics that have occurred in Iraq's past, both relating to the emergence of regionalism, with one focusing on the north, and the other on the south. With regard to what is happening in Kurdistan, in the north, does the fact that, throughout Iraq's modern history, several powerful and prominent Kurdish tribes and leaders (including both Massoud Barzani and Jalal Talabani) have sought alliance with the Iraqi government, thereby weakening the Kurdish nationalist movement, mean that this will happen in the future when difficult choices perhaps have to be made? Or has the de facto state in Kurdistan now become so institutionalized within Kurdish political culture that it is now a permanent feature of the political map? If our geographical gaze moves to the south and considers historical occurrences of separatism, is it possible to infer that because regionalism in Basra was overshadowed by Iraqi nationalism in the 1920s, then so too the current trend among Shi'i elites, of considering more fully than at any other time the possibility of breaking Iraq's integrity and using their own oil wealth to benefit themselves, is doomed to fail? Arguably, the drivers of Shi'i political aspirations are are now very different. Their leaders increasingly see the dangers of advancing into IS-controlled lands, as well as the difficulties in negotiating with the independence-minded Kurds, and they view the possibility of becoming a smaller state with vast oil wealth under their control as preferable to the alternative of having to hold Iraq together by force. For the leaders of the Islamic State, the concept of the Middle Eastern state system is deemed invalid and already has been declared obsolete as they seek to build their new Islamic Caliphate, ignoring former boundaries of the states. The Kurdish leaders, and especially those around Barzani, see the problems of being tied into a state in which they will always be a minority, and always viewed with suspicion. Some of them will think, understandably so, that it would be far better to secure their own economic livelihood and build their own regional relationships according to their own interests.

Of course, this presents a heavily generalized view, driven by the political aspirations of certain elites, of what is happening in Iraq and what may unfold in the future. Within each of these three communities exists a range of political currents and powerholders and, of course, there is also the great swathe of unpolitically connected people that exist across each of these territories. Yet it seems that, in post-2014 Iraq, political power and the agency to control, effect and change Iraq's political direction is very much in the hands of those groups best placed to control coercion across society, and to project their power as and when needed. Indeed, the notion that the institutions of the government of Iraq, or the Kurdistan Regional Government – as the two 'legal' governing entities in Iraq and Kurdistan respectively – are the ultimate arbiters of power in their lands is very much incorrect. Today, in the Baghdad-Basra region, the government of Iraq is not only merely one coercive actor among many. It is also an actor that has itself seen its institutions 'captured' by other sub-state forces, including militias, political groups and powerful politicians, many of which are influenced by external state actors. The Kurdistan Region is also not immune to this tendency, with the KRG being very much subservient to the political whims of the two leading parties – the KDP and PUK – which themselves remain aware of the wishes and expectations of Turkey and Iran respectively. Perhaps surprisingly, the Islamic State can claim more independence in deciding what its aims are, and how they will be achieved – not least because they are so grand and non-negotiable (basically, the furthering of the Caliphate across the globe). Yet even within the Islamic State, it would seem that they too have to be very much aware of internal balances, the need to maintain tribal allegiances and the necessity of ensuring that their informal relationships that maintain whatever support and supply network is in place remain operational. In short, these three entities have highly complex dynamics within them that makes predicting how they will act very difficult indeed.

At what point does a society become transformed to the point whereby the legacies of the past can no longer be utilized as variables in predicting what might, or should, happen in the future? Could it be the case that scenarios built upon viewing historical patterns are now largely specious due to the possibility that *thresholds have been and are being passed*. Put simply, the 'order' that characterized Iraqi society, especially before 1991, has now been destroyed in the post-2003 period, and particularly since the rise of IS. With every terrorist atrocity that causes the death of scores of Shiʿi, each retaliation by the Shiʿi militia, and all the actions taken by Kurdish forces to secure their hold over the disputed territories in the north, the nebulous thresholds that contained the 'rules' that governed Iraqi society are weakened, and new, clearer, but harder rules are being formulated.

These new rules are those of communalization, identity-based politics, chauvinism, religious exclusivism and ethnically based nationalism. Iraq is now in a period where these new patterns have formed. This is clear. What is not so clear is whether these new patterns have become permanent because the societal thresholds of twentieth-century Iraq have been passed, or whether the 'old' rules have survived and their patterns of social and political development will make a comeback. Personally, I do not see how the situation can be engineered in order to allow a return to the situation as it once was. But this is only an opinion. What can be stated as fact is that Iraqi society is undergoing a profound transformation, one that started decades ago, which is now reaching its critical final moments. If these nebulous thresholds have not been crossed, then the survival of Iraq and the rebuilding of it as a multi-communal and federal state are still possibilities. This is, however, a very big 'if'.

Notes

Introduction: Artificiality, Identity, Dictatorship and State-Building

1 The lineage of Sunni *jihadist* organizations in Iraq will be looked at in detail in Chapter 9, where the rise of the Islamic State of Iraq and al-Sham (ISIS) and the subsequent declaration of the Islamic State (IS) of 2014 are considered.

2 The White House, 'Highlights of the Iraq Strategy Review', January 2007. Available at: <http://2001-2009.state.gov/p/nea/rls/78589.htm>.

3 There has been an inordinate amount of attention paid to naming the Islamic State, and its predecessor ISIS. Not wanting to legitimize the organization as a 'state', or acknowledge any Islamic association, the term 'daesh' has often been used, which is itself an acronym derived from the Arabic name for the Islamic State of Iraq and al-Sham, al-Dawla al-Islamiyya fi al-Iraq wa al-Sham. In this book, in order to facilitate a clear understanding of the chronology of events, I use the following names/acronyms: ISI (2006–13), ISIS (2013–14), and IS (2014–).

4 The formal name of Iraqi Kurdistan, as recognized in the Constitution of Iraq of 2005 is the Kurdistan Region of Iraq (KRI). Its legislature is the Kurdistan National Assembly (KNA) and its executive is the Kurdistan Regional Government (KRG), and both sit in the region's capital of Erbil. While it is common to refer to the Kurdistan Region as 'KRG', it is more accurate to refer to it as 'the KRI', using the name 'KRG' to refer to the Kurds' government.

5 While literature discussing Iraqi society in the mid-twentieth century would tend to extol the non-sectarian nature of Iraqi

political culture and society, describing in the main an educated people (and especially in the major cities) that were increasingly of a secular outlook, these references would rarely focus upon the Kurdish situation, and also tended to build a picture of Iraqi society by extrapolating from the urbane middle classes of the major cities – a middle class that was very much tied to the patronage of the state.

Chapter 1 Legacies of Civilizations and Empires

1 L. Paul Bremer, administrator of the Coalition Provisional Authority, speaking at the Police Academy Commencement, Baghdad, 1 April 2004; available at: <http://www.cpa-iraq.org/transcripts/20040401_bremer_police.html>.
2 Cuneiform was used widely across the Mesopotamian region for nearly 3,000 years, and the script was used by different peoples to write their own languages, including the Akkadians, Hittites, Assyrians and (old) Persians. It was only in 1835 that cuneiform was rediscovered by Henry Rawlinson, a British Army officer, when he happened upon undeciphered inscriptions to King Darius (522–486 BC) on a cliff face in Behistun, Iran. Rawlinson succeeded in translating the script by 1850 (Couture 1984: 143–4).
3 The Kurds claim ancestry from a variety of different peoples. The most common claim is that they are descendants of the Medes. However, there is a tendency among some Kurdish academics to think about their identity in a 'primordial' manner and to claim that their ancestry can be traced to ever earlier peoples, including the Hittites and Hurrians. Merhdad Izady, for example, makes the astonishing claim that a link can be made between the Kurds and the period of the Ubaid culture (5000 BC), and even before this to the Halaf period (6000 BC) (Izady 2004a). It is fair to say that such linkages, made across timescales of several millennia, are highly problematic to prove or disprove, and I am in no position to add to the debate one way or the other apart from remarking that the actual utility of such claims, whether right or wrong, is questionable. Kurdish ancestral claims are important to note, however, as they show clearly how historical links are used to promote myths of nationhood, no matter how tenuous the links with the past actually are. The Kurds are also not the only practitioners of this within Iraq. Most notably, the 'claiming' of Mesopotamian civilizations as part of the national myths of Arab and Assyrian peoples in

Iraq is commonly acknowledged, and I have also met with Turkmen who make similar claims with regard to Sumer.

4 The rise to prominence of the *mamluks* can be traced to the end of the seventeenth century. Around 1700, the ruler of Baghdad, Hasan Pasha, imported slave boys (*mamluks*) from Circassia and Georgia (in the Caucases) to form a loyal military and administrative elite. They were given preferential education and training in preparation for important positions in the military and in the civil service. The policy was continued by Hasan's son, Ahmad Pasha, who increased his dependency upon the *mamluks*. When a *mamluk* leader, Sulayman Abu Laylah, married Ahmad's daughter, he soon seized power to become the first of the *mamluk* pashas. The Ottoman Sultan was forced to accept this reality, and the new pasha in turn recognized the sultan as his master (see Nieuwenhuis 1982; Salman 1992).

Chapter 2 State Formation, Monarchy and Mandate, 1918–1932

1 A counter to the argument presented in the text is provided by Dina Rizk Khoury, who argues that the eighteenth century was not one of decline for the Ottoman empire, but one of decentralization. Rather than weakening the empire, it is suggested with reference to Mosul that the process of decentralization strengthened it through a transformation, or Ottomanization, of regional elites occurring (Khoury 1997).

2 In addition to these powerful external stimuli causing transformation within the empire, Kamal Karpat also notes that there existed equally powerful internal stimuli that are often overlooked when addressing the changes that occurred in the nineteenth century (Karpat 1972). These changes were of a socio-economic nature and included economic liberalization and the encroachment of external powers into Ottoman markets, and the emergence of a new middle class that was the product of trade and business activities.

3 The Entente Powers were an alignment of France, Russia and Britain. It was not specifically a military alliance, but a collection of bilateral agreements that linked the interests of the three together. The Franco-Russian alliance had been signed in 1894, in response to the appearance of the Triple Alliance of Germany, Austro-Hungary and Italy in 1882. Britain signed the Entente Cordiale with France in 1904, and the signing of the Anglo-Russian Entente in 1907 brought Britain, Russia and France together in an informal association that would form the basis of the alliance that entered the First World War.

4 One of the most important figures in the creation of the Iraqi state, Gertrude Bell was born in County Durham in 1868. She graduated from Oxford University with a first-class degree in history, before embarking on a series of overseas trips, which included destinations in Persia and a stay in Jerusalem in 1900. Due to her knowledge of the Arab world, she was recruited by British Intelligence in the First World War, before serving as a political officer in Mesopotamia as the British forces advanced from Basra to Baghdad. Her diaries, photographs and letters can be accessed at the University of Newcastle's 'Gertrude Bell Project'; available at: <http://www.gerty.ncl.ac.uk/>. Other sources on her life and activities in Iraq include Janet Wallach, *Desert Queen* (London: Weidenfeld and Nicholson, 1996); and Liora Lukitz, *A Quest in the Middle East: Gertrude Bell and the Making of Modern Iraq* (London: I. B. Taurus, 2005).

5 For Wilson's detailed account of his career in Iraq, see his *Loyalties, Mesopotamia 1914–1917: A Personal and Historical Record* (London: Oxford University Press, 1930), and *Mesopotamia 1917–1920: A Clash of Loyalties: A Personal and Historical Record* (London: Oxford University Press, 1931).

Chapter 3 Conceptualizing Political Mobilization in Iraq

1 Considerable tension exists between Shiʿi political parties over whether or not there should be a region in the south. Some groups, including the Sadr Movement led by Muqtada al-Sadr remained resolutely opposed to the concept of federalism, viewing it as a scheme by which Iraq would ultimately be partitioned into smaller independent states. Other groups, most notably the Supreme Council for Islamic Revolution in Iraq (SCIRI), led by Abd al-Aziz al-Hakim, advocated the establishment of a 'super-province' of the nine governorates in the south in which the Shiʿi are in a majority. Such a province would spread to the environs of Baghdad and encompass most of the central and the entirety of the southern region of Iraq. A further viewpoint, held particularly by the Fadilah Party, remained focused upon the immediate south and the city of Basra. Each of these groups had their own political reasons for promoting their agendas.

2 The concept of 'dominant nation' is explained by Andreas Wimmer as being a product of political modernity: 'Political modernity – democracy, constitutionalism, and citizenship – had its price...Inclusion into the national community of solidarity, justice, and democracy went along with exclusion and

domination of those not considered to be true members of the sovereignty/citizenry/nation…we may call the constellation of power in fully nationalised states one of 'dominant nationhood' (Wimmer 2004: 44).

3 Hanna Batatu notes that Mohammed Hadid of the al-Ahali movement had studied at the London School of Economics between 1928 and 1931 and had been influenced by the ideas of Professor Harold Laski, a 'widely known socialist and agnostic' (Batatu 1978: 301).

4 The most notable example of this occurred during the elections of January 2005. Organized by the Kurdistan Referendum Movement, an informal poll was taken of voters that asked 'What do you want?', with the choice being either an Iraqi or Kurdish flag on a ballot paper. Although a rather crude way of surveying public opinion, the result was striking – out of 2.1 million people who participated in the poll, 1.9 million of these had ticked the Kurdish flag. See 'Kurdish Party Says Self-rule is inevitable', Al-Jazeera.net, 2 February 2005. Available at: <http://www.thewe.cc/contents/more/archive2005/february/kurd_independence.htm>.

5 I am choosing to include the Assyrians in the listing of 'ethnic' groups as this is how they themselves choose to be identified. There has been considerable debate, even argument, within the Christian community of Iraq, and particularly between Chaldeans and Assyrians, over whether the Christian community should be recognized in religious or ethnic terms. Generally speaking, Chaldeans have preferred to discuss their identity primarily in confessional terms, whereas the Assyrian community has favoured a focus upon being a distinct nation. The two main churches of the Christian community in Iraq, the Church of the East and the Chaldean Catholic Church, reached agreement in 1994 when the Church of the East Patriarch and Pope John Paul II issued a joint declaration on the doctrine of Christ, followed by an agreement that allowed for mutual admission to the Eucharist between the two churches, signed in 2001. Following this alignment in the religious sphere, the political movements came closer together when, on 24 October 2003, the *Final Declaration of the Chaldean Syriac Assyrian General Conference* stressed the unity of all Christians in Iraq, agreeing to the name 'Chaldoassyrian', recognizing that they are 'an indigenous nationality (people) on a par with the rest of the Iraqi ethnic nationalities'. For further information on this subject, see O'Mahony 2004, and materials in *The Mesopotamian*, the

newsletter of the Assyrian Democratic Movement (ADM); available at: <www.themesopotamian.org>.

6 See *The Mesopotamian*, vol. 1, issue 2, December 2004.

Chapter 4 From Authoritarian to Totalitarian State, 1933–1979

1 Ja'far Pasha was born in Baghdad in 1885. He graduated from Baghdad military college in 1904 before joining the army. He spent three years training with the German army in Berlin, before returning to Constantinople where he and other politicized Arab officers formed the nucleus of the al-Ahd Party (Tarbush 1982: 75). Ja'far Pasha's involvement in the formative years of the Iraqi state illustrates the influences acting upon prominent military figures and Arab nationalists. His memoirs have been published under the title of *A Soldier's Story: From Ottoman Rule to Independent Iraq: The Memoirs of Jafar Pasha Al-Askari* (London: Arabian Publishing, 2003).

2 King Ghazi died on the evening of 3 April 1939, with the official communiqué stating that the king lost control of his car while driving at high speed. The car then crashed into an electricity pylon, which broke and fell on the king's head, causing his death (Khadduri 1951: 137–8).

3 For an outstanding account of the Ba'th Party, see Joseph Sassoon, *Saddam Hussein's Ba'th Party: Inside an Authoritarian Regime* (Cambridge: Cambridge University Press, 2012).

4 Extensive original documents illustrating the mechanisms and actions of the Iraqi security services can be found at the Iraq Research and Documentation Project (IRDP); available at: <http://www.fas.harvard.edu/~irdp/>.

Chapter 5 Iraq at War, 1979–1989

1 The rationale for this was that Iran already had a long coastline on the northern shore of the Gulf, whereas Basra's only access to the sea was via the Shatt (Bakhash 2004: 13).

2 For a first-hand account of the Kurdish rebellion, see Adamson 1964.

3 Following the end of the Kurdish revolution in 1975, Mustafa Barzani lived in exile in Tehran. He flew to the US in August 1975 for health tests which revealed that he was suffering from lung cancer. He spent the next four years lobbying the US government. He died in Washington DC in March 1979. See Korn 1994 for a detailed account of Barzani's final years.

4 For a vivid account of the fate of the Barzanis, and the discovery of their graves following the US-led invasion of Iraq in 2003, see the documentary *Saddam's Road to Hell* made by Gwynne Roberts and Mohammed Ihsan. A transcript of the programme is available at: <http://www.pbs.org/frontlineworld/stories/iraq501/ transcript.html>.

5 For a disturbing account of how the *Anfal* campaign was implemented, see the account of Taimour 'Abdallah, a survivor from the village of Qulatcho, in Kanan Makiya, *Cruelty and Silence: War, Tyranny, Uprising and the Arab World* (London: Penguin Books, 1993).

6 The reflagging of Kuwaiti vessels was, from the US perspective, part of a wider geopolitical move aimed at preventing Soviet naval forces from increasing their presence in the region (Gross Stein 1988: 148).

7 The Iran-Contra affair (otherwise known as Irangate) broke in 1986 after it became apparent that members of the US government, under President Ronald Reagan, had been secretly selling weapons to Iran in order to secure the release of US hostages seized in Lebanon, and using the proceeds to support the Contra rebels in Nicaragua.

8 Marion Farouk-Sluglett and Peter Sluglett note that the Iraqi leadership allocated $5 billion per year to rearmament over the period 1988–92, and $2.5 billion for the construction of 'victory' monuments and a new presidential palace (1990b: 23).

Chapter 6 The Pariah State, 1989–2003

1 A letter from Tariq Aziz to Chadli Kilbi, the Arab League Secretary-General on 15 July 1990 (Hiro 2001: 28; Mohamedou, 1997: 128).

2 UN Department of Humanitarian Affairs (1995), *UN Consolidated Inter-Agency Humanitarian Cooperation Programme for Iraq: Mid-term Review*, 21 September.

3 For a comprehensive account of the impact of UN-imposed sanctions on Iraq, see Graham-Brown 1999.

4 The Kurdish regions were unaffected by this economic volatility. After the uprising and the withdrawal of Saddam's forces from the north, the Kurds chose to keep the old Iraqi dinar (OID) rather than use Saddam's new Iraqi dinar (NID). This elegant solution to their currency predicament meant that the Kurds had a natural anti-inflation mechanism, as it was impossible to print any more OIDs. The 'Kurdish dinar' remained relatively stable, trading at anywhere between 15

and 30 dinar to the dollar over the decade (Stansfield 2003: 49–50).

5 Figures from the UN Office of the Iraqi Programme website; available at: <http://www.un.org/depts/oip>. Also see Niblock 2001, Chapter 14, for an assessment of the oil-for-food programme.

6 Freedman and Stecklow, 'How Iraq Reaps Illegal Oil Profits', *Wall Street Journal*, 2 May 2002, quoted in *Sources of Revenue for Saddam & Sons: A Primer on the Financial Underpinnings of the Regime in Baghdad* (Washington DC: The Coalition for International Justice, September 2002), p. 15.

7 *Sources of Revenue*, pp. 27–35.

8 *Sources of Revenue*, pp. 35–49.

9 See <http://www.whitehouse.gov/news/releases/2002/01/20020129-11.html> for the 2002 'State of the Union' address, which refers to Iraq as being a member of the 'axis of evil'.

10 While impressive in terms of the number of nations it included, the 'Coalition of the Willing' was far less impressive in terms of the military expertise of the majority of its members. Of the forty-five nations supporting the US, only thirty were prepared to do so publicly – Afghanistan, Albania, Australia, Azerbaijan, Bulgaria, Colombia, the Czech Republic, Denmark, El Salvador, Eritrea, Estonia, Ethiopia, Georgia, Hungary, Italy, Japan, Latvia, Lithuania, Macedonia, the Netherlands, Nicaragua, the Philippines, Poland, Romania, Slovakia, South Korea, Spain, Turkey, UK and Uzbekistan. However, many of these countries simply did not have the capacity to send troops to Iraq, with the result that virtually all of the Coalition combat forces were Anglo-American. For example, after the 260,000 Americans and 40,000 British, the next largest contingent was the 2,000 Australians. Unlike 1991, no Arab state openly supported the invasion of Iraq, and the Turkish legislature refused to allow US forces to enter Iraq from Turkish territory to establish a second, northern front in the war. The war split the traditional Western alliance created after the Second World War, with North Atlantic Treaty Organization (NATO) members Belgium, Canada and Norway, as well as France and Germany, refusing to join the US-led coalition.

11 See Dawood 2003 for a discussion about Iraqi tribes.

Chapter 7 Regime Change, 2003–2007

1 There is an obvious problem with describing Iraq as 'multi-ethnic', as this term can only accurately reflect ethnic divisions

in society, and does not adequately portray different religions (i.e., Islam and Christianity), nor sectarian differences within religions (e.g., between Sunni and Shi'i Muslims, and Assyrian and Chaldean Christians). This is particularly problematic as religious association exists irrespective of ethnic origin (e.g., approximately 15 per cent of Kurds are Shi'i, 80 per cent are Sunni). The term *plural society*, developed by Arend Lijphart, is perhaps more appropriate to the situation of Iraq. He defines plural societies in such a way 'that political parties, interest groups, media of communication, schools, and voluntary associations tend to be organized along the lines of segmental cleavages… [such] cleavages may be of a religious, ideological, linguistic, regional, cultural, racial, or ethnic nature' (Lijphart 1977: 3–4, quoted by Steiner 1981: 340). Most literature, however, employs the term 'multi-ethnic', incorporating ethnic and sectarian groups irrespectively.

2 For news reports about the killing of Uday and Qusay Saddam Hussein, see Julian Borger and Gary Younge, 'Dead: The Sons of Saddam' in the *Guardian*, 23 June 2003 (available at: <http://www.guardian.co.uk/Iraq/Story/0,,1004168,00.html>); and 'The Brothers Grim' in *The New York Times*, 23 June 2003. For reports on the capture of Saddam Hussein, see 'Saddam Hussein Arrested in Iraq', posted on the BBC website on 14 December 2003, available at: <http://news.bbc.co.uk/1/hi/world/middle_east/3317429.stm>;, and Peter Grier, 'Anatomy of Saddam Hussein's Capture', *The Christian Science Monitor*, 15 December 2003, available at: <http://www.csmonitor.com/2003/1215/p01s01-woiq.html>.

3 For a graphic description of the US drive towards Baghdad, and the problems faced by 'bypassing' territory, see Wright 2004.

4 It is not totally true to say that no planning had taken place; rather, it seems, planning had occurred only to be discarded later. As far back as 2002, the State Department had organized workshops of more than 200 Iraqi exiles and US officials. This 'Democratic Principles Working Group' met under the auspices of the 'Future of Iraq Project', and drafted a fifteen-volume study covering the range of issues to be faced in the immediate post-Saddam environment, including transitional justice, economy and infrastructure, and public health. The Pentagon effectively shelved the report, ignoring its recommendations. However, in his account of his year in Iraq, Paul Bremer claims that the report was never intended to act as a plan, but was, rather bizarrely, merely a strategy to 'engage Iraqi-Americans to think about

their country's future' (ICG 2004; Bremer 2006: 25; Diamond 2005: 28). The final report of the group can be found at: <www.iraqfoundation.org/studies/2002/dec/study.pdf>.

5 The Shi'i members of the IGC were: Abd al-Aziz al-Hakim (SCIRI); Mohammed Bahr al-Ulloum (Najaf cleric); Ezzadine Salim (Da'wa); Ibrahim al-Ja'afari (Da'wa); Abd al-Karim al-Mohammedawi (Iraqi Hizballah); Mouwafak al-Ruba'i; Ahmed Chalabi (INC); Ahmed al-Barak; Hamid Majid Mousa (ICP); Raja Habib al-Khuza'i; Aquila al-Hashimi (assassinated 23 September 2003); Iyad Allawi (INA); Wael Abd al-Latif. The Sunni members of the IGC were: Adnan Pachachi; Nasser al-Chaderchi (National Democratic Party); Samir Shakir Mahmoud; Ghazi Al-Yawer; Muhsin Abd al-Hamid (Iraqi Islamic Party); Dara a Noor al-Zin. The Kurdish members of the IGC were: Jalal Talabani (PUK); Massoud Barzani (KDP); Mahmoud Othman (independent); Salahadin Ba'ahadin (Kurdistan Islamic Union). The Assyrian member was Younadam Kana (Assyrian Democratic Movement), and the Turkmen representative was Sondul Chapouk (Anderson and Stansfield 2005: 252–3).

6 See Askold Krushelnycky, 'Iraq: At Least 11 Dead In Jordanian Embassy Bombing In Baghdad', *Radio Free Europe/Radio Liberty*, 7 August 2003; 'Top UN Official among Dead in Baghdad Blast', *Guardian*, 19 August 2003, available at: <http://www.guardian.co.uk/international/story/0,,1021792,00.html>.

7 See Anton La Guardia, 'Charismatic Cleric was Central to US Strategy', *Telegraph*, 30 August 2003; available at: <http://www.telegraph.co.uk/news/main.jhtml?xml=/news/2003/08/30/wirq230.xml>. Indicating the complexity of the political situation in Iraq, virtually every Iraqi political grouping and intelligence service of the Middle East region and the occupying powers was implicated in a series of conspiracy theories surrounding the assassination of Ayatollah Mohammed Bakr al-Hakim. The involvement of Iran was speculated, with the move being a warning to SCIRI not to get too close to the US. The hand of Israel's Mossad was seen by some as being behind the attack, in an attempt to provoke further instability in Iraq, and Muqtada Sadr was of course blamed in certain quarters.

8 The Transitional Administrative Law can be accessed at: <http://www.cpa-iraq.org/government/TAL.html>.

9 The spread of the Sadr Movement was remarkable. Even in the north, Sadr's representatives had managed to assemble

significant forces. I met with one of Sadr's lieutenants, Sayyid Abd al-Fattah al-Mousawi, in Kirkuk the day before the rebellion broke out. The presence of Jaish al-Mahdi units this far north, and in considerable numbers, suggests that the Sadr Movement had strong support among Turkmens and Arab Shiʿi in Kirkuk, if not the Kurds.

10 This information comes from interviews with IMK members in London and Iraq.

11 See John F. Burns, 'The Conflict in Iraq: Threats to Voters', in the *New York Times*, 24 January 2005; available at: <http://query.nytimes.com/gst/fullpage.html?res=9B05E1D81E38F937A15752COA9639C8B63&pagewanted=all>.

12 See Lionel Beehner, 'Iraq: Cabinet Ministers', *Council on Foreign Relations*, 12 May 2005, for a full listing of the ministers of the Jaʿafari cabinet; available at: <http://www.cfr.org/publication.html?id=8061#1>.

13 For analyses of the federal possibilities for Iraq's future, see Anderson and Stansfield (2005), 'The Implications of Elections for Federalism in Iraq: Toward a Five-Region Model', *Publius: The Journal of Federalism* 35/3: 1–24; and contributions in Brendan O'Leary et. al. (eds) (2005), *The Future of Kurdistan in Iraq* (Philadelphia, PA: University of Pennsylvania Press).

14 See Jonathan Steele, 'Iraq Constitution Yes Vote Approved by UN', *Guardian*, 26 October 2005; available at: <http://www.guardian.co.uk/Iraq/Story/0,,1600512,00.html>.

15 Simon Freeman, 'Sunnis and Kurds Plot to Oust Iraqi Leader', in *The Times*, 2 March 2006; available at: <http://www.timesonline.co.uk/article/0,,7374-2066102_1,00.html>.

Chapter 8 From the Brink to the Brink, 2007–2014

1 Stephen Biddle, Jeffrey A. Friedman and Jacob N. Shapiro, 'Testing the Surge: Why Did Violence Decline in Iraq in 2007?', *International Security* 37/1 (summer 2012): 7–40.

2 See James Baker and Lee Hamilton, *Iraq Study Group Report* (New York: Random House, 2006); available at: <http://media.usip.org/reports/iraq_study_group_report.pdf>.

3 Toby Dodge, *Iraq: From War to a New Authoritarianism* (London: International Institute for Strategic Studies/Routledge, 2012), pp. 75–6.

4 Ibid., p. 80.

5 For further details on the concepts of hybridity and compromised peacebuilding, see Michael Barnett, Songying Fang and

Christoph Zurcher, 'Compromised Peacebuilding', *International Studies Quarterly* 58 (2014): 608–20; Roger MacGinty, 'Hybrid Peace: The Interaction Between Top-Down and Bottom-Up Peace', *Security Dialogue* 41/4 (August 2010): 391–412.

6 Department of the Army, *Counter-Insurgency Field Manual*, FM 3–24 (Washington DC: Headquarters, Department of the Army, 2006), quoted in Dodge 2012, *Iraq: From War to a New Authoritarianism*, p. 81.

7 See Nir Rosen, 'The Great Divide', *The National*, 5 June 2008; available at: <http://www.thenational.ae/news/world/middle-east/the-great-divide>.

8 For a fast-paced account of the life and career of Abu Bakr Al-Baghdadi, see William McCants, 'The Believer: How an Introvert with a Passion for Religion and Soccer Became Abu Bakr Al-Baghdadi, Leader of the Islamic State', *Brookings Essay*, 1 September. Washington DC: The Brookings Institute, 2015a; available at: <http://www.brookings.edu/research/essays/2015/thebeliever>.

9 For highly detailed accounts of the circumstances that led to the Anbar Awakening and the US military involvement, see Timothy Williams and Kurtis Wheeler (eds), *Al-Anbar Awakening: Volume I: American Perspectives: US Marines and Counterinsurgency in Iraq, 2004-2009* (Quantico, VA: Marine Corps University, 2009); Gary Montgomery and Timothy Williams (eds), *Al-Anbar Awakening: Volume II: Iraqi Perspectives: From Insurgency to Counterinsurgency in Iraq* (Quantico, VA: Marine Corps University, 2009).

10 For the importance of the 1920 revolution as a founding myth of the modern state of Iraq, see Abbas Khadhim, *Reclaiming Iraq: The 1920 Revolution and the Founding of the Modern State* (Austin, TX: University of Texas Press, 2012).

11 For an enlightening account of Maliki's background, see Ali Khedery, 'Why We Stuck with Maliki – and Lost Iraq', *Washington Post*, 3 July 2014. Available at: <https://www.washingtonpost.com/opinions/why-we-stuck-with-maliki–and-lost-iraq/2014/07/03/0dd6a8a4-f7ec-11e3-a606-946fd632f9f1_story.html>.

12 Ibid.

13 Nicholas Krohley, *The Death of the Mahdi Army: The Rise, Fall, and Revival of Iraq's Most Powerful Militia* (London: C. Hurst & Co., 2015), p. 3. Maliki's complicity in the Jaish al-Mahdi's role in the conflict of 2007 was strongly evidenced by

his blocking of the US military's ability to target key Sadr lieutenants, banning operations against them without his consent. See Dodge (2012), *Iraq: From War to a New Authoritarianism*, p. 102.

14 Krohley (2015), *The Death of the Mahdi Army*, p. 3; David Ucko, 'Militias, Tribes and Insurgents: The Challenge of Political Reintegration in Iraq', *Conflict, Security & Development*, October 2008, pp. 361–2.

15 Richard Iron, 'The Charge of the Knights', *The RUSI Journal* 158/1 (2013): 54–62.

16 Ibid.

17 Dodge (2012), *Iraq: From War to a New Authoritarianism*, pp. 149–50.

18 See Leila Fadel and Karen de Young, 'Ayad Allawi's Bloc Wins Most Seats in Iraqi Parliamentary Elections', *Washington Post Foreign Service*, 27 March 2010. Available at: <http://www.washingtonpost.com/wpdyn/content/article/2010/03/26/AR2010032602196.html>.

19 See Gareth Stansfield, 'Reading the Elections in Iraq', *RUSI Newsbrief*, 19 May 2014a. Available at: <https://www.rusi.org/go.php?structureID=articles_newsbrief&ref=A537A2607577F6#.VA2Aq0u0bfM>.

20 Dodge (2012), *Iraq: From War to a New Authoritarianism*, p. 162.

21 Dexter Filkins, 'Is Bush Right about Clinton and Iraq?', *New Yorker*, 13 August 2015. Available at: <http://www.newyorker.com/news/daily-comment/is-bush-right-about-clinton-and-iraq>.

22 Barbara F. Walter, 'The Critical Barrier to Civil War Settlement', *International Organization* 51/3 (1997): 335–64, quoted at p. 336.

23 For differing analyses of the Constitution, see Brendan O'Leary, *How To Get Out of Iraq with Integrity* (Philadelphia, PA: University of Pennsylvania Press, 2009), particularly Chapter 6; and Haider Ala Hamoudi, *Negotiating in Civil Conflict: Constitutional Construction and Imperfect Bargaining in Iraq* (Chicago, IL: University of Chicago Press, 2014).

24 Dodge (2012), *Iraq: From War to a New Authoritarianism*, p. 164.

25 Adrian Blomfield and Damien McElroy, 'Iraq in Fresh Turmoil as Prime Minister Nouri al-Maliki Orders Arrest of Vice President', *Telegraph*, 19 December 2011; available at: <http://www.telegraph.co.uk/news/worldnews/middleeast/iraq/8966587/Iraq-in-fresh-turmoil-as-Prime-Minister-Nuri

-al-Maliki-orders-arrest-of-vice-president.html>; 'Iraq: Maliki Power Grab Risks Fresh Civil War', *Strategic Comments* 18/3, 4 May 2012; available at: <http://www.iiss.org/en/publications/strategic%20comments/sections/2012-bb59/iraq--maliki-power-grab-risk-fresh-civil-war-0818>.

26 See text of Article 58 of the TAL, in Liam Anderson and Gareth Stansfield, *Crisis in Kirkuk: The Ethnopolitics of Conflict and Compromise* (Philadelphia, PA: University of Pennsylvania Press, 2009), p. 114. For further discussion of the politics surrounding Article 140, see Rex Zedalis, *Oil and Gas in the Disputed Kurdish Territories: Jurisprudence, Regional Minorities and Natural Resources in a Federal System* (London: Routledge, 2012).

27 Ibid., p. 179.

28 See Wisam Mohammed and Sherko Maruf, 'Iraq Kurds and Government End Standoff over Northern Town', *Reuters*, 3 September 2008; available at: <http://uk.reuters.com/article/2008/09/03/us-iraq-khanaqin-idUKL365141120080903>.

29 For an analysis tying the oil dispute to the question of federalism, see Raad Alkadiri, 'Oil and the Question of Federalism in Iraq', *International Affairs* 86/6 (November 2010): 1315–28.

30 See, for example, Ned Parker, 'Kurdish Leader Sees Authoritarian Drift in Iraq', *Los Angeles Times*, 11 January 2009, available at: <http://articles.latimes.com/2009/jan/11/world/fg-iraq-barzani11>; Quil Lawrence, 'A Precarious Peace in Northern Iraq', *MERIP Middle East Report*, 1 October 2009, available at: <http://www.merip.org/mero/mero100109>.

31 See Yaniv Voller, 'Kurdish Oil Politics in Iraq: Contested Sovereignty and Unilateralism', *Middle East Policy* XX/1 (spring 2013), pp. 68–82; and 'Chevron Acquires Interest in Kurdistan Concessions', *Chevron Press Release*, 19 July 2012, available at: <http://www.chevron.com/chevron/pressreleases/article/07192012_chevronacquiresinterestinkurdistanconcessions.news>.

32 See Gareth Stansfield, 'Tension on the Trigger-Line', *RUSI Analysis*, 26 November 2012, available at: <https://www.rusi.org/analysis/commentary/ref:C50B3567FBD21E/#.VdM0pni1hRo>; and 'The Unravelling of the post-First World War State System? The Kurdistan Region of Iraq and the Transformation of the Middle East', *International Affairs* 89/2 (2013): 259–82.

33 See Gareth Stansfield (2014b), 'Kurdistan Rising: To Acknowledge or Ignore the Unraveling of Iraq', *Brookings Institute Middle East Memo* 33 (July). Available at: <http://www.brookings.edu/~/media/research/files/papers/2014/07/kurdistan-iraq-isis-0731/kurdistan-iraq-isis-stansfield-0731.pdf>.

34 See 'Iraqi President Jalal Talabani "in Coma after Stroke" ', *BBC News Middle East*, 18 December 2012; available at: <http://www.bbc.co.uk/news/world-middle-east-20766435>.

35 See Kamal Naama, 'Sunni Protesters Attack Iraq Official's Convoy, Guards Wound Two', *Reuters*, 30 December 2012; available at: <http://uk.reuters.com/article/2012/12/30/uk-iraq-protests-idUKBRE8BT04A20121230>.

36 The term *safavi* refers to the Safavid dynasty of Iran that enforced the conversion of Iran to Shiʿism in the sixteenth century. Patrick Cockburn notes that Sunni militants have used the term to refer to Iraqi Shiʿi in general, and to the *safavi* Iraqi government, as 'a derogatory term... to imply that Iraqi Shia are Iranian pawns. Saddam Hussein spat out the words at his tormentors before he went to the gallows.' See Patrick Cockburn, *Muqtada: Muqtada al-Sadr, the Shia Revival, and the Struggle for Iraq* (New York: Simon & Schuster, 2008), p. 25.

37 See, for example, a video uploaded by Sunni demonstrators at Hawijah on 23 April 2014, showing Iraqi security forces desecrating the bodies of Sunni protestors; available at: <http://www.youtube.com/watch?v=VcpVS7J-Rks>.

Chapter 9 The Islamic State, the Kurdistan Region and Shiʿi Iraq

1 While its violently exclusionist behaviour has rendered detailed research on ISIS near impossible to undertake, several detailed analyses of ISIS have emerged in the months following the taking of Mosul. Some of the most insightful of these early attempts to make sense of ISIS include: Patrick Cockburn, *The Rise of Islamic State: ISIS and the New Sunni Revolution* (London: Verso, 2014); Charles Lister, 'Profiling the Islamic State', *Analysis Paper* 13 (Doha: Brookings Doha Center, November 2014); Charles Lister, *The Syrian Jihad: Al-Qaeda, the Islamic State and the Evolution of an Insurgency* (London: Hurst & Co., 2015); Ahmed S. Hashim, 'The Islamic State: From Al-Qaeda Affiliate to Caliphate', *Middle East Policy* XXI/4 (winter 2014): 69–83; Michael Weiss and Hassan Hassan, *ISIS: Inside the Army of Terror* (New York: Regan Arts, 2015); Jessica Stern and J. M. Berger, *ISIS: The State of Terror* (London: William Collins, 2015); William McCants, *The ISIS Apocalypse: The History, Strategy, and Doomsday Vision of the Islamic State* (New York: St Martin's Press, 2015b).

2 Tawhid was originally named Jund al-Sham. See Lister (2015), *The Syrian Jihad*, p. 6.
3 The KRI has always had Islamist parties in its political mix, with the Islamic Movement of Kurdistan (IMK) being the strongest of these until the late 1990s. Extremist, militant Islamist groups emerged in 2001. Following the splintering of the relatively mainstream Islamic Movement of Kurdistan (IMK) in 2001, a grouping of younger members demanded that a *jihad* be launched against the KDP and PUK. These extremists, led by Abu Abdullah al-Shafiʿi formed the Jund al-Islam in August 2001, which then merged with a range of other Kurdish militant groups opposed to the KDP and PUK, including Kurdish HAMAS, Islamic Tawhid, and Hezi Du Soran. Together, these groups united to form Ansar al-Islam under the leadership of Mulla Krekar, with funds reportedly coming from Osama bin Laden himself. See Gareth Stansfield, 'Finding a Dangerous Equilibrium: Internal Politics in Iraqi Kurdistan – Parties, Tribes, Religion and Ethnicity Reconsidered', in Faleh Jabar and Hosham Dawod (eds), *The Kurds: Nationalism and Politics* (London: Saqi, 2006), pp. 258–76.
4 Lister (2015), *The Syrian Jihad* p. 7.
5 Ibid., p. 8.
6 Ibid., and Weiss and Hassan (2015), *ISIS: Inside the Army of Terror*, p. 62.
7 Weiss and Hassan (2015), *ISIS: Inside the Army of Terror*, p. 61.
8 Patrick Cockburn, 'Middle East Leader of the Year? You'd Be Surprised…', *Independent*, 22 December 2013; available at: <http://www.independent.co.uk/voices/comment/middle-east-leader-of-the-year-youd-be-surprised-9020089.html>.
9 William McCants, 'The Believer: How an Introvert with a Passion for Religion and Soccer became Abu Bakr al-Baghdadi, Leader of the Islamic State', *The Brookings Essay* (Washington DC: The Brookings Institution, 2015a); available at: <http://www.brookings.edu/research/essays/2015/thebeliever>.
10 Stern and Berger (2015), *ISIS: The State of Terror*, p. 38.
11 Lister (2015), *The Syrian Jihad*, p. 12.
12 For a comprehensive account of Syria's involvement with *jihadist* movements in Iraq, see Charles Lister, *The Syrian Jihad: Al-Qaeda, the Islamic State and the Evolution of an Insurgency* (London: Hurst & Co., 2015), pp. 31–50.
13 See Hannah Smith, 'Warnings on Iraq ISIS Attack Ignored – KRG Official', *Asharq al-Awsat*, 20 June 2014; available at:

<http://www.aawsat.net/2014/06/article55333445/warnings-on-iraq-isis-attack-ignored-krg-official>.

14 Gareth Stansfield (2014c), 'The New Rules of the Game in Iraq', *RUSI Analysis*, 18 June; available at: <https://www.rusi.org/go.php?structureID=commentary&ref=C53A1ADAD87078#.VdXWo3i1hRo>.

15 Gareth Stansfield (2014d), 'The Islamic State, the Kurdistan Region, and the Future of Iraq: Assessing UK Policy Options', *International Affairs* 90/6 (November): 1329–50.

16 The People's Protection Units and the Democratic Union Party are commonly referred to by their Kurdish-derived acronyms of the YPG (Yekîneyên Parastina Gel) and PYD (Partiya Yekîtiya Demokrat) respectively. For more information concerning Syrian Kurdish political parties and militias, see Harriet Allsopp, *The Kurds of Syria: Political Parties and Identity in the Middle East* (London: I. B. Tauris, 2014); Michael Gunter, *Out of Nowhere: The Kurds of Syria in Peace and War* (London: Hurst & Co., 2014); Robert Lowe, 'The Emergence of Western Kurdistan and the Future of Syria', in David Romano and Mehmet Gurses (eds), *Conflict, Democratization and the Kurds in the Middle East* (New York: Palgrave Macmillan, 2014). For an analysis of the Kurds of Syria in a broader historical context, see Jordi Tejel, *Syria's Kurds: History, Politics and Society* (London: Routledge, 2009).

17 Rick Noack, 'Here's how the Islamic State compares with real states', *Washington Post*, 12 September 2014; available at: <https://www.washingtonpost.com/blogs/worldviews/wp/2014/09/12/heres-how-the-islamic-state-compares-to-real-states>.

18 See 'da'ish tu'linu qiyam al-khilafa al-islamiya wa tabaya'u al-Baghdadi khalifa' [ISIS announces the Caliphate and pledges allegiance to Baghdadi as the Caliph], *Al-Quds Al-Arabi*, 29 June 2014; available at: <http://www.alquds.co.uk/?p=186538>.

19 See 'Iraq: Kurdish President Proposes Independence Referendum', *Guardian*, 3 July 2014, available at: <http://www.theguardian.com/world/2014/jul/03/iraq-kurdish-president-barzani-proposes-independence-referendum>.

20 Personal communication to the author.

21 See Mustafa al-Kadhimi, 'Will Sistani be able to Control Popular Mobilization Forces?', *Al-Monitor*, 12 March 2015; available at: <http://www.al-monitor.com/ pulse/originals/2015/03/iraq-sistani-righteous-jihad-fatwa-popular-mobilization.html#>.

Chronology

Before 1920

9000–5000 BC	Early farming communities begin cultivation of wild wheat and barley and domestication of animals
5000–3500 BC	Ubaid people develop villages and build first religious shrines
3500–1900 BC	Sumerians settle on the banks of the Euphrates; develop kingships and hereditary monarchies
1900–500 BC	Babylonian and Assyrian period
550 BC	Rise of the Persian Achaemenid empire
247 BC–224 AD	Parthian empire rules today's Iran and Iraq
224–661	Sasanian period
610	Prophet Mohammed experienced his first revelations from God
632	Mohammed dies
637	Battle of Qadisiyya; Islamic conquest of Iraq
750–1258	Abbasid Caliphate
1258–1353	Ilkhanate period
1411–1469	Qara Qoyunlu dynasty
1465–1508	Aq Qoyunlu dynasty
1508–1534	Safavid rule
1534–1918	Ottoman rule

First World War and After

November 1914	British forces occupy Basra and Fao
1915	Constantinople Agreement between Britain, France and Russia

3 January 1916	'Sykes-Picot' Agreement planning the partition of the Ottoman empire
1917	Baghdad falls to British forces
22 May 1919	Kurdish Sheikh Mahmoud Barzinji rebels against the British in Suleimaniyya
April 1920	San Remo Peace Conference; mandate power granted to Britain over Palestine, Transjordan and Mesopotamia
2 June 1920	Start of the 1920 Revolt
10 August 1920	Treaty of Sèvres, recognizing Kurdistan
March 1921	Cairo Conference
July 1921	Plebiscite on King Faisal I
27 August 1921	Faisal I installed as king
July 1923	Treaty of Lausanne, reneging upon the Treaty of Sèvres
16 December 1925	League of Nations awards the Mosul *vilayet* to Iraq
1927	British strike oil at Kirkuk
16 November 1930	Anglo-Iraqi Treaty ratified
October 1932	Iraq becomes formally independent
8 September 1933	King Faisal I dies; succeeded by his son, Ghazi
1933	Massacre of Assyrians at Sumayl, headed by Bakr Sidqi
October 1936	Bakr Sidqi military coup
11 August 1937	Bakr Sidqi assassinated
December 1938	Nuri al-Sa'id made prime minister
April 1939	Death of King Ghazi in a car crash; his four-year-old son crowned as Faisal II, with his uncle, Abd al-Illah, appointed regent
September 1939	Second World War commences
1 April 1 1941	Rashid Ali coup
2 May 1941	Britain invades Iraq; Rashid Ali flees to Tehran
14 July 1958	Qasim coup; King Faisal, Abd al-Illah and Nuri al-Sa'id killed; Brigadier Abd al-Karim Qasim made prime minister of Iraq
1959	Return to Iraq of Kurdish leader Mulla Mustafa Barzani, previously exiled in the USSR

July 1959	Qasim's alliance with the ICP breaks down; fighting in Kirkuk; ICP members persecuted
7 October 1959	Failed Ba'th assassination attempt on Qasim; Saddam Hussein involved and flees to Egypt
September 1961	Kurdish autonomy plan proposed by Barzani and KDP rejected by Qasim; Kurdish rebellion commences
8 February 1963	Qasim overthrown by military-Ba'th Party coup led by Abd al-Salim Arif; Qasim executed
18 November 1963	Arif removes Ba'th Party from positions of power
18 April 1966	Arif dies in helicopter crash; his brother, Abd al-Rahman Arif, succeeds him as president
17 July 1968	Second Ba'th coup led by Ahmed Hassan al-Bakr
November 1969	Saddam Hussein appointed deputy chair of the RCC
11 March 1970	Kurdish autonomy agreed by the 'March 11 manifesto'
1 December 1971	Britain withdraws from the Gulf
March 1974	Negotiations with Kurds collapse; Kurds rebel with Iranian support
6 March 1975	Algiers Agreement between Iraq and Iran ends Iranian support to Kurds and reaches agreement on Shatt al-Arab waterway that is favourable to Iran
16 July 1979	Saddam Hussein succeeds al-Bakr as president; Bakr dies in 1982
8 April 1980	Iraqi security services arrest the leader of Hizb al-Da'wa, Ayatollah Mohammed Bakr al-Sadr, and his sister, Bint al-Huda, following assassination attempt on Deputy Prime Minister Tariq Aziz; 40,000 Shi'is expelled to Iran; Ayatollah Khomeini calls for the Ba'th regime to be overthrown
September 1980	Start of the Iran–Iraq War
4 September 1980	Iran shells Iraqi border towns

17 September 1980	Iraq abrogates the 1975 treaty with Iran
22 September 1980	Iraq attacks Iranian air bases
7 June 1981	Israel attacks an Iraqi nuclear research centre near Baghdad
February 1986	Iran captures Fao peninsula
16 March 1988	Iraqi military attacks Kurdish town of Halabja with chemical weapons, killing an estimated 4,000 people; the *Anfal* Campaign of 1988–89 kills an estimated 180,000 Kurds and destroys some 4,000 villages
16 April 1988	Iraq recaptures Fao peninsula, using chemical weapons
20 July 1988	Iran accepts UN-brokered ceasefire; Iran–Iraq War ends
2 August 1990	Iraq invades Kuwait; UN SCR 660 calls for Iraq's immediate withdrawal
6 August 1990	UN SCR 661 is passed placing Iraq under sanctions
8 November 1990	US troop presence in Saudi Arabia increased to 400,000
29 November 1990	UN SCR 678 authorizes member states to use 'all means necessary' to impose earlier resolutions once a deadline of 15 January 1991 has passed
12 January 1991	US Senate authorizes use of force by US military
15 January 1991	UN issues Iraqi government with an ultimatum to withdraw from Kuwait
17 January 1991	Operation Desert Storm – the liberation of Kuwait – commences
28 February 1991	Desert Storm ceasefire
March–April 1991	Shi'i *intifadah* and Kurdish *rapareen* break out in south and north of the country; revolts crushed by Iraqi Republican Guard; 1.5 million Kurds flee to the mountainous areas of the Iraq–Turkey border
3 April 1991	UN SCR 687 establishes terms of ceasefire and stipulates the formation of UNSCOM to ensure Iraq's WMD programmes are terminated

May 1992	Elections held for the Kurdistan National Assembly (KNA); Kurdistan Regional Government (KRG) formed by an alliance of the KDP and PUK
June 1992	Iraqi National Congress (INC) established in Vienna, Austria
May 1994	KDP and PUK fall into civil war in Kurdistan; KDP expelled from the Kurdish capital Erbil
14 April 1995	UN SCR 986 establishes the terms of the 'oil-for-food' programme
7 August 1995	Defection of Hussein and Saddam Kamil to Jordan
26 June 1996	Attempted INA coup fails
28 June 1996	Iranian incursion into Kurdistan Region attacks Iranian Kurdish group based in Koysanjaq
31 August 1996	KDP invites Iraqi government into Kurdistan to remove Iranian threat; KDP occupies Erbil; Iraqi forces destroy INC base at Qushtapa, killing several hundred militiamen; PUK leadership evacuates to Iran
September, 1996	PUK counterattacks; peace process brokered by US; KDP left in control of Erbil; PUK maintains hold over Suleimaniyya
10 December 1996	First oil flows as part of UN SCR 986
29 October 1997	Iraq demands withdrawal of UNSCOM inspectors
13 November 1997	Inspectors withdrawn (but return one month later)
October 1998	UNSCOM report shows that Iran has weaponized VX nerve agent
1 November 1998	Iraq ceases cooperation with UNSCOM
17–20 December 1998	Operation Desert Fox – US and British aerial bombardment of Iraq following UNSCOM reporting Iraq's failure to cooperate with inspectors
19 February 1999	Grand Ayatollah Mohammad Sadiq al-Sadr assassinated in Najaf
17 December 1999	UN SCR 1284 establishes UNMOVIC
November 2000	Iraq refuses to allow UNMOVIC inspectors into country

11 September 2001	Attacks by al-Qaeda on US; speculation grows about Iraq's involvement – later shown to be false
October 2001	*Tawhid* organization of Abu Musab al-Zarqawi relocates to Afghanistan from Jordan
29 January 2002	Iraq identified by US President George W. Bush as being part of the 'axis of evil', along with Iran and North Korea
March–August 2002	Talks take place regarding allowing UNMOVIC inspectors into Iraq
September 2002	Iraq allows inspections on the condition that they are not tied to new resolutions
22 September 2002	UK Prime Minister Tony Blair releases dossier showing that Iraq has significant WMD capabilities
8 November 2002	UN SCR 1441 calls on Iraq to cooperate with UNMOVIC inspectors; Iraq must also declare all WMD by 8 December; UNMOVIC enters Iraq and begins work
7 December 2002	Iraq submits documentation to satisfy UN SCR 1441 claiming that Iraq has disposed of its WMD; US remains unconvinced

After 2003

7 March 2003	UNMOVIC chief Hans Blix reports to UN Security Council
19 March 2003	'Second Iraq War' begins with US raid on Baghdad; US ground forces invade from south
9 April 2003	Baghdad falls to US forces
April–May 2003	*Tawhid* of Zarqawi emerges as a prominent insurgent group
1 May 2003	President Bush declares 'mission accomplished'
14 July 2003	First meeting of US-appointed Iraqi Governing Council (IGC)
22 July 2003	Uday and Qusay Saddam Hussein killed in action against US troops in Mosul

19 August 2003	UN compound in Baghdad destroyed by suicide bomber from al-Qaeda in Iraq, led by Abu Musab al-Zarqawi; head of UN mission Sergio Vieira de Mello killed
29 August 2003	Explosion in Najaf kills leader of SCIRI, Ayatollah Mohammed Bakr al-Hakim; *Tawhid* of Zarqawi claims responsibility for the attack
16 October 2003	UN SCR 1511 recognizes legitimacy of the US-supported provisional Iraqi government
14 December 2003	Saddam Hussein captured
February 2004	More than 100 killed in Erbil in suicide attacks on offices of KDP and PUK
1 March 2004	Transitional Administrative Law (TAL) agreed by interim government
2 March 2004	Suicide bombings kill 140 Shiʿi worshippers in Baghdad and Karbala during *Ashura*
April 2004	First Sadr uprising led by Muqtada al-Sadr; fighting breaks out in Fallujah
28 June 2004	Prime Minister Iyad Allawi receives Iraq's sovereignty from Paul Bremer of the CPA
September 2004	Zarqawi pledges allegiance of *Tawhid* to al-Qaeda, creating al-Qaeda Iraq (AQI)
November 2004	Coalition forces attack Fallujah
30 January 2005	Elections held for the Transitional National Assembly
April 2005	Jalal Talabani selected by the TNA to be president of Iraq; Ibrahim al-Jaʿafari named as prime minister
June 2005	Massoud Barzani sworn in as president of the Kurdistan Region
July 2005	Study assembled by the Iraqi Body Count organization estimates that as many as 25,000 Iraqi civilians have been killed since March 2003
October 2005	Trial of Saddam Hussein begins; new constitution approved by referendum
November 2005	Suicide bombers target mosques in Khanaqin, killing at least seventy-four people

15 December 2005	Iraqis vote for the first full-term government and parliament since the US-led invasion
4–5 January 2006	More than 150 people are killed in suicide bombings and attacks targeting Karbala, Ramadi, Miqdadiya and Baghdad
20 January 2006	Shia-led United Iraqi Alliance emerges as the winner of December's parliamentary elections, but fails to gain an absolute majority
February 2006 onwards	Bomb attack on the Shiʿi Askariyya shrine in Samarra unleashes a wave of sectarian violence in which hundreds of people are killed
7 April 2006	More than seventy people killed when three suicide bombers attack a Shiʿi mosque in Baghdad
22 April 2006	Newly re-elected President Talabani asks Shiʿi compromise candidate Jawad al-Maliki to form a new government, ending four months of political deadlock
6 June 2006	AQI leader Zarqawi killed by US air strike; replaced by Abu Omar al-Baghdadi
Summer 2006	AQI renamed the Islamic State of Iraq (ISI); no pledge of allegiance given to al-Qaeda
October 2006	ISI declares an Islamic emirate in Iraq
30 December 2006	Saddam Hussein executed by hanging, in front of a baying crowd of supporters chanting Muqtada al-Sadr's name
31 December 2006	Total of American military deaths since the March 2003 invasion reaches 3,000
10 June 2007	US commanders unveil a strategy to arm Sunni Arab groups fighting al-Qaeda, otherwise known as the Awakening Movement
29 August 2007	Muqtada al-Sadr announces six-month suspension of military activities of the Jaish al-Mahdi militia
31 December 2007	Deadline expires for implementing Article 140 of the Constitution, to resolve the status of Kirkuk and other disputed territories

24 March 2008	Prime Minister Maliki orders the ISF 'Charge of the Knights' operation against the Jaish al-Mahdi in Basra
30 June 2009	US troops withdraw from Iraqi cities into remote bases
7 March 2010	Parliament elections across Iraq gives a narrow victory to the Iraqiyya coalition, but incumbent Prime Minister Maliki of the dawlat al-qanun coalition refuses to hand over power
18 April 2010	Leader of ISI, Abu Omar al-Baghdadi, killed in Tikrit; replaced by Abu Bakr al-Baghdadi
31 August 2010	President Obama declares an end to US combat missions in Iraq
11 November 2010	Post-March election government formed under Prime Minister Maliki
27 October 2011	Salahadin provincial council votes to hold a referendum on forming a region
15 December 2011	US forces declare a formal end to operations in Iraq; Prime Minister Maliki targets leading Sunni politicians for arrest
February 2012	Iraqiyya withdraws ministers from the government
July 2012	ISI begins the 'Breaking the Walls' campaign, releasing Sunni insurgents from prison
July 2013	ISI assaults Abu Ghraib prison, releasing several hundred fighters; they begin the 'Soldiers Harvest' campaign, targeting the ISF
18 December 2012	President Jalal Talabani suffers a massive stroke, ending his political career
9 April 2013	Abu Bakr al-Baghdadi announces ISI has become ISIS
19 April 2013	ISF forces suppress Sunni demonstrators in Hawijah
December 2013	ISIS captures Fallujah and Ramadi
April 2014	Iraq parliamentary elections
4 June 2014	ISIS begins assault on Mosul
9 June 2014	Mosul falls to ISIS; Kurdish leadership orders occupation of the disputed territories by the *peshmerga*

11 June 2014	ISIS attacks and captures the refinery town of Baiji
13 June 2014	Ayatollah Sistani proclaims the 'righteous *jihad*' fatwa, calling for Iraqis to fight IS, furthering formation of Shi'i militia under the umbrella of the Hashed al-Sha'bi
29 June 2014	Abu Bakr proclaims himself Caliph of the Islamic State
3 July 2014	Kurdistan Region President Massoud Barzani instructs the Kurdistan parliament to prepare for a referendum on independence
5 August 2014	ISIS attacks the Kurdistan Region
7 August 2014	President Obama orders air strikes against ISIS as a means of protecting the Kurdistan Region
14 August 2014	Prime Minister Maliki steps down and is replaced by Haidar al-Abadi, also of the Da'wa Party

Sources

<http://news.bbc.co.uk/1/hi/world/middle_east/737483.stm>
<http://www.mideastweb.org/iraqtimeline.htm>
<http://www.juancole.com>
<http://www.nytimes.com/interactive/2010/08/31/world/middleeast/20100831-Iraq-Timeline.html?_r=0#/#time111_3295>

Internet Links

Media Outlets and Summaries

Iraqi News: <http://www.iraqinews.com>
Kurdish Media: <www.kurdishmedia.org>
Kurdistan Observer: <www.kurdistanobserver.com>
Institute for War and Peace Reporting: <www.iwpr.net>
Az-Zaman (Iraqi newspaper) archives: <http://www.azzaman.com/pdfarchive/>
Rudaw (Kurdish) newspaper: <http://rudaw.net/english>

NGOs and Think Tanks

Iraq Revenue Watch: <http://www.iraqrevenuewatch.org/reports/>
Iraq Body Count: <http://www.iraqbodycount.net/>
Iraq Research and Documentation Project (IRDP): <http://www.fas.harvard.edn/~irdp/>
International Crisis Group: <www.crisisgroup.org>
Royal Institute of International Affairs: <www.chathamhouse.org.uk>
United States Institute for Peace: <www.usip.org>
Carnegie Endowment for International Peace: <http://www.carnegieendowment.org>
Institute for the Study of War: <http://www.understandingwar.org/sub-page-slider/iraq-research>
Brookings Institution: <http://www.brookings.edu/research/topics/iraq>
Royal United Services Institute: <http://www.rusi.org>

Wilson Center: <https://www.wilsoncenter.org/program/middle-east -program>
Middle East Research Institute, Erbil: <http://www.meri-k.org>

Weblogs

Historiae.org (weblog of Dr Reidar Visser, focusing upon southern Iraq): <http://www.historiae.org>
Informed Comment (weblog of Professor Juan Cole): <www.juancole.com>
Aymenn Jawad Al-Tamimi, observer of IS activities: <http://www.aymennjawad.org>
Musings on Iraq, weblog of Joel Wing: <http://musingsoniraq.blogspot.co.uk>

Government and International Organizations

Iraqi Presidency: <http://en.presidency.iq>
Iraqi Prime Minister's Office: <http://pmo.iq/pme/indexe.htm>
Iraqi Ministry of Foreign Affairs: <http://www.mofa.gov.iq/en/>
Kurdistan Region Presidency Council: <http://www.presidency.krd/english/> Kurdistan Regional Government: <www.krg.org>
UK Foreign and Commonwealth Office page on Iraq: <https://www.gov.uk/government/world/iraq>
UN Assistance Mission for Iraq: <http://www.uniraq.org/>
US State Department Iraq page: <http://www.state.gov/r/pa/ei/bgn/6804.htm>

Political Parties and Movements

Ayatollah Ali al-Sistani: <www.sistani.org>
Hizb al-Da_wa site (in Arabic): <http://www.islamicdawaparty.org/>
ISCI (in Arabic): <http://www.almejlis.org>
Kurdistan Democratic Party: <http://www.kdp.info>
Patriotic Union of Kurdistan: <http://pukmedia.com/EN/EN_Sereta.aspx>
Gorran Movement: <https://www.gorran.net/En/Default.aspx>

References

Abdullah, Thabit (2003) *A Short History of Iraq*. London: Pearson Longman.

Abu Galal, Saif (2002) *UN Economic Sanctions and Iraq: A Critical Analysis of a Failed Policy*. Durham Middle East Paper No. 69. University of Durham: Institute of Middle East & Islamic Studies.

Aburish, Said K. (2000) *Saddam Hussein: The Politics of Revenge*. New York: Bloomsbury.

Adamson, David (1964) *The Kurdish War*. London: George Allen and Unwin.

Agnew, John and Stuart Corbridge (1995) *Mastering Space: Hegemony, Territory and International Political Economy*. London: Routledge.

Ala Hamoudi, Haider (2014) *Negotiating in Civil Conflict: Constitutional Construction and Imperfect Bargaining in Iraq*. Chicago, IL: University of Chicago Press.

Alkadiri, Raad (2010) 'Oil and the Question of Federalism in Iraq', *International Affairs* 86/6: 1315–28.

Allsopp, Harriet (2014) *The Kurds of Syria: Political Parties and Identity in the Middle East*. London: I. B. Tauris.

Alnasrawi, Abbas (1994) *The Economy of Iraq: Oil, Wars, Destruction of Development and Prospects, 1950–2010*. Westport, CT: Greenwood Press.

Anderson, Benedict (1984) *Imagined Communities: Reflections on the Origin and Spread of Nationalism*. London: Verso.

Anderson, Liam and Gareth Stansfield (2004) *The Future of Iraq: Dictatorship, Democracy or Division?* 2nd edn. New York: Palgrave Macmillan.

Anderson, Liam and Gareth Stansfield (2005) 'The Implications of Elections for Federalism in Iraq: Toward a Five-Region Model', *Publius: The Journal of Federalism* 35/3: 1–24.

Anderson, Liam and Gareth Stansfield (2009) *Crisis in Kirkuk: The Ethnopolitics of Conflict and Compromise*. Philadelphia, PA: University of Pennsylvania Press.

Ansari, Ali (2003) *Modern Iran Since 1921: The Pahlavis and After*. London: Longman.

Arendt, Hannah (1962) *The Origins of Totalitarianism* (first published in 1951). New York: Meridian.

al-Askari, Jafar Pasha (2003) *A Soldier's Story: From Ottoman Rule to Independent Iraq: The Memoirs of Jafar Pasha Al-Askari*. London: Arabian Publishing.

Atwan, Abdel Bari (2015) *Islamic State: The Digital Caliphate*. London: Saqi.

Ayubi, Nazih (1995) *Overstating the Arab State*. London: I. B. Taurus.

Aziz, T. M. (1993) 'The Role of Muhammad Baqir al-Sadr in Shii Political Activism in Iraq from 1958–1980', *International Journal of Middle East Studies* 25/2: 207–22.

Bagg, Ariel (2000) 'Irrigation in Northern Mesopotamia: Water for the Assyrian Capitals (12th–7th centuries BC)', in *Irrigation and Drainage Systems* 14: 301–24.

Baker, James and Lee Hamilton (2006) *Iraq Study Group Report*. New York: Random House.

Bakhash, Shaul (2004) 'The Troubled Relationship: Iran and Iraq, 1930–80', in Lawrence Potter and Gary Sick (eds), *Iran, Iraq, and the Legacies of War*, pp. 11–28.

Baram, Amatzia (1989) 'The Ruling Political Elite in Bathi Iraq, 1968–1986: The Changing Features of a Collective Profile', *International Journal of Middle East Studies* 21/4: 447–93.

Baram, Amatzia (1994) 'A Case of Imported Identity: The Modern Secular Ruling Elites of Iraq and the Concept of Mesopotamian-Inspired Territorial Nationalism, 1922–1992', *Poetics Today* 15/2 (Cultural Processes in Muslim and Arab Society: Modern Period II): 279–319.

Baram, Amatzia (1997) 'Neo-Tribalism in Iraq: Saddam Hussein's Tribal Policies 1991–96', *International Journal of Middle East Studies* 29/1: 1–31.

Baram, Amatzia (1998) *Building Toward Crisis: Saddam Hussein's Strategy for Survival*. Washington DC: Washington Institute for Near East Policy.

Baram, Amatzia (2003) 'Saddam's Power Structure: The Tikritis Before, During and After the War', in Toby Dodge and Steven

Simon (eds), *Iraq at the Crossroads: State and Society in the Shadow of Regime Change*. International Institute of Strategic Studies (IISS) Adelphi Paper 354. London: Oxford University Press and IISS, pp. 93–114.

Barnett, Michael, Songying Fang and Christoph Zurcher (2014) 'Compromised Peacebuilding', *International Studies Quarterly* 58: 608–20.

Batatu, Hanna (1978) *The Old Social Classes and the Revolutionary Movements of Iraq: A Study of Iraq's Old Landed and Commercial Classes and of its Communists, Ba'thists and Free Officers*. Princeton, NJ: Princeton University Press (reprinted by Saqi Books, London, 2004).

Beck, Peter (1981) '"A Tedious and Perilous Controversy": Britain and the Settlement of the Mosul Dispute, 1918–1926', *Middle Eastern Studies* 17/2: 256–76.

Bengio, Ofra (1992) *Baghdad Between Shi'a and Kurds*. Washington Institute for Near East Policy, Policy Focus no. 18, pp. 7–8.

Biddle, Stephen, Jeffrey Friedman and Jacob Shapiro (2012) 'Testing the Surge: Why Did Violence Decline in Iraq in 2007?', *International Security* 37/1: 7–40.

Blomfield, Adrian and Damien McElroy (2011) 'Iraq in Fresh Turmoil as Prime Minister Nouri al-Maliki Orders Arrest of Vice President', *Telegraph*, 19 December; available at <http://www.telegraph.co.uk/news/worldnews/middleeast/iraq/8966587/Iraq-in-fresh-turmoil-as-Prime-Minister-Nuri-al-Maliki-orders-arrest-of-vice-president.html>.

Bluth, Christoph (2004) 'The British Road to War: Blair, Bush and the Decision to Invade Iraq', *International Affairs* 80/5: 871–92.

Bossuyt, Audrey, Broze, Laurence and Victor Ginsburgh (2001) 'On Invisible Trade Relations Between Mesopotamian Cities During the Third Millennium B.C.', *The Professional Geographer* 53/3: 374–83.

Boyne, Sean (1997/8) 'Inside Iraq's Security Network, Part One', *Jane's Intelligence Review* 9/7 (July 1997) and 8 (August 1998).

Bremer, L. Paul (with Malcolm McConnell) (2006) *My Year in Iraq: The Struggle to Build a Future of Hope*. New York: Simon & Schuster.

Brooker, Paul (2000) *Non-Democratic Regimes: Theory, Government & Politics*. Basingstoke: Macmillan.

Brown, Stuart (1986) 'Media and Secondary State Formation in the Neo-Assyrian Zagros: An Anthropological Approach to an Assyriological Problem', *Journal of Cuneiform Studies* 38/1: 107–19.

Busch, Briton (1976) *Mudros to Lausanne: Britain's Frontier in West Asia 1918–1923*. Albany, NY: SUNY Press.

Butler, Richard (2000) *Saddam Defiant: The Threat of Weapons of Mass Destruction and the Crisis of Global Security*. London: Weidenfeld & Nicolson.

Camus, Albert (1960) *The Plague*. Harmondsworth: Penguin.

Carothers, Thomas (2002) 'The End of the Transition Paradigm', *Journal of Democracy* 13/1: 5–21.

Catherwood, Christopher (2004) *Churchill's Folly: How Winston Churchill Created Modern Iraq*. New York: Carroll and Graf Publishers.

Center for Economic and Social Rights (CESR) (1996) *UN-Sanctioned Suffering: A Human Rights Assessment of United Nations Sanctions on Iraq*. New York: CESR. Available at: <http://cesr.org/node/393>.

Çetinsaya, Gokhan (1994) *Ottoman Administration of Iraq, 1890–1908*. PhD thesis, University of Manchester.

Çetinsaya, Gokhan (2003) 'The Ottoman View of the British Presence in Iraq and the Gulf: The Era of Abdulhamid II', *Middle Eastern Studies* 39/2: 194–203.

Chatham House (2004) *Iraq Scenarios: Transition to Elections*. Briefing Paper No. 5. London: The Royal Institute of International Affairs.

Chubin, Shahram (1989) 'Iran and the War: From Stalemate to Ceasefire', in Efraim Karsh (ed.), *The Iran/Iraq War: Impact and Implications*, pp.13–25.

Chubin, Shahram and Charles Tripp (1991) *Iran and Iraq at War*. Boulder, CO: Westview Press.

(The) Coalition for International Justice (2002) *Sources of Revenue for Saddam & Sons: A Primer on the Financial Underpinnings of the Regime in Baghdad*. Washington DC: The Coalition for International Justice, 2002. Available at: <http://www.iraqwatch.org/perspectives/cij-saddammoney-091802.pdf>.

Cockburn, Andrew and Patrick Cockburn (1999) *Out of the Ashes: The Resurrection of Saddam Hussein*. New York: HarperCollins.

Cockburn, Patrick (2008) *Muqtada: Muqtada al-Sadr, the Shia Revival, and the Struggle for Iraq*. New York: Simon & Schuster.

Cockburn, Patrick (2013) 'Middle East Leader of the Year? You'd Be Surprised …' *Independent*, 22 December. Available at: <http://www.independent.co.uk/voices/comment/middle-east-leader-of-the-year-yard-be-surprised-9020089.html>.

Cockburn, Patrick (2014) *The Rise of Islamic State: ISIS and the New Sunni Revolution*. London: Verso.

Cohen, Saul (1976) *British Policy in Mesopotamia, 1903–1914*. Oxford: Ithaca Press.

Cole, Juan (2003) 'The United States and Shi'ite Religious Factions in Post-Ba'thist Iraq', *Middle East Journal* 57/4: 543–66.
Cole, Juan (2004) 'The Three State Solution,' *The Nation*, 29 March. Available at: <http://www.thenation.com/doc/20040329/cole>.
Coughlin, Con (2002) *Saddam: The Secret Life*. London: Macmillan.
Couture, Philip G. (1984) 'Sir Henry Creswicke Rawlinson: Pioneer Cuneiformist', *Biblical Archaeologist* 47/3 (September): 143–5.
Crawford, Harriet (2004) *Sumer and the Sumerians*, 2nd edn. Cambridge: Cambridge University Press.
Crystal, Jill (1994) 'Authoritarianism and its Adversaries in the Arab World', *World Politics* 46/2: 262–89.
Danchev, Alex and John Macmillan (eds) (2004) *The Iraq War and Democratic Politics*. London: Routledge.
Davidson, Nigel (1933) 'The Termination of the "Iraq Mandate" ', *International Affairs* 12/1: 60–78.
Davis, Eric (2005) *Memories of State: Politics, History, and Collective Identity in Modern Iraq*. Berkeley, CA: University of California Press.
Dawod, Hosham (2003) 'The "State-ization" of the Tribe and the Tribalization of the State: The Case of Iraq', in Faleh A. Jabar and Hosham Dawood (eds), *Tribes and Power: Nationalism and Ethnicity in the Middle East*. London: Saqi Books, pp. 110–35.
Department of the Army (2006) *Counter-Insurgency Field Manual*. Washington DC: Department of the Army.
Diakonoff, I. M. (1985) 'Media', in Ilya Gershevitch (ed.), *The Cambridge History of Iran: Volume 2: The Median and Achaemenian Periods*. Cambridge: Cambridge University Press, pp. 36–148.
Diamond, Larry (2005) *Squandered Victory: The American Occupation and the Bungled Effort to Bring Democracy to Iraq*. New York: Times Books.
Dodge, Toby (2003) *Inventing Iraq: The Failure of Nation Building and a History Denied*. New York: Columbia University Press.
Dodge, Toby (2005) *Iraq's Future: The Aftermath of Regime Change*. Adelphi Paper 372. London: International Institute for Strategic Studies.
Dodge, Toby (2012) *Iraq: From War to a New Authoritarianism*. London: International Institute for Strategic Studies/Routledge.
Dodge, Toby and Steven Simon (eds) (2003) *Iraq at the Crossroads: State and Society in the Shadow of Regime Change*. International Institute of Strategic Studies (IISS) Adelphi Paper 354. London: Oxford University Press and IISS.
Donner, Fred (1981) *The Early Islamic Conquests*. Princeton, NJ: Princeton University Press.

Dunne, Michael (2003) 'The United States, the United Nations, and Iraq', *International Affairs* 79/2: 257–77.

Elphinston, W. G. (1946) 'The Kurdish Question', *International Affairs* 22/1: 91–103.

Eppel, Michael (2004) *Iraq from Monarchy to Tyranny: From the Hashemites to the Rise of Saddam*. Gainesville, FL: University Press of Florida.

Eskander, Saad (2000) 'Britain's Policy in Southern Kurdistan: The Formation and the Termination of the First Kurdish Government, 1918–1919', *British Journal of Middle Eastern Studies* 27/2: 139–63.

Etherington, Mark (2005) *Revolt on the Tigris: The Al-Sadr Uprising and the Governing of Iraq*. London: Hurst & Co.

Etzioni, Amitai (2004) 'A Self-Restrained Approach to Nation-Building by Foreign Powers', *International Affairs* 80/1: 1–17.

Fadel Leila, and Karen de Young (2010) 'Ayad Allawi's Bloc Wins Most Seats in Iraqi Parliamentary Elections', *Washington Post Foreign Service*, 27 March. Available at: <http://www.washingtonpast.com/wp-dyn/content/article/2010/03/26/Ar2010032602196.html>.

Fattah, Hala (2003) 'The Question of the "Artificiality" of Iraq as a Nation-State', in Shams Inati (ed.), *Iraq: Its History, People, and Politics*. New York: Humanity Books.

Farouk-Sluglett, Marion and Peter Sluglett (1978) 'Some Reflections on the Sunni/Shi'i Question in Iraq', *The Bulletin of the British Society for Middle Eastern Studies* 5/2: 79–87.

Farouk-Sluglett, Marion and Peter Sluglett (1990a) *Iraq Since 1958: From Revolution to Dictatorship*. London: I. B. Taurus.

Farouk-Sluglett, Marion and Peter Sluglett (1990b) 'Iraq Since 1986: The Strengthening of Saddam', *Middle East Report* 167: 19–24.

Farouk-Sluglett, Marion and Peter Sluglett (1991) 'The Historiography of Modern Iraq', in *American History Review* 96/5: 1408–21.

Fernea, Robert A. (1970) *Shaykh and Effendi: Changing Patterns of Political Authority among the El-Shabana of Southern Iraq*. Cambridge, MA: Harvard University Press.

Fieldhouse, D. K. (ed.) (2002) *Kurds, Arabs and Britons: The Memoir of Wallace Lyon in Iraq, 1918–44*. London: I. B. Taurus.

Filkins, Dexter (2015) 'Is Bush Right about Clinton and Iraq?', *New Yorker*, 13 August. Available at: <http://www.newyorker.com/news/daily-comment/is-bush-right-about-clinton-and-iraq>.

Fitzgerald, Edward P. (1994) 'France's Middle Eastern Ambitions, the Sykes-Picot Negotiations, and the Oil Fields of Mosul, 1915–1918', *The Journal of Modern History* 66/4: 697–725.

Fromkin, David (1991) *A Peace to End All Peace: Creating the Modern Middle East, 1914–1922*. Harmondsworth: Penguin.

Galbraith, Peter W. (2006) *The End of Iraq: How American Incompetence Created a War Without End*. New York: Simon & Schuster.

Gasiorowski, Mark (2002) 'The Nuzhih Plot and Iranian Politics', in *International Journal of Middle Eastern Studies* 34: 645–66.

Graham-Brown, Sarah (1999) *Sanctioning Saddam: The Politics of Intervention in Iraq*. London: I. B. Taurus.

Gregory, Derek (2004) *The Colonial Present*. Oxford: Blackwell Publishing.

Gross Stein, Janice (1988) 'The Wrong Strategy in the Right Place: The United States in the Gulf', *International Security* 13/3: 142–67.

Gunter, Michael M. (1999) *The Kurdish Predicament in Iraq: A Political Analysis*. London: Macmillan Press.

Gunter, Michael M. (2014) *Out of Nowhere: The Kurds of Syria in Peace and War*. London: Hurst & Co.

Halpern, Manfred (1962) 'Middle Eastern Armies and the New Middle Class', in John Johnson (ed.), *The Role of the Military in Under-Developed Countries*. Princeton, NJ: Princeton University Press, pp. 277–316.

Hashim, Ahmed (2003a) 'Military Power and State Formation in Modern Iraq', in *Middle East Policy* 10/4: 29–47.

Hashim, Ahmed (2003b) 'Saddam Husayn and Civil–Military Relations in Iraq: The Quest for Legitimacy and Power', in *Middle East Journal* 57/1: 9–41.

Hashim, Ahmed (2006) *Insurgency and Counter-Insurgency in Iraq*. London: Hurst & Co.

Hashim, Ahmed (2014) 'The Islamic State: From Al-Qaeda Affiliate to Caliphate', *Middle East Policy* XXI/4 (winter): 69–83.

Hazelton, Fran (1989) 'Iraq to 1963', in Committee Against Repression and for Democratic Rights in Iraq (CARDRI), *Saddam's Iraq: Revolution or Reaction?* London: Zed Books, pp. 1–29.

Hemphill, Paul (1979) 'The Formation of the Iraqi Army, 1921–1933', in Abbas Kelidar (ed.), *The Integration of Modern Iraq*. London: Croom Helm, pp. 88–110.

al-Hirmizi, Ershad (2003) *The Turkmen and Iraqi Homeland*. Istanbul: Kerkük Vakfi.

al-Hirmizi, Arshad (2005) *The Turkmen Reality in Iraq*. Istanbul: Kerkük Vakfi.

Hiro, Dilip (1989) *The Longest War: The Iran–Iraq Military Conflict*. London: Grafton.

Hiro, Dilip (2001) *Neighbours, Not Friends: Iraq and Iran After the Gulf Wars*. London: Routledge.

Hobsbawm, Eric (1990) *Nations and Nationalism Since 1780*. Cambridge: Cambridge University Press.

Hopwood, Derek, Habib Ishow and Thomas Koszinowski (eds) (1993) *Iraq: Power and Society*. Reading: Ithaca Press.

Horowitz, S. (2004) 'Identities Unbound: Escalating Ethnic Conflict in Post-Soviet Azerbaijan, Georgia, Moldova, and Tajikistan', in S. Lobell and P. Mauceri (eds), *Ethnic Conflict and International Politics: Explaining Diffusion and Escalation*. New York: Palgrave, pp. 51–74.

Human Rights Watch (1990) *Human Rights in Iraq*. New Haven, CT: Yale University Press.

Human Rights Watch (1992) *Endless Torment: The 1991 Uprising in Iraq and its Aftermath*. New York: Human Rights Watch.

Human Rights Watch (1993) *Genocide in Iraq: The Anfal Campaign Against the Kurds*. New York: Human Rights Watch.

Human Rights Watch (1994) *Bureaucracy of Repression: The Iraqi Government in its Own Words*. New York: Human Rights Watch.

Human Rights Watch (2003) *Iraq: Forcible Expulsion of Ethnic Minorities*, vol. 15, no. 3(E). Washington DC: Human Rights Watch.

Hünseler, Peter (1984) 'The Historical Antecedents of the Shatt al-Arab Dispute', in M. S. El-Azhary (ed.), *The Iran Iraq War: An Historical, Economic and Political Analysis*, pp. 8–19.

Hurewitz, J. C. (1962) 'Russia and the Turkish Straits: A Revaluation of the Origins of the Problem', *World Politics* 14/4: 605–32.

Hurewitz, J. C. (1979) *The Middle East and North Africa in World Politics: A Documentary Record, Vol. 2*. New Haven, CT: Yale University Press.

Husry, Khaldun S. (1974) 'The Assyrian Affair of 1933 (I)', *International Journal of Middle East Studies* 5/2: 161–76.

International Crisis Group (ICG) (2004) *Reconstructing Iraq*. ICG Middle East Report no. 30.

International Crisis Group (ICG) (2006) *In Their Own Words: Reading the Iraqi Insurgency*. ICG Middle East Report no. 50.

Iron, Richard (2013) 'The Charge of the Knights', *The RUSI Journal* 158/1: 54–62.

Izady, Merhdad (2004a) 'Kurdish History and Culture', posted on the website of the Kurdistan Regional Government, 18 December 2004. Available at: <www.krg.org>.

Izady, Merhdad (2004b) 'Kurds and the Formation of the State of Iraq, 1917–1932', in Reeva Simon and Eleanor Tejirian (eds), *The*

Creation of Iraq, 1914–1921. New York: Columbia University Press, pp. 95–109.

Jabar, Faleh A. (1992) 'Why the Uprisings Failed', *Middle East Report*, pp. 2–14.

Jabar, Faleh A. (2003a) 'Sheikhs and Ideologues: Deconstruction and Reconstruction of Tribes Under Patrimonial Totalitarianism in Iraq, 1968–1998', in Faleh Jabar and Hosham Dawod (eds), *Tribes and Power: Nationalism and Ethnicity in the Middle East*. London: Saqi Books, pp. 69–109.

Jabar, Faleh A. (2003b) *The Shiʿite Movement in Iraq*. London: Saqi Books.

Jawad, Saʿad (1982) 'Recent Developments in the Kurdish Issue', in Tim Niblock (ed.), *Iraq: The Contemporary State*, pp. 47–61.

Jhaveri, Nayna (2004) 'Petroimperialism: US Oil Interests and the Iraq War,' *Antipode* 36/1: 2–11.

Jwaideh, Wadie (1960) *The Kurdish Nationalist Movement: Its Origins and Development*. PhD dissertation, Syracuse University.

al-Kadhimi, Mustafa (2015) 'Will Sistani Be Able to Control Popular Mobilization Forces?', *Al-Monitor*, 12 March. Available at: <http://www.al-monitor.com/pulse/originals/2015/03/iraq-sistani-righteous-jihad-fatwa-popular-mobilization.html>.

Karpat, Kemal (1972) 'The Transformation of the Ottoman State, 1789–1908,' *International Journal of Middle East Studies* 3/3: 243–81.

Karsh, Efraim (ed.) (1989a) *The Iran/Iraq War: Impact and Implications*. Basingstoke: Macmillan.

Karsh, Efraim (1989b) 'From Ideological Zeal to Geopolitical Realism: The Islamic Republic and the Gulf', in Efraim Karsh (ed.), *The Iran/Iraq War: Impact and Implications*, pp. 26–41.

Keating, Michael and John McGarry (eds) (2001) *Minority Nationalism and the Changing International Order*. Oxford: Oxford University Press.

Kedourie, Elie (1970) *The Chatham House Version and Other Middle-Eastern Studies*. London: Weidenfeld and Nicolson.

Kelidar, Abbas (ed.) (1979) *The Integration of Modern Iraq*. London: Croom Helm.

Kelidar, Abbas (1993) 'States Without Foundations: The Political Evolution of State and Society in the Arab East', in *Journal of Contemporary History* 28/2: 315–39.

Kennedy, Hugh (1981) *The Early Abbasid Caliphate*. London: Croom Helm.

Kennedy, Hugh (2004) *The Court of the Caliphs: The Rise and Fall of Islam's Greatest Dynasty*. London: Weidenfeld & Nicolson.

Kent, Marian (1976) *Oil and Empire: British Policy and Mesopotamian Oil, 1900–1920*. London: Macmillan.

Kerr, Malcolm (1971) *The Arab Cold War: Gamal 'Abd al-Nasir and His Rivals, 1958–1970*, 3rd edn. London: Oxford University Press.

Khadduri, Majid (1951) *Independent Iraq*. London: Oxford University Press.

Khadduri, Majid (1969) *Republican Iraq: A Study in Iraqi Politics Since the Revolution of 1958*. London: Oxford University Press.

Khadduri, Majid (1978) *Socialist Iraq: A Study in Iraqi Politics Since 1968*. Washington DC: Middle East Institute.

Khadduri, Majid and Edmund Ghareeb (1997) *War in the Gulf 1990–91: The Iraq–Kuwait Conflict and its Implications*. New York and Oxford: Oxford University Press.

Khadhim, Abbas (2012) *Reclaiming Iraq: The 1920 Revolution and the Founding of the Modern State*. Austin, TX: University of Texas Press.

al-Khafaji, Isam (1992) 'State Terror and the Degradation of Politics in Iraq', *Middle East Report*, no. 176, *Iraq in the Aftermath*, pp. 15–21.

al-Khafaji, Isam (2000) 'The Myth of Iraqi Exceptionalism', *Middle East Policy* 7/4: 62–91.

al-Khafaji, Isam (2003) 'A Few Days After: State and Society in a Post-Saddam Iraq', in Toby Dodge and Steve Simon (eds), *Iraq at the Crossroads: State and Society in the Shadow of Regime Change*. Oxford: Oxford University Press/International Institute for Strategic Studies, pp. 77–92.

Khedery, Ali (2014) 'Why We Stuck with Maliki – and Lost Iraq', *Washington Post*, 3 July. Available at: <https://www.washingtonpost.com/opinions/why-we-stuck-with-maliki–and-lost-iraq/2014/07/03/0dd6a8a4-f7ec-11e3-a606-946fd632f9f1_story.html>.

Khoury, Dina Rizk (1997) *State and Provincial Society in the Ottoman Empire*. Cambridge: Cambridge University Press.

Klingner, D. E. and L. R. Jones (2005) 'Learning from the Philippine Occupation: Nation-Building and Institutional Development in Iraq and Other High Security Risk Nations', in *Public Administration and Development* 25: 145–56.

Korn, David (1994) 'The Last Years of Mustafa Barzani', *Middle East Quarterly* 1/2. Available at: <http://www.meforum.org/220/the-last-years-of-mustafa-barzani>.

Krohley, Nicholas (2015) *The Death of the Mahdi Army: The Rise, Fall, and Revival of Iraq's Most Powerful Militia*. London: C. Hurst & Co.

Lapidus, Ira (2002) *A History of Islamic Societies*. Cambridge: Cambridge University Press.

Laubell S. and P. Mauceri (2004) 'Diffusion and Escalation of Ethnic Conflict', in S. Lobell and P. Mauceri (eds), *Ethnic Conflict and International Politics: Explaining Diffusion and Escalation*. New York: Palgrave Macmillan, pp. 1–10.

Lawrence, Quil (2009) 'A Precarious Peace in Northern Iraq', *MERIP Middle East Report*, 1 October. Available at: <http://www.merip.org/mero/mero100109>.

Leaman, George (2004) 'Iraq, American Empire, and the War on Terrorism', *Metaphilosophy* 35/3: 234–48.

Lijphart, Arend (1977) *Democracy in Plural Societies*. New Haven, CT: Yale University Press.

Linz, Juan J. (1964) 'An Authoritarian Regime: Spain', in Erik Allardt and Yrjő Littunen (eds), *Cleavages, Ideologies and Party Systems*. Helsinki: The Westermarck Society, pp. 291–341. Reprinted in Erik Allardt and Stein Rokkan (eds) (1970), *Mass Politics: Studies in Political Sociology*. New York: The Free Press, pp. 251–83.

Lister, Charles (2014) 'Profiling the Islamic State', *Analysis Paper*, no. 13, Doha: Brookings Doha Center, November.

Lister, Charles (2015) *The Syrian Jihad: Al-Qaeda, the Islamic State and the Evolution of an Insurgency*. London: Hurst & Co.

Liverani, Mario (1995) 'The Medes at Esarhaddon's Court', *Journal of Cuneiform Studies* 47: 57–62.

Lloyd, H. I. (1926) 'The Geography of the Mosul Boundary', *The Geographical Journal* 68/2: 104–13.

Lobell, S. and Mauceri, P. (eds) (2004) *Ethnic Conflict and International Politics: Explaining Diffusion and Escalation*. New York: Palgrave.

Longrigg, Stephen M. (1953) *Iraq, 1900–1950: A Political, Social and Economic History*. Oxford: Oxford University Press.

Louis, Wm R. and R. Fernea (eds) (1991) *The Iraqi Revolution of 1958: The Old Social Classes Revisited*. London: I. B. Taurus.

Lowe, Robert (2014) 'The Emergence of Western Kurdistan and the Future of Syria', in David Romano and Mehmet Gurses (eds), *Conflict, Democratization and the Kurds in the Middle East*. New York: Palgrave Macmillan, pp. 225–48.

Lukitz, Liora (2005) *A Quest in the Middle East: Gertrude Bell and the Making of Modern Iraq*. London: I. B. Taurus.

McCants, William (2015a) 'The Believer: How an Introvert with a Passion for Religion and Soccer Became Abu Bakr Al-Baghdadi,

Leader of the Islamic State', *The Brookings Essay*, 1 September. Washington DC: The Brookings Institution. Available at: <http://www.brookings.edu/research/essays/2015/thebeliever>.

McCants, William (2015b) *The ISIS Apocalypse: The History, Strategy, and Doomsday Vision of the Islamic State*. New York: St Martin's Press.

MacGinty, Roger (2010) 'Hybrid Peace: The Interaction Between Top-Down and Bottom-Up Peace', *Security Dialogue* 41/4: 391–412.

Machinist, Peter (1983) 'Assyria and its Image in the First Isaiah,' *Journal of the American Oriental Society* 103/4: 719–37.

Mahdi, Kamil (2005) 'What are the Real Divisions in Iraq?' *Socialist Worker Online* 1936. Available at: <http://www.socialistworker.co.uk/article.php?article_id=5721>.

Makiya, Kanan (1993) *Cruelty and Silence: War, Tyranny, Uprising and the Arab World*. Harmondsworth: Penguin.

Makiya, Kanan (1998) *Republic of Fear: The Politics of Modern Iraq*, 2nd edn. Berkeley: UCLA Press.

Malkasian, Carter (2006) 'Signaling Resolve, Democratization and the First Battle of Fallujah', *The Journal of Strategic Studies* 29/3 (June): 423–52.

Malone, David M. (2006) *The International Struggle Over Iraq: Politics in the UN Security Council 1980–2005*. Oxford: Oxford University Press.

Marashi, Ibrahim (2003) 'Iraq's Security and Intelligence Network: A Guide and Analysis', *Middle East Review of International Affairs Journal* 6/3. Available at: <http://www.rubincenter.org/2002/09/al-marashi-2002-09-01/>.

Marr, Phebe (2004) *The Modern History of Iraq*, 2nd edn. Boulder, CO: Westview Press.

Meriage, Lawrence (1978) 'The First Serbian Uprising (1804–1813) and the Nineteenth Century Origins of the Eastern Question', *Slavic Review* 37/3: 421–39.

Mofid, Kamran (1990) *The Economic Consequences of the Gulf War*. London: Routledge.

Mohamedou, M. (1997) *Iraq and the Second Gulf War: State Building and Regime Security*. Bethesda, MD: Austin & Winfield.

Mohammed, Wisam and Sherko Maruf (2008) 'Iraq Kurds and Government End Standoff Over Northern Town', *Reuters*, 3 September. Available at: <http://uk.reuters.com/article/us-iraq-khanaqin-idUKL365141120080903>.

Montgomery, Gary and Timothy Williams (eds) (2009) *Al-Anbar Awakening: Volume II: Iraqi Perspectives: From Insurgency to Counterinsurgency in Iraq*. Quantico, VA: Marine Corps University.

Morony, Michael (1984) *Iraq after the Muslim Conquest*. Princeton, NJ: Princeton University Press.

Morozova, Galina (2005) 'A Review of Holocene Avulsions in the Tigris and Euphrates Rivers and Possible Effects on the Evolution of Civilizations in Lower Mesopotamia', *Geoarchaeology: An International Journal* 20/4: 401–23.

Moss Helms, Christine (1984) *Iraq: Eastern Flank of the Arab World*. Washington DC: The Brookings Institution.

Mufti, Malik (1996) *Sovereign Creations: Pan-Arabism and Political Order in Syria and Iraq*. London: Cornell University Press.

Murray, Williamson and Robert Scales (2003) *The Iraq War: A Military History*. Cambridge, MA: Harvard University Press.

Naama, Kamal (2012) 'Sunni Protesters Attack Iraq Official's Convoy, Guards Wound Two', *Reuters*, 30 December. Available at: <http://uk.reuters.com/article/uk-iraq-protests-idUKBRE8BT04A20121230>.

Nakash, Yitzhak (1994) *The Shi'is of Iraq*. Princeton, NJ: Princeton University Press.

Nakash, Yitzhak (2006) *Reaching for Power: The Shi'a in the Modern World*. Princeton, NJ: Princeton University Press.

Napoleoni, Loretta (2005) *Insurgent Iraq: Al Zarqawi and the New Generation*. London: Constable.

al-Naqeeb, Khaldoun (1990) *Society and State in the Gulf and Arab Peninsula: A Different Perspective*. London: Routledge.

Natali, Denise (2001) 'Manufacturing Identity and Managing Kurds in Iraq,' in Brendan O'Leary, Ian Lustick and Thomas Callaghy (eds), *Right-Sizing the State: The Politics of Moving Borders*. Oxford: Oxford University Press, pp. 253–88.

Niblock, Tim (ed.) (1982) *Iraq: The Contemporary State*. London: Croom Helm.

Niblock, Tim (2001) *"Pariah States" and Sanctions in the Middle East: Iraq, Libya, Sudan*. London: Lynne Reinner Publishers.

Nieuwenhuis, Tom (1982) *Politics and Society in Early Modern Iraq: Mamluk Pashas, Tribal Shayks and Local Rule Between 1802 and 1831*. The Hague: Martinus Nijhoff Publishers.

Noack, Rick (2014) 'Here's How the Islamic State Compares with Real States', *Washington Post*, 12 September. Available at: <http://www.washingtonpost.com/news/worldviews/wp/2014/09/12/heres-how-the-islamic-state-compares-to-real-states>.

Oğuzlu, H. Tarik (2002) 'The "Turkomans" as a Factor in Turkish Foreign Policy', *Turkish Studies* 3/2: 139–48.

O'Leary, Brendan (2009) *How To Get Out of Iraq with Integrity*. Philadelphia, PA: University of Pennsylvania Press.

O'Leary, Brendan and Khaled Saleh (2005) 'The Denial, Resurrection, and Affirmation of Kurdistan', in Brendan O'Leary et al. (eds) (2005), *The Future of Kurdistan in Iraq*, pp. 3–43.

O'Leary, Brendan, Ian Lustick and Thomas Callaghy (eds) (2001) *Right-Sizing the State: The Politics of Moving Borders*. Oxford: Oxford University Press.

O'Leary, Brendan, John McGarry and Khaled Saleh (eds) (2005) *The Future of Kurdistan in Iraq*. Philadelphia, PA: University of Pennsylvania Press.

Olson, Robert (1993) 'The Battle for Kurdistan: The Churchill–Cox Correspondence Regarding the Creation of the State of Iraq, 1921–1923', in *The International Journal of Turkish Studies* 5/1: 121–36.

O'Mahony, Anthony (2004) 'Christianity in Modern Iraq', *International Journal for the Study of the Christian Church* 4/2: 121–42.

Packer, George (2006) *The Assassins' Gate: America in Iraq*. London: Faber and Faber.

Paris, Timothy (1998) 'British Middle East Policy-Making After the First World War: The Lawrentian and Wilsonian Schools', *The Historical Journal*, 41/3: 773–93.

Parker, Ned (2009) 'Kurdish Leader Sees Authoritarian Drift in Iraq', *Los Angeles Times*, 11 January. Available at: <http://articles.latimes.com/2009/jan/11/world/fg-iraq-barzani11>.

Pasha, M. (2002) 'Predatory Globalization and Democracy in the Islamic World,' *The Annals of the American Academy of Political and Social Science*, vol. 581, pp. 121–32.

Patton, John S. (1963) *The Historical Background of the 'Iraqi Revolution, International and Internal Problems: 1918–1945*. PhD dissertation, American University.

Pei, M. and S. Kasper (2003) 'The "Morning After" Regime Change: Should US Force Democracy Again?', *Christian Science Monitor*, 15 January. Available at: <http://www.csmonitor.com/2003/0115/p09s02-coop.html>.

Péteri, György (2000) 'Between Empire and Nation-State: Comments on the Pathology of State Formation in Eastern Europe during the "Short Twentieth Century"', *Contemporary European History* 9/3: 367–84.

Pinault, David (1992) *The Shiʿites: Ritual and Popular Piety in a Muslim Community*. New York: St Martin's Press.

Pollack, Susan (1999) *Ancient Mesopotamia: The Eden that Never Was*. Cambridge: Cambridge University Press.

Pool, David (1980) 'From Elite to Class: The Transformation of Iraqi Leadership, 1920–1939,' *International Journal of Middle Eastern Studies* 12: 331–50.

Postgate, J.N. (1994) *Early Mesopotamia: Society and Economy at the Dawn of History*, revised edn. London: Routledge.

Potter, Lawrence and Gary Sick (eds) (2004) *Iran, Iraq, and the Legacies of War*. York: Palgrave Macmillan.

Preston, Zoë (2003) *The Crystallization of the Iraqi State: Geopolitical Function and Form*. Bern: Peter Lang.

Rae, Heather (2002) *State Identities and the Homogenisation of Peoples*. Cambridge: Cambridge University Press.

Rangwala, Glen (2005) 'The Democratic Transition in Iraq and the Discovery of its Limitations', in Alex Danchev and John Macmillan (eds), *The Iraq War and Democratic Politics*. London: Routledge, pp. 160–80.

Resool, Shorsh Haji (2003) *Anfal: Kurd u Dawlati Iraq* [Anfal: The Kurds and the Iraqi State] London.

Rieff, David (2004) 'Focus on Iraq: Blueprint for a Mess', in *Foreign Service Journal* (March): 22–8.

Rosen, Nir (2008) 'The Great Divide', *The National*, 5 June. Available at: <http://www.thenational.ae/news/world/middle-east-the-great-divide>.

Rothman, Mitchell S. (2001) 'The Local and the Regional: An Introduction', in Mitchell Rothman (ed.), *Uruk Mesopotamia and its Neighbors: Cross-Cultural Interactions in the Era of State Formation*. Santa Fe, NM: School of American Research Press, pp. 3–26.

Rothwell, V. (1970) 'Mesopotamia in British War Aims', *The Historical Journal* 13/2: 273–94.

Roux, Georges (1980) *Ancient Iraq*, 2nd edn. London: Pelican Books.

Salman, Kamal Abdal-Rahman (1992) *The Ottoman and British Policies Toward Iraqi Tribes: 1831 to 1920*. PhD dissertation, University of Utah.

Sambanis, Nicholas (2004) 'What is Civil War? Conceptual and Empirical Complexities of an Operational Definition', in *Journal of Conflict Resolution* 48/6: 814–58.

Sassoon, Jospeh (2012) *Saddam Hussein's Ba'th Party: Inside an Authoritarian Regime*. Cambridge: Cambridge University Press.

Schapiro, Leonard (1972) *Totalitarianism*. London: Pall Mall

Schofield, Richard (2004) 'Position, Function, and Symbol: The Shatt al-Arab Dispute in Perspective', in Lawrence Potter and Gary Sick (eds), *Iran, Iraq, and the Legacies of War*, pp. 29–70.

El-Shazly, Nadia El-Sayed (1998) *The Gulf Tanker War: Iran and Iraq's Maritime Swordplay*. Basingstoke: Macmillan.

Shourush, Sami (2002) 'The Religious Composition of the Kurdish Society: Sufi Orders, Sects and Religions', in Faleh Jabar (ed.), *Ayatollahs, Sufis and Ideologues: State, Religion and Social Movements in Iraq*. London: Saqi, pp. 114–39.

Simon, Reeva and Eleanor Tejirian (eds) (2004) *The Creation of Iraq, 1914–1921*. New York: Columbia University Press.

Simons, Geofficy (1994) *Iraq: From Sumer to Saddam*, 2nd edn. New York: St Martin's Press.

Sirriyeh, Hussein (1985) 'Development of the Iraqi–Iranian Dispute, 1847–1975', in *Journal of Contemporary History* 20/3: 483–92.

Small, Melville and J. David Singer (1982) *Resort to Arms: International and Civil War, 1816–1980*. Beverly Hills, CA: Sage.

Smith, Anthony (2004) 'Ethnic Cores and Dominant Ethnies', in Eric Kaufman (ed.), *Rethinking Ethnicity: Majority Groups and Dominant Minorities*. London: Routledge, pp. 17–30.

Smith, Hannah (2014) 'Warnings on Iraq ISIS attack ignored – KRG official', *Asharq al-Awsat*, 20 June. Available at: <http://english.aawsat.com/2014/06/article55333445/warning-on-iraq-isis-attack-ignored-krg-official>.

Smith, Steve (2002) 'The End of the Unipolar Movement? September 11 and the Future of World Order', *International Relations* 16/2: 171–83.

Stafford, Ronald S. (1935) *The Tragedy of the Assyrians*. London: George Allen and Unwin.

Stansfield, Gareth R. V. (2003) *Iraqi Kurdistan: Political Development and Emergent Democracy*. London: RoutledgeCurzon.

Stansfield, Gareth R. V. (2005a) 'Political Life and the Military', in Youssef Choueiri (ed.), *A Companion to the History of the Middle East*. Oxford: Blackwell, pp. 355–71.

Stansfield, Gareth R. V. (2005b) 'The Transition to Democracy in Iraq: Historical Legacies, Resurgent Identities and Reactionary Tendencies', in Alex Danchev and John Macmillan (eds), *The Iraq War and Democratic Politics*. London: Routledge, pp. 134–59.

Stansfield, Gareth R. V. (2006) 'Finding a Dangerous Equilibrium: Internal Politics in Iraqi Kurdistan – Parties, Tribes, Religion and Ethnicity Reconsidered', in Faleh Jabar and Hosham Dawod (eds), *The Kurds: Nationalism and Politics*. London: Saqi, pp. 258–76.

Stansfield, Gareth R. V. (2012) 'Tension on the Trigger-Line', *RUSI Analysis*, 26 November. Available at: <https://rusi.org/commentary/tension-trigger-line>.

Stansfield, Gareth R. V. (2013) 'The Unravelling of the post-First World War State System? The Kurdistan Region of Iraq and the Transformation of the Middle East', *International Affairs* 89/2: 259–82.

Stansfield, Gareth R. V. (2014a) 'Reading the Elections in Iraq', *RUSI Newsbrief*, 19 May. Available at: <https://rusi.org/publication/newsbrief/reading-elections-iraq>.

Stansfield, Gareth R. V. (2014b) 'Kurdistan Rising: To Acknowledge or Ignore the Unraveling of Iraq', *Brookings Institute Middle East Memo*, No. 33, July. Available at: <http://www.brookings.edu/~/media/research/files/papers/2014/07/kurdistan-iraq-isis-0731/kurdistan-iraq-isis-stansfield-0731.pdf>.

Stansfield, Gareth R. V. (2014c) 'The New Rules of the Game in Iraq', *RUSI Analysis*, 18 June. Available at: <https://rusi.org/commentary/briefing-new-rules-game-iraq>.

Stansfield, Gareth R. V. (2014d) 'The Islamic State, the Kurdistan Region, and the Future of Iraq: Assessing UK Policy Options', *International Affairs* 90/6 (November): 1329–50.

Stansfield, Gareth and Shorsh Haji Resool (2006) 'The Tortured Resurgence of Kurdish Nationalism, 1961–1990', in Michael Gunter and Mohammed Ahmed (eds), *The Evolution of Kurdish Nationalism*. Costa Mesa, CA: Mazda Press, pp. 98–122.

Steiner, J. (1981) 'The Consociational Theory and Beyond', *Comparative Politics* 13/3: 339–54.

Stern, Jessica and J. M. Berger (2015) *ISIS: The State of Terror*. London: William Collins.

Stivers, William (1982) *Supremacy and Oil: Iraq, Turkey, and the Anglo-American World Order, 1918–1930*. Ithaca, NY: Cornell University Press.

Stork, Joe (1982) 'State Power and Economic Structure: Class Determination and State Formation in Contemporary Iraq', in Tim Niblock (ed.), *Iraq: The Contemporary State*. London: Croom Helm, pp. 27–46.

Swearingen, Will (1988) 'Geopolitical Origins of the Iran–Iraq War', *Geographical Review* 78/4: 405–16.

al-Tabari, M. J. (1989) *The History of al-Tabari, Volume XIII: The Conquest of Iraq, Southwestern Persia, and Egypt*, trans. Gautier H.A. Juynboll. Albany, NY: State University of New York Press.

al-Tabari, M. J. (1992) *The History of al-Tabari, Volume XII: The Battle of Qadisiyyah and the Conquest of Syria and Palestine*, trans. Yohanan Friedmann. Albany, NY: State University of New York Press.

al-Tabari, M. J. (1993) *The History of al-Tabari, Volume XI: The Challenge to the Empires*, trans. Khalid Y. Blankinship. Albany, NY: State University of New York Press.

Tarbush, Mohammad (1982) *The Role of the Military in Politics: A Case Study of Iraq to 1941*. London: Kegan Paul.

Tejel, Jordi (2009) *Syria's Kurds: History, Politics and Society*. London: Routledge.

Tejirian, Eleanor H. (1972) *Iraq, 1932–1963: Politics in a Plural Society*. PhD dissertation, Columbia University.

Tripp, Charles (2000) *A History of Iraq*. Cambridge: Cambridge University Press.

Tripp, Charles (2003) 'The Imperial Precedent,' *Le Monde Diplomatique*, January. Available at: <https://mondediplo.com/2003/01/02empire>.

Ucko, David (2008) 'Militias, Tribes and Insurgents: The Challenge of Political Reintegration in Iraq,' *Conflict, Security & Development*, October 8/3: 341–73.

Van Bruinessen, Martin (1986) 'The Kurds between Iran and Iraq', *MERIP Middle East Report*, no. 141, *Hidden Wars*, pp. 14–27.

Van Bruinessen, Martin (1992) *Agha, Shaikh and State: The Social and Political Organization of Kurdistan*. London: Zed Books.

Vinogradov, Amal (1972) 'The 1920 Revolt in Iraq Reconsidered: The Role of Tribes in National Politics', *International Journal of Middle East Studies* 3: 123–9.

Visser, Reidar (2005) *Basra, the Failed Gulf State: Separatism and Nationalism in Southern Iraq*. Berlin: LIT Verlag.

Voller, Yaniv (2013) 'Kurdish Oil Politics in Iraq: Contested Sovereignty and Unilateralism', *Middle East Policy* XX/1. Available at: <http://www.mepc.org/journal/middle-east-policy-archives/kurdish-oil-politics-iraq-contested-sovereignty-and-unilateralism>.

Wallach, Janet (1996) *Desert Queen: The Extraordinary Life of Gertrude Bell: Adventurer, Adviser to Kings, Ally of Lawrence of Arabia*. London: Weidenfeld and Nicolson.

Walter, Barbara F. (1997) 'The Critical Barrier to Civil War Settlement', *International Organization* 51/3: 335–64.

Weiss, Michael and Hassan Hassan (2015) *ISIS: Inside the Army of Terror*. New York: Regan Arts.

Williams, K. (2004) 'Internationalization of Ethnic Conflict in the Balkans: The Breakup of Yugoslavia', in S. Lobell and P. Mauceri (eds), *Ethnic Conflict and International Politics: Explaining Diffusion and Escalation*. New York: Palgrave, pp. 75–84.

Williams, Timothy and Kurtis Wheeler (eds) (2009) *Al-Anbar Awakening: Volume I: American Perspectives: US Marines and Counterinsurgency in Iraq, 2004–2009*. Quantico, VA: Marine Corps University.

Wilson, Arnold T. (1930) *Loyalties, Mesopotamia 1914–1917: A Personal and Historical Record*. London: Oxford University Press.

Wilson, Arnold T. (1931) *Mesopotamia 1917–1920: A Clash of Loyalties: A Personal and Historical Record*. London: Oxford University Press.

Wimmer, Andreas (2002) *Nationalist Exclusion and Ethnic Conflict: Shadows of Modernity*. Cambridge: Cambridge University Press.

Wimmer, Andreas (2004) 'Dominant Ethnicity and Dominant Nationhood', in Eric Kaufman (ed.), *Majority Groups and Dominant Minorities: Conceptualizing Dominant Ethnicity*. London: Routledge. Available at: <http://www.sscnet.ucla.edu/soc/faculty/wimmer/B64.pdf>.

Wittfogel, Karl (1981) *Oriental Despotism: A Comparative Study of Total Power*. New York: Vintage Books.

Woodward, Bob (2008) *The War Within: A Secret White House History 2006–2008*. New York: Simon & Schuster.

Wright, Evan (2004) *Generation Kill: Living Dangerously on the Road to Baghdad with the Ultraviolent Marines of Bravo Company*. London: Bantam Press.

Yaphe, Judith (2003) 'War and Occupation in Iraq: What Went Right? What Could Go Wrong?', *Middle East Journal* 57/3: 381–99.

Yaphe, Judith (2004) 'The View From Basra: Southern Iraq's Reaction to War and Occupation, 1915–1925', in Reeva S. Simon and Eleanor H. Tejirian (eds), *The Creation of Iraq, 1914–1921*. New York: Columbia University Press, pp. 19–35.

Yoffee, Norman (1995) 'Political Economy in Early Mesopotamian States', *Annual Review of Anthropology* 24: 281–311.

Yordan, Carlos L. (2004) 'Failing to Meet Expectations in Iraq: A Review of the Original U.S. Post-War Strategy', in *Middle East Review of International Affairs* 8/1: 52–68.

Young, T. Cuyler (1988) 'The Early History of the Medes and the Persians and the Achaemid Empire to the Death of Cambyses', in John Boardman, N. G. L. Hammond, D. M. Lewis and M. Ostwald (eds), *The Cambridge Ancient History: Volume*

IV: Persia, Greece and the Western Mediterranean, 2nd edn. Cambridge: Cambridge University Press, pp. 1–52.

Zawadzki, Stefan (1988) *The Fall of Assyria and Median-Babylonian Relations in Light of the Nabopolassar Chronicle*. Uniwersytet Im. Adama Mickiewicza w Poznaniu, Seria Historia, Nr. 149. Poznan: Eburon-Deeft.

Zedalis, Rex (2012) *Oil and Gas in the Disputed Kurdish Territories: Jurisprudence, Regional Minorities and Natural Resources in a Federal System*. London: Routledge.

Zubaida, Sami (1991) 'Community, Class and Minorities in the 1958 Iraqi revolution', in Louis, R. and R. Fernea (eds), *The Iraqi Revolution of 1958: The Old Social Classes Revisited*. London: I. B. Taurus, pp. 197–210.

Zubaida, Sami (2000) 'Contested Nations: Iraq and the Assyrians', *Nations and Nationalism* 6/3: 363–82.

Zubaida, Sami (2002) 'The Fragments Imagine the Nation: the case of Iraq', in *International Journal of Middle East Studies* 34: 205–15.

Index